Management Studies in Crisis

More students study business and management than ever, the number of business schools worldwide continues to rise, and more management research is being published in a greater number of journals than could have been imagined twenty years ago. Dennis Tourish looks beneath the surface of this progress to expose a field in crisis, and in need of radical reform. He identifies the ways in which management research has lost its way, including a remoteness from the practical problems that managers and employees face, a failure to replicate key research findings, poor writing, endless obscure theorizing, and an increasing number of research papers being retracted for fraud and other forms of malpractice. Tourish suggests fundamental changes to remedy these issues, enabling management research to become more robust, more interesting and more valuable to society. This is a must-read for academics, practising managers, university administrators and policy makers within higher education.

DENNIS TOURISH is Professor of Leadership and Organization Studies at the University of Sussex. He is editor of the journal *Leadership*, and is closely associated with the emerging area of critical leadership studies. His most recent authored book was *The Dark Side of Transformational Leadership: A Critical Perspective* (2013).

Management Studies in Crisis

Fraud, Deception and Meaningless Research

DENNIS TOURISH
University of Sussex

CAMBRIDGE
UNIVERSITY PRESS

CAMBRIDGE
UNIVERSITY PRESS

University Printing House, Cambridge CB2 8BS, United Kingdom

One Liberty Plaza, 20th Floor, New York, NY 10006, USA

477 Williamstown Road, Port Melbourne, VIC 3207, Australia

314-321, 3rd Floor, Plot 3, Splendor Forum, Jasola District Centre, New Delhi - 110025, India

79 Anson Road, #06-04/06, Singapore 079906

Cambridge University Press is part of the University of Cambridge.

It furthers the University's mission by disseminating knowledge in the pursuit of education, learning and research at the highest international levels of excellence.

www.cambridge.org
Information on this title: www.cambridge.org/9781108480475
DOI: 10.1017/9781108616669

First published 2019

A catalogue record for this publication is available from the British Library

Library of Congress Cataloging in Publication data
Names: Tourish, Dennis, author.
Title: Management studies in crisis : fraud, deception and meaningless research / Dennis Tourish, University of Sussex.
Description: Cambridge, United Kingdom ; New York, NY : Cambridge University Press, 2019. | Includes bibliographical references.
Identifiers: LCCN 2018055111 | ISBN 9781108480475 (hardback)
Subjects: LCSH: Management – Research – Evaluation. | Management – Study and teaching. | Research – Moral and ethical aspects.
Classification: LCC HD30.4 .T68 2019 | DDC 658.0072–dc23
LC record available at https://lccn.loc.gov/2018055111

ISBN 978-1-108-48047-5 Hardback
ISBN 978-1-108-72748-8 Paperback

This book is dedicated to my wife, Naheed Tourish. I am eternally grateful for all her love, support and understanding as I worked on this book. Her presence in my life makes everything possible.

Contents

Tables

Acknowledgements

I owe a debt to Professor Russell Craig, whose collaboration and friendship over many years has been stimulating, productive and, above all, fun. Some of the chapters that follow have their origins in papers that I co-wrote with him. In addition, Russell patiently read several others, and always offered invaluable feedback and criticism. I am also indebted to my good friend Professor Paul Robson, for his expert insights into statistics.

Introduction: the Crisis in Management Studies

I moved to Australia from Northern Ireland in 1999, to work in one of the country's leading business schools. Moving continents was a challenge. But it also involved relocating from the social science discipline of communication and into the new and unfamiliar world of management studies. In truth, both were nerve-shredding prospects. Yet this book has its origins in a conversation that took place during my time in Australia.

My colleagues and I were visited by a senior management academic from the USA for the usual research seminar, lunch and debate. Over coffee, talk turned to the state of research. Our visitor remarked casually, as if stating a well-known fact: 'Of course, most management research is rubbish.' Everyone laughed, although a little nervously. The view seemed to be that he was quite right, but he was saying things that shouldn't be said in sophisticated company, like someone who blurts out a preference for the bagpipes rather than opera. I remember feeling shocked at his nonchalance. It is a feeling that has long since worn off.

I have grown increasingly alarmed at the state of management research, the unreadability of our journals, the triviality of the topics that they mostly address, and the importance of the many issues that they ignore. As John Mingers reported in 2015:

> A very quick check in *Web of Science* (WoS) shows that out of 115,000 papers in management ... published since 1990 only 328 (0.28 percent) were concerned with climate change, and that out of 222,500 papers in management, business and finance only 292 (0.13 percent) were concerned with the financial crises. Interestingly, the first paper on this subject was not published until

2008 (it was the only one in that year) which shows how little foresight there was before the actual events happened.[1]

If this isn't a crisis, I don't know what is. It is also astonishing and disgraceful. To this day, none of the major journals issued by the Academy of Management have published a substantive paper dealing with the Great Recession of 2008. Remarkably enough, even top finance journals have published very little serious work examining the 2008 crisis, and the type of research that they publish remains pretty much as it was before the crash.[2] Perhaps what happened just wasn't important enough to discuss. Yet there is scant evidence that the banking and finance systems have been radically reformed. This offers the appalling prospect that another financial crisis is a matter of when rather than if. The consequences could be even more cata-strophic, economically, socially and politically. In largely ignoring these issues, both mainstream and critically oriented management scholars have shown a diligent spirit of due negligence.

This sort of problem has been long recognised but still endures. Bill Starbuck complained as far back as 2003 that 'few organization theorists have focused on connections between organizations and social problems, although long-standing social problems persist and new ones appear'.[3] From his perspective, it follows that 'Organization theory can and should contribute more to human welfare. Efforts to make such contributions can inject vitality into organization theory as well as benefit our neighbors, our societies, and people far away.' Yet management scholars seem to engage with bigger issues in the same spirit that many of us approach visiting the dentist. We know that it is good for us and we know that we should. But we really don't want to do it. Why is this? It is a question I return to throughout this book.

Concerns of this kind are now widespread, and are increasingly articulated in our journals. For example, Bill Harley writes of what he terms 'an emerging crisis of confidence in management studies'. He goes on to say: 'Why might management scholars feel that their research and publishing activities were unsatisfying or even meaningless? To put it bluntly, this is a completely reasonable response to the fact that most of the research and publishing that most of us do has little or no impact.'[4]

In addition, many of our papers seem to be written by sadists who enjoy inflicting pain on masochists. To take a random example from the *Academy of Management Journal*, I find a paper entitled 'When does Medici hurt da Vinci? Mitigating the signaling effect of extraneous stakeholder relationships in the field of cultural production'.[5] Good luck to anyone trying to figure out what this is about from its title. Soldiering on through its abstract I find the following:

> We ... confirm that the salience of the relationship with extraneous stakeholders – operationalized as the number of corporate donors – has a negative effect on peer recognition ... We contribute to both the institutional logics perspective and stakeholder literatures by bringing in a signalling perspective: we show that peer recognition, upon which the maintenance of a dominant logic lies, is directly impacted by the nature of relationships with extraneous stakeholders.

And so on. This paper has value and even contains some lucid passages. But its abstract is the main part that most people will read. Why does it have to be written in such a way that only those already on the inside of the debates it refers to can understand it?

It has also become evident that various forms of research malpractice are common in our field. I discuss these throughout this book. I am talking about outright fraud such as inventing data, but also about plagiarism, self-plagiarism, poor-quality statistical analysis and *p*-hacking. The last-named involves such practices as dropping variables from analysis, terminating a study before it is completed, and 'rounding off' numbers obtained from statistical tests in order to obtain results that are statistically significant. The number of retractions in our field as a result of these practices is rising, while the volume of papers making extravagant claims that may be fatally flawed is also growing.

I offer one example of the latter from psychology. This is an adjacent discipline to management. Many of its findings have implications for management practice as well as theory, and our journals often overlap in the topics that they address. In 2010, Amy Cuddy was an upcoming scholar at Harvard Business School. With two colleagues, she published a paper entitled 'Power posing: brief nonverbal displays affect neuroendocrine levels and risk tolerance'.[6] The paper proposed that 'a person can, by assuming two simple 1-min poses, embody power and instantly become more powerful'. By adopting a particular posture that imitates power you seem more powerful to yourself and others. The researchers summarised some of the effects as follows: 'Results of this study confirmed our prediction that posing in high-power nonverbal displays (as opposed to low-power nonverbal displays) would cause neuroendocrine and behavioral changes for both male and female participants: High-power posers experienced elevations in testosterone, decreases in cortisol, and increased feelings of power and tolerance for risk; low-power posers exhibited the opposite pattern.' As they noted, this 'has real-world, actionable implications'.[7] I can, for example, imagine significant implications for leadership research and leadership development programmes.

Others thought likewise. Cuddy went on to do a TED talk that has become one of the most watched ever.[8] In 2014 the *New York Times* published an article about her work that reads like the profile of a Hollywood movie star. It reported that she 'has attracted lucrative speaking invitations from around the world, a contract from Little, Brown & Co. for a book to be published next year, and an eclectic army of posture-conscious followers'. According to the article, the implications of her work are boundless. It claimed that 'Elementary school students, retirees, elite athletes, surgeons, politicians, victims of bullying and sexual assault, beleaguered refugees, people dealing with mental illness or physical limitations (including a quadriplegic): they have all written to say that adopting a confident pose – or simply

THE CRISIS IN MANAGEMENT STUDIES 5

visualizing one, as in that last case – delivers almost instant self-assurance.' The article includes a picture captioned 'Amy Cuddy strikes a winning pose outside her Harvard office'.[9] Her book was duly published in 2015 and garnered glowing reviews from readers on Amazon's website. Its title, *Presence: Bringing Your Boldest Self to Your Biggest Challenges*, chimes with the positive psychology movement.[10] This seeks to convince us that if we only developed the right mental attitude then many of our problems would disappear.

There is only one slight problem. The study that led to all this exposure was replicated by another team of researchers with a sample five times bigger than the original.[11] It did not find any of the effects that had been claimed. Yet, as Andrew Gelman and Kaiser Fung reported in 2016, the original findings continue to be widely publicised by the mass media.[12] By comparison, the failed replication has been virtually ignored.

Now, there may be many reasons for this failure, and no one has suggested that the original findings were faked. Researchers, like everyone else, like to show that their hunches are correct. We seek out evidence that confirms them and downplay the importance of evidence that does not. Perhaps further work will vindicate the original claims that were made. But it is clear that academic careers can be enormously advanced when people make what appear to be ground-breaking claims that also appeal to a media on the lookout for the latest sensational 'discoveries'. How many such claims rest on inadequate sample sizes, insufficiently rigorous analyses, over-hyping by authors keen to make an impact, and on occasion outright fraud? It is questions like these that led me to write the book you are now reading.

In Chapter 1, I look at the historical roots of some of these issues. In my view, there never was a 'golden age' of management research to which we can return. Many of our current problems were there from the outset, in one form or another. However, the never-ending processes of measurement and audit that now infect universities have made all these problems worse, as well as adding some new ones to keep them company. I examine these dynamics in Chapter 2.

The effects on the quality of academic life are severe, as I outline in Chapter 3. In Chapter 4 I discuss the different forms of research misconduct and malpractice that can be found throughout academic research, and in Chapter 5 look in detail at how these are manifest in management studies.

A particular problem within management studies is that much of our research is far too preoccupied with creating the illusion of theory development, much of which is pretentious nonsense. I discuss this in Chapter 6, and in Chapter 7 illustrate it in depth by looking at an example of so-called 'theory development' in leadership studies. Some prominent researchers, such as Denise Rousseau and Jeffrey Pfeffer, have argued that one answer to the problem of irrelevance in management research is what they have termed 'evidence-based management'. Chapter 8 offers my take on this suggestion, and in particular argues that the poor state of management research makes it problematic. As computer scientists have long delighted in telling us, garbage in equals garbage out (GIGO). In Chapter 9 I suggest that our research should make a greater effort to address important issues, and offer some examples of what these could be. Lastly, I look in Chapter 10 at what we can do individually and collectively to reclaim traditional academic values of disinterested inquiry, and commit ourselves to doing research with a greater purpose than publication for its own sake.

I should also say that I am not putting myself forward here as a paragon of virtue. I have committed many of the faults discussed in this book, including poor writing and wasting time on topics that I should have ignored. In a sinful world, none of us are entirely free from sin. Nor do I want this book to be just a series of complaints. I offer suggestions throughout about what we can do to move forward. My premise, fundamentally, is that the world faces major challenges across numerous issues. Many of these are organisational. How can we respond to the introduction of new technologies that are transforming the nature of work? How should we deal with the changing culture within universities, where academics are pressurised more than ever to produce at least the appearance of ground-breaking research? They are rewarded handsomely if they do and penalised if they don't – a classic incentive for misconduct. What is the purpose of universities generally and business schools in particular in this ever-changing world that we inhabit?

It is my belief that management scholars can make important contributions to these issues. At present, we generally don't. Most managers don't read our research and most of the public is unaware that it even exists. Their instincts are sound. Turning this around is of course in our own interests. More importantly, we are missing tremendous opportunities to influence debate around us on a range of exciting, terrifying and important questions. Is the current state of affairs really what we want? Is it the best that we can do?

In the hope that your answer to both these questions is 'No', I offer the book that follows.

I Flawed from the Get-Go: the Early Misadventures of Management Research

INTRODUCTION

In this chapter, I outline two main arguments. Delving into our history, and particularly the work of Frederick Taylor that led to scientific management and the famous Hawthorne Studies that laid the foundations for the human relations school, I argue that many of the problems now confounding management research were present from the origins of the discipline. These include poorly designed studies, an extravagant tendency to generalise from small samples to a population consisting of everyone who has a job (everywhere in the world), and a blatantly political agenda that obscures issues of power and so serves dominant interests. This is not a purely historical exercise. Rather, it illuminates the weak foundations on which much of our scholarship rests and reveals the extent of the challenges we face if we really wish to do better.

Second, I address the vexed issue of the relevance and rigour of our research.[1] Ever since the key Ford and Carnegie Foundation reports on American business schools in the late 1950s, management researchers have been fixated on rigour, particularly in terms of quantitative studies.[2] Arguably, much that passed for management research before then was high in relevance. It consisted largely of reports by practitioners in the few journals then generally available to them. But it lacked theoretical or methodological sophistication and was as likely to be wrong as it was to be right. This needed fixing. That said, we have now reached an opposite extreme in which only a handful of devotees can understand most of our ideas, and fewer still can find any application for them beyond academic conferences and journals. Establishing why this is the case tells us troubling truths about our research and raises fundamental issues about what business schools are and, more importantly, about what they should become.

THE LEGEND OF BETHLEHEM IRON COMPANY AND THE RIGOURS OF SCIENTIFIC MANAGEMENT

People are fond of origin stories. These are embellished in folklore, fantasies and myths. So it is with management studies. The generally accepted picture is that in The Beginning was The Word, and that word was Scientific Management. This is, of course, associated with the work of Frederick Taylor and his 1911 book *The Principles of Scientific Management*.[3] A review of Taylor's life and work in *The Oxford Handbook of Management Theorists* by Robert Conti rightly notes that Taylor 'evokes the most emotional and polarized responses of any management theorist. He is both revered and reviled.'[4] Revered, because he appeared to produce a systematic account of how management could maximise productivity and thus profits; reviled, because it is said that in doing so he reduced workers to the status of mechanical body parts whose emotional and social needs could be disregarded. It is this deficiency that the human relations school purported to fix.

In essence, Taylorism relied on measuring the amount of time required to carry out particular pieces of work. This enabled managers to match the capabilities of workers to the needs of the job. Management and workers, Taylor suggested, were on the same side, even if, like squabbling siblings, they sometimes failed to recognise it. Scientific management's influence today can be seen in the ongoing attention to efficiency and in associated attempts to overcome employee resistance to the multitudinous change programmes that regularly sweep through corporations.

Himself an engineer who had forgone the opportunity to attend Harvard, instead becoming an apprentice patternmaker and machinist, Taylor identified 'soldiering' as a problem early in his career. This was the restriction of output by workers, enforced through peer pressure. In his words, it was 'the greatest evil with which the working-people of both England and America are afflicted'.[5] It is perhaps obvious why workers acted in this way. Increased productivity could lead to job losses and did not necessarily earn higher pay. Taylor therefore advocated incentive systems. But managers often reduced the rate per piece of work when wages rose, frustrating the intention. Overcoming these obstacles was Taylor's lifelong mission.

The archetypical image of Taylorism is of a factory assembly line, where a vast army of human robots mechanically repeat the same task to maximise efficiency. It has been endlessly parodied, including by Charlie Chaplin in his classic movie *Modern Times*. The US TV series *I Love Lucy* also did so in a famous skit where Lucille Ball and her friend work on a chocolate assembly line. Their job is to wrap each chocolate as it whizzes past. As they start, their supervisor yells that they will be fired if even one chocolate slips by unwrapped. At first all goes well. Then the line speeds up, forcing them to eat pieces of chocolate and frantically conceal others in their hats and pockets. When the supervisor reappears, she tells them that they are doing splendidly – and shouts for the line to be speeded up yet further.[6]

One study was central to Taylor's claims to have established a new way of thinking about management. In 1899, he and some colleagues studied how pig-iron bars were being loaded on to rail cars at the Bethlehem Iron Company. Taylor claimed that they studied seventy-five men for several days, and then picked a handful who seemed physically up to the task of loading greater volumes of pig-iron. Chief among them was Henry Noll, whom Taylor called 'Schmidt'. Carefully designed rest periods were factored into the experiment and helped improve productivity. Schmidt was central, and Taylor reports this infamous version of an early dialogue with him. I have edited it here for length:

> 'Schmidt, are you a high-priced man?'
> 'Vell, I don't know vat you mean ... '
> 'Oh, come now, you answer my questions. What I want to find out is whether you are a high-priced man or one of these cheap fellows

here. What I want to find out is whether you want to earn $1.85 a day or whether you are satisfied with $1.15, just the same as all those cheap fellows are getting.'

'Did I vant $1.85 a day? Vas dot a high-priced man? Vell, yes, I vas a high-priced man.'

'Oh, you're aggravating me. Of course you want $1.85 a day— every one wants it! You know perfectly well that that has very little to do with your being a high-priced man. For goodness' sake answer my questions, and don't waste any more of my time. Now come over here. You see that pile of pig iron? ... Well, if you are a high-priced man, you will load that pig iron on that car tomorrow for $1.85. Now do wake up and answer my question. Tell me whether you are a high-priced man or not.'

'Vell, did I got $1.85 for loading dot pig iron on dot car to-morrow?'

'Yes, of course you do, and you get $1.85 for loading a pile like that every day right through the year. That is what a high-priced man does, and you know it just as well as I do.'

'Vell, dot's all right. I could load dot pig iron on the car to-morrow for $1.85, and I get it every day, don't I?'

'Certainly you do – certainly you do.'

'Vell, den, I vas a high-priced man.'

'Now, hold on, hold on. You know just as well as I do that a high-priced man has to do exactly as he's told from morning till night ... Well, if you are a high-priced man, you will do exactly as this man tells you tomorrow, from morning till night. When he tells you to pick up a pig and walk, you pick it up and you walk, and when he tells you to sit down and rest, you sit down. You do that right straight through the day ... Now a high-priced man does just what he's told to do, and no back talk. Do you understand that? When this man tells you to walk, you walk; when he tells you to sit down, you sit down, and you don't talk back at him.'[7]

Taylor seemed to view Schmidt as a semi-imbecile. Their reported dialogue drips with condescension. Schmidt is little more than a beast of burden, to be manipulated by his betters in pursuit of an aim whose importance and virtue is assumed to be self-evident – loading more pig-iron. Taylor himself remarked:

> This seems to be rather rough talk. And indeed it would be if applied to an educated mechanic, or even an intelligent laborer. With a man of the mentally sluggish type of Schmidt it is appropriate and not unkind, since it is effective in fixing his attention on the high wages which he wants and away from what, if it were called to his attention, he probably would consider impossibly hard work.[8]

Schmidt is here reduced to a childlike status that as, Bill Cooke argues, bears comparison to the relationship between slaves and their masters in the old American South.[9] And, indeed, Taylor proposes a similar division between those who can plan and think and those who actually do the hard graft of heavy lifting. In his view, the job required little more than a combination of brute force and ignorance: 'The work is so crude and elementary that the writer firmly believes that it would be possible to train an intelligent gorilla so as to become a more efficient pig-iron handler than any man can be.'[10] He later returned to this theme, explaining in detail what attributes were needed in someone able to do the job:

> [He] shall be so stupid and so phlegmatic that he more nearly resembles in his mental make-up the ox rather than any other type . . . He is so stupid that the word 'percentage' has no meaning to him, and he must consequently be trained by a man more intelligent than himself into the habit of working in accordance with the laws of this science before he can be successful.[11]

Taylor's system therefore separated management from workers. It put all control of the labour process in the hands of the former and sought to ensure that a worker had no more knowledge or skill than was needed to perform the particular task which scientific management had allocated him.[12] The assumption seemed to be that although both sides had a unitarist interest, nevertheless workers had an intrinsic interest in getting the maximum rate of pay for the minimum amount of work, while management had an intrinsic interest in securing the greatest amount of work for the minimum amount of pay. This circle has never been squared. It puts management and labour on a collision course. Speaking many years after the event, to a special committee of the US House of Representatives, Taylor testified that his first attempts as a 'gang boss' to increase output and establish piecework led to a battle that lasted three years.[13] Compulsion was thus hard-wired into his system: 'It is only through *enforced* standardization of methods, *enforced* adoption of the best implements and working conditions, and *enforced* cooperation that this faster work can be assured. And the duty of enforcing the adoption of standards and enforcing this cooperation rests with *management* alone.'[14]

This approach implied a vast expansion in surveillance and in the managerial class needed to administer it. Here Taylor describes how pig-iron was loaded and the manner in which rest periods were prescribed:

> Schmidt started to work, and all day long, and at regular intervals, was told by the man who stood over him with a stop watch, 'Now pick up a pig and walk. Now sit down and rest. Now walk – now rest', etc. He worked when he was told to work, and rested when he was told to rest.[15]

Taylor assumed the interests of all these managers would align naturally with those of owners. But the Roman expression *Quis custodiet ipsos custodes*? ('Who will guard the guardians?') comes to mind. Managers, it turned out, had their own set of interests and didn't hesitate to advance them. There is no escape from the law of unintended consequences. James Burnham's *The Managerial Revolution*, published in 1941 and hugely influential in its day, reflected the apocalyptic nature of the times and the widespread fear that everything which had previously appeared everlasting, such as capitalism and democracy, were collapsing into ruin.[16] Burnham foresaw their end, but in predicting that the new class of managers would assume power he was also acknowledging the growth of their status, authority and numbers. Sovereignty, he argued, was slipping from parliaments and representative institutions generally, and into the hands of a new managerial class who would reshape the world in their own interests. Leaving aside the specifics of Burnham's prophecy (capitalism and its institutions proved much more resilient than anyone at that time could have imagined), the problem of containing the power of managers still preoccupies us today.

It is no surprise that the most important thing, from Taylor's standpoint, was that Schmidt and his co-workers were able to increase the amount of pig-iron they loaded from 12 tons to over 47 in each shift. Schmidt, Taylor suggested, exceeded even this on some shifts. Taylor also claimed that he sought outside workers to come and join his efforts at the Bethlehem plant, helped by coverage in local newspapers. The story of Schmidt is now the stuff of legend, retold in countless textbooks and discussed in classrooms throughout the world for many decades. But, as Charles Wrege and Amedeo Perroni point out, the killer is that it is 'more fiction than fact', to the extent that some of its key ingredients are little more than falsification.[17]

Taylor was an enthusiastic salesman for his ideas, and as he retold them for different audiences he embellished the stories on which they were based. The Bethlehem Iron Company certainly existed, as did 'Schmidt'. But much of the rest is fantasy. Rather than Schmidt and others being carefully selected, it appears that there was widespread opposition to any kind of piecework. No story about the plant or Taylor appeared at the time in local newspapers, and the carefully calibrated rest periods that he described didn't exist. Rather, when men walked back empty-handed after loading pig-iron their walk was regarded as a rest period. It seems that there never were seventy-five men carrying pig-iron whose work could be observed. Rather, there were a couple of dozen who did this and other work as needed. From this group Taylor selected some large Hungarian workers, on the scientific basis that they looked strong. Initially keen to impress, they managed to shift 16.5 tons in double-quick time. Their work rate would have equated to 71 tons over a ten-hour day, but Taylor rounded this up to 75 tons, figured that such sustained work was impossible, and reduced the target by 40 per cent. This is a scientific process known by experts as 'conjuring figures out of thin air'.

Even so, as Matthew Stewart puts it, 'To have suggested that the workers could sustain such a rate throughout the day, every day of their pig-iron lifting careers . . . would have been as fatuous as estimating a marathon runner's time by extrapolating from the results of a 100-meter dash.'[18] No wonder that the Hungarians revolted when they realised that they might be expected to keep working at this rate indefinitely. Some random 'volunteers' then emerged. One senses that Taylor and his associates would at this stage have gratefully involved anyone whose knuckles cleared the ground. In all probability, the much-reported dialogue between Taylor and Schmidt was invented. Several of this new group dropped out in exhaustion, leaving Schmidt to carry the flame for scientific management. All this rather takes the shine off the massive improvements that Taylor claimed his approach had created.

It seems that the guru of scientific management had a footloose relationship with facts. He was determined not to let them stand in the way of a good story. I am reminded of John Ford's classic Western, *The Man Who Shot Liberty Valance*. James Stewart plays Ranse Stoddard, a US senator who may yet become vice-president and whose reputation rests on having killed the outlaw Valance. In a long interview with a newspaper reporter, where events are depicted in flashback, Stewart reveals that Valance was actually shot by Tom Doniphon, played by John Wayne. The reporter famously ends the interview by throwing his notes into the fire and says: 'This is the West, sir. When the legend becomes fact, print the legend.' Taylor pocketed his generous consulting fees, and determined to do precisely that.

Is management scholarship shot through with a similar 'creative' mentality? It is surely fortunate that we can turn to the Hawthorne Studies for reassurance. Or is it?

THE HAWTHORNE STUDIES: A DREADFUL WARNING, OR AN EXAMPLE TO FOLLOW?

Elton Mayo, the man most associated with the Hawthorne Studies, was a self-publicist in search of a convincing story to publicise. Born in Australia, he flunked out of three medical schools but passed up on every opportunity to correct the impression that he possessed a medical degree. So far as I can see, his only true degree was a BA in psychology and philosophy from the University of Adelaide; his one higher degree was an honorary MA obtained from the University of Queensland, where he at one time lectured. But it is his time in the US, where he moved in 1922, that sets the scene for the Hawthorne Studies and their importance in the field of management research.

Mayo's career would be unimaginable today. Possessing little more than charm and a letter of endorsement from Australia's prime minister, he had an uncanny ability to convince benefactors, business-men and politicians that he was uniquely deserving of their support. He persuaded John D. Rockefeller to himself finance Mayo's appointment at the Wharton School in 1923, in the face of opposition from the trustees of the fund Rockefeller had set up in his mother's name to 'improve the well-being of humanity around the world'. In 1926 Mayo moved to Harvard, personally recruited by the business school's second dean, Wallace Donham. Again, there was considerable opposition. Once more Mayo's Fairy Godmother, the Rockefeller Foundation, came to his rescue. It agreed to underwrite the costs of his appointment for a period of four years with the possibility of more to come.

Context is everything: without taking it into account, much about the impact of the Hawthorne Studies and the willingness of Rockefeller to bankroll them would be unfathomable. Strikes were widespread. Four million American workers went on strike in 1919. There was a general strike in Canada. Boston police also went on strike, inflation was rampant, and an influenza pandemic that killed millions contributed to widespread panic about the future of civilisa-tion. Mayo had dabbled in psychoanalysis and now applied this approach to industrial strife. Writing in 1922, he argued that 'It may be that wages and working conditions are not the real question at issue, but some dissatisfaction that is concealed within the "twilight" areas of the human mind.' It followed that

> 'industrial unrest' is not caused by mere dissatisfaction with wages and working conditions, but by the fact that a conscious dissatisfaction serves to 'light up', as it were, the hidden fires of mental uncontrol. Passionate emotions run wildly through the industrial group; tales of capitalistic conspiracy are eagerly accepted, and dispassionate logic is contemptuously spurned.[19]

Resentment on the part of workers is depicted here as an irrational pathology that required treatment and rendered them 'unfit for "voice" in the workplace'.[20] The possibility that managers might sometimes act irrationally is not considered. This is a powerful ideological argument. To my mind, it has echoes of a disease diagnosed by the US physician Samuel Cartwright in 1851. This was drapetomania, a term derived from conjoining two Greek words meaning 'a runaway slave' and 'mad' or 'crazy'.[21] Its main symptom was an irrational desire on the part of slaves to escape from their masters. Cartwright, like many of his contemporaries, believed that the Bible sanctioned slavery. It reflected the notion that blacks were inferior to whites. Freedom would only make them miserable. As Cartwright wrote, in terms that Mayo would surely have recognised: 'The "cure" for drapetomania was a firm, kindly master, who provided decent necessities and a structured work environment.' If this failed to subdue slaves' spirit of revolt,

> humanity and their own good require that they should be punished until they fall into that submissive state which it was intended for them to occupy in all after-time, when their progenitor received the name of Canaan or 'submissive knee-bender'. They have only to be kept in that state and treated like children, with care, kindness, attention and humanity, to prevent and cure them from running away.[22]

From the standpoint of power, what's not to like? As John Van Maanen puts it:

> What could be more attractive to owners and managers than to be repeatedly told that one's employees or direct reports are really irrational and illogical; that their lack of cooperation is but a frustrated urge to cooperate; that their economic wants mask a need to be consulted and listened to in the workplace; that these needs are best met by a more or less therapeutic regime that pays close attention to the social and emotional needs of employees; and that you – as owner or manager – are charged with a historical mandate (or destiny) to bring social harmony to the workplace?[23]

Elton Mayo now had a theory. All he needed was some evidence to back it up. Enter Hawthorne.

The Hawthorne Works factory in Cicero, Illinois, was run by Western Electric. Initially, the company commissioned a study into the effects of illumination guided by a simple technocratic question: does better lighting increase productivity? The claimed results still echo in our textbooks and remain a cause of wonder. Whether the lighting was raised or lowered, productivity went up, reinforcing the view that simply paying attention to people, even remotely, was what mattered in improving productivity. How marvellous. Perhaps improving productivity would not be such a hard task after all.

Mayo's own direct involvement in the Hawthorne experiment was minimal. In 1928 and 1929 he spent a total of six days at the site of the experiments, busying himself in the interim with securing funding and appointing and managing his research associates. Two of them, Fritz Roethlisberger and William Dickson, published the key account of the study in 1939.[24] Mayo himself published a short book in 1933 that devoted two chapters to Hawthorne. Together, these books report five stages of the study conducted between 1927 and 1932. After that, the Depression led to the suspension of the research and the investigators had to pack up and go home. They took with them a mountainous volume of data and, it seems, an even greater volume of half-baked speculations to assist in their analysis.

Stage 1 of the studies rested on a two-year study of five women assembling telephone relays. The workers were separated from the rest of the factory and received special attention from both the experimenters and the management of the plant. Their rest periods also permitted greater than usual social interaction among themselves. It was, so the experimenters claimed, these social conditions that explained the increases in production that they breathlessly reported. Roethlisberger and Dickson's chief conclusion, popularised in numerous management textbooks ever since, was that 'none of the results give the slightest substantiation to the theory that the worker is primarily motivated by economic interest. The evidence indicated that the efficacy of a wage incentive is so dependent on its relation to other factors that it is impossible to separate it out as a thing in itself having an independent effect.'

But problems with this interpretation are boundless. Consider that only five women were involved. Even this is an exaggeration. Elton Mayo's own account discloses that 'the work of numbers one and five shows a pronounced irregularity which at no time characterises the work of numbers two, three and four'.[25] It seems that the 'pronounced irregularity' consisted largely of 'excessive' talking, on such topics as movies, boyfriends and clothes. 'One' and 'five' were replaced by two more compliant workers who behaved much more as the experimenters expected them to, and the disconfirming data from the others were discarded.[26] This selective approach is a preposterous basis on which to claim anything, let alone to suggest that such findings can be applied to virtually all work situations in the world. Mayo's justification for keeping the group small is also fatuous. It was that 'changes were more likely to be noticed by the official observers if the group were small'.[27] That this would render the sample size insignificant and invalidate any generalisations he made does not seem to have occurred to him.

It is now known that an experimenter's expectations help to produce anticipated effects.[28] Recall the phenomenon of Hans 'the talking horse'. He acquired fame in early-twentieth-century Berlin by being able to count. His ability extended to solving maths problems such as 'What is the sum of three plus two?' Hans signalled his answers by tapping numbers or letters with his hoof. Closer study revealed that he accomplished these miracles by responding to expressions on the face of his trainer.[29] When no one present knew the answers to the questions being posed, neither did Hans. Richard Gillespie's forensic analysis of the Hawthorne experiments makes it clear that this contaminating process was a key factor in the 'Hawthorne effect'.[30] Thus:

> Before each experimental stage was introduced, the workers met with ... experimenters ... where a discussion would be held regarding the progress of the tests to date, the factors affecting production, and whether the workers thought they could increase production despite the reduction of working hours through rests and a shorter day.

This is a violation of the most elementary experimental protocols. You have to wonder here who was experimenting on who. Of course, it can be argued that we shouldn't expect the level of sophistication we find in studies today compared to work carried out ninety and more years ago. This may be a valid argument. But it surely follows that neither should we treat the results of such studies with the veneration they have traditionally received.

Mayo's description of the women whose work showed a 'pronounced irregularity' is also noteworthy:

> [O]ne and five had been characterized from the first as 'nervous'. Their ages and experiences are widely different: number one was about forty years of age, a widow with two children both doing well at school, she has had five years' experience of splitting mica; number five is eighteen, unmarried, and lives at home, she is 'restrained by severe parental discipline, especially from her

mother' ... The older woman is intelligent and conscientious, reads and thinks of 'child-welfare', has few friends and is inordinately anxious about her children; in a word, she 'overthinks' her situation in true obsessive fashion.[31]

Even allowing for the norms of his time this is crass and demeaning stuff. Despite the humanistic halo attached to his image, Mayo did not seem to have a much higher opinion of working people than Frederick Taylor. Gerard Hanlon has criticised the simplistic view that scientific management and the human relations school were somehow 'opposites'. Rather, they shared the aim of subordinating the will of workers to whatever management deemed necessary in the interests of profitability. A disrespectful, even contemptuous, attitude to employees was hardwired into both. As Hanlon notes, each believed that 'the worker was incapable of managing because of his or her political, moral and character failings'.[32]

One of the earliest critical reviews of Hawthorne, published by Alex Carey in 1967, still remains one of its most powerful.[33] He points out that numerous changes occurred to the working conditions of the women involved throughout Stage 1 of the study. These included shorter hours, rest pauses, more friendly supervision and an incentive system. There was no control group with whom comparisons could be drawn. By the end of two years their productivity had gone up by 30 per cent. Among the most likely explanations of this were that rest pauses and/or new incentive systems had stimulated greater effort. Roethlisberger and Dickson consider these explanations, only to dismiss them on the questionable grounds that neither work curves nor medical examinations provided evidence for the presence of fatigue effects, and that the impact of social considerations and incentives made it impossible to establish whether rest pauses and incentives had any independent effects. Oddly enough, they did not apply the same logic to the effects of social situations. But then that would have invalidated their starting assumptions.

However, an even more fundamental flaw lies at the heart of the study. Let Alex Carey explain it for us. In Stage 3,

> To obtain the percentage increase to be attributed to each girl the investigators chose, for each girl, a 'peak' output period within the study period and measured her increase as the difference between this peak and her output rate at the outset of the study. These peaks occur at different rates for different girls. To secure the 15 percent increase that is claimed, the study is, in effect, terminated at different conveniently selected dates for different girls. There is no one period over which the group achieved the 15 per cent average increase claimed.[34]

This was a stunningly selective use of data. But, if anything, Carey's verdict may be too generous. Stephen Jones looked again in 1992 at the data for the employees' productivity. His conclusion is devastating:

> Relative to the week preceding the change, mean output falls slightly in the week of the change for each of the core group of workers on the narrow definition, but the pattern is mixed for the changes within the broad category. In both cases, however, the changes are numerically very small. For subsequent weeks, there is similarly no clear pattern, and the movement is once again slight. At conventional significance levels, one certainly could not reject the hypothesis that output had the same mean in each of the weeks surrounding the experimental change.[35]

It is also worth returning to the original 'illumination experiments' that stimulated the Hawthorne studies in the first place. Recall the finding that productivity improved whether lighting was turned up or down. But this conclusion may have rested on a misconception. Steven Levitt and John List reanalysed the data in the illumination experiments in 2011. They found that the lighting was only ever changed on Sundays when *there were no workers in the factory*. Productivity was then measured on Monday. As they report: 'The empirical fact is that productivity is higher on Mondays than

on Fridays and Saturdays. Output on Mondays is equally high, however, whether or not a lighting change occurs on that particular
Monday. Thus, researchers seemingly misinterpreted the day of
week effect with the Hawthorne effect.'[36]

This is a sorry saga by any measure, and in drawing it to a close
we should consider its wider implications for today. We are left with
little more than two banal insights. First, people carry their non-work
needs, such as the desire for respect, love and comradeship, into the
workplace with them. Second, if we are nice to people instead of rude
they feel better about themselves and may function more effectively.
Should we really be surprised by any of this? And do these propositions
warrant acclaim for the depth of the theorising and data collection
that led to them? Management research continues to couch obvious
points in convoluted language (see Chapter 6), and many of its preten-
sions to profundity are deflated when they are translated into everyday
language.

I also believe that we should give more weight to the political
and ideological assumptions that drove Mayo. I pointed out earlier
that he saw conflict as the product of irrational mind-sets, particularly
on the part of employees. As John Van Maanen puts it, 'That one can
be both highly rational and highly uncooperative was a non-sequitur
for Mayo.'[37] This unwarranted notion hobbles management theorising and distorts much of its empirical work even today, and it is time
our discipline outgrew it.

We need to be more sceptical of big claims and question the data
on which they purport to rest. Mayo and his colleagues kept their data
to themselves for many years, during which time their authenticity
and the reliability of their analysis were taken on trust. Fortunately,
a lot of the data survived for further inspection. But what if they
hadn't? I return to this problem in Chapter 5, where I argue that we
need much greater transparency with data than in the past. Like
Frederick Taylor, Elton Mayo had a creative relationship to empirical
evidence. His commitment to pre-existing theories also tainted his
analysis, leading him to confirm what he thought he already knew

rather than study the evidence dispassionately. These problems still bedevil our research today. In seeking to improve what we do, we may learn much more from the writings of both Taylor and Mayo than they ever intended.

RIGOUR AND RELEVANCE IN MANAGEMENT RESEARCH

All this begs a key question: what, really, is the point of management research? For most of the twentieth century this question was rarely asked because there was very little management research to think about. The Ford Foundation's report in 1959 was particularly scathing. It urged business schools to create 'a more stimulating intellectual atmosphere, to bring the less progressive faculty members up to date with the latest scientific literature and business practice in their own and related fields, and to generate the capacity and desire to ask more probing questions and to engage in more significant research'.[38] It went on to say:

> In many schools, no more than lip service is paid to the need for research. In those schools that emphasize undergraduate teaching, little time, energy, or resources are left for research activity ... many deans have little conception of what might be significant lines of research. To some, it is important only that enough of something be published to make a respectable list in the reports prepared for the central university administration.

Ouch. Publication outlets were also few. The *Academy of Management Journal* (*AMJ*) only began publishing in 1958, and *Administrative Science Quarterly* (*ASQ*) in 1956. The *Academy of Management Review* appeared as recently as 1976. The quality of some of these early efforts can be gleaned by looking at the first issue of *AMJ*. It contains an article entitled 'Executive decision making' by Richard Schmidt.[39] This tells us that 'Executives have, as part of their problem solving activities, the responsibility of making decisions.' It goes on:

The life cycle of the typical firm is marked by a series of problems. The question is: Why do problems arise? The answer lies in that all businesses are in some stage of growth. Growth implies positive, zero or negative change, either absolutely or relatively, or both. But growth is not automatic nor routine and because of this, problems arise and decisions must be made.

This may well be relevant. But it is hardly profound, and is certainly not rigorous. The paper consists of little more than statements of the blindingly obvious. Nor is my unflattering assessment only the benefit of hindsight. Such articles aroused disquiet even at the time they were published. The first issue of *ASQ* in 1956 carried an article by James Thompson entitled 'On building an administrative science'. He argued that:

> Much of our literature is lore, spelling out how a procedure or technique is carried out in current practice or proclaiming that 'this is the way to do it.' This material contains rather bold and often implicit assumptions about the relationships between the procedure or technique under consideration and other things which take place within the organization. This type of literature frequently asserts that a certain device is proper, i.e., gets desired results on the grounds that 'General Motors has it' or that the one hundred 'best-managed companies' use it. But ... any particular item ... may show a high correlation with 'success' when imbedded in one context but show a low correlation in a different context.[40]

The approach that Thompson criticised is still prevalent, and not just in popular books such as *In Search of Excellence*, written by Tom Peters and Robert Waterman in 1982.[41] Nevertheless, there was now a greater tendency to show that management studies could be rigorous, and could therefore develop compelling theories that would constitute a new science of organisations. Writing in 2007, Ken Starkey and Nick Tiratsoo stress the role of academics who joined business schools in the 1980s and 1990s with a background in other disciplines such as sociology and psychology. These had a

> growing interest in designing 'appropriate experiments', and much greater emphasis on quantification. Business school faculty now wrote what they termed 'papers', which, like those in the natural science journals, featured specialist language, and a rigidly prescribed format ... Older traditions, such as qualitative investigations of messy but real human situations, were increasingly viewed as inferior ... More and more articles involved the micro-analysis of obscure aspects of firm or management performance, while the study of broader controversies and pressing issues languished.[42]

This suggests that as the rigour of research improved, so its relevance to practitioners declined. Looking at the extent to which ideas from academia influence management practice, Jeffrey Pfeffer and Christina Fong concluded, in 2002, that 'less than one third of the tools and ideas that companies are paying money to implement came out of academia and those that originated in universities were used less often and were abandoned more often'.[43]

Increasingly, it seems, we write for ourselves and the micro-tribes with which we most closely identify. Our research is bland, pernickety and keen to avoid some of the biggest challenges that society faces. Here is the verdict from Anne Tsui, a former president of the Academy of Management:

> Around the ivory tower, an impenetrable wall keeps outsiders from accessing the mystery within. Many scientists in business schools either do not care or only pretend to care about the practical value of their work. Their research fills journal space and books that only other scientists working on the same esoteric problems can understand or read. Occupying the inner circle are the successful scholars whose work appears in the exclusive, mostly A-ranked journals. Neophytes admire them as definers of the theoretical and

methodological rigor. Junior scholars must follow their methods and standards or risk being rejected by the prestigious journals. Non-academic outsiders (managers and the public), though mystified by and even dissatisfied with what happens inside the ivory towers, do not have the scientific expertise to question why or to whom such research is valuable.[44]

Leaving aside the dubious proposition that staff who work in business schools are 'scientists', is more relevant research the answer? Donald Hambrick is among those who have argued that it is. Here is an extract from his 1993 presidential address to the Academy of Management:

> We must recognise that our responsibility is not to ourselves, but rather to the institutions around the world that are in dire need of improved management, as well as to those individuals who seek to be the most effective managers they possibly can be. It is time for us to break out of our closed loop. It is time for us to matter.[45]

To see what might be wrong with this, let us return to 'Executive decision making'. For all the changes to our scholarship that have occurred, there is one constant. Richard Schmidt aimed his counsel, of course, at managers – or, as he calls them, 'executives'. Naturally, these are always described as 'he'. But what is striking is the assumption that managers make all important decisions. There is no consideration of how to leverage the expertise of anyone outside the managerial cadre. Managers either already know everything about a problem, or can find out, and once they do will then be able to identify a way forward that others can implement. Frederick Taylor would have been delighted. The idea of relevance, here, suggests that what scholars publish should serve the immediate needs of managers, to help them make better decisions. It is a view that still dominates much of our research (see Chapter 8, on evidence-based management).

However, managers are themselves only one constituency within organisations and society. But what they do, and how our organisations function, thrive and fail, impacts on all of us. With due respect to Fredrick Taylor, other voices are entitled to a hearing. They also have important things to say.

Give the frantic nature of their jobs, managers understandably tend to be focused on immediate problems and priorities. Many look for 'best practices' that they can act on, and rarely pause to evaluate the evidence on which these are based.[46] We have had a proliferation of quack remedies masquerading as best practice. Recall business process reengineering, the wunderkind of 1990s management consulting.[47] It took off like a rocket. Even Peter Drucker, perhaps the most famous of all management writers, was quoted as saying that 'Reengineering is new, and it has to be done.'[48] Sadly, for all involved, it almost immediately plummeted back to earth like a dud firework. Eileen Shapiro memorably described the frenzy these crazes often unleash as 'Fad surfing in the boardroom'.[49] As Martin Kilduff and Mihaela Kelemen argue, if managers with this mind-set are accorded a central role in the research process it is likely that research will focus on short-run issues rather than deeper and perhaps more important processes.[50] It would certainly skew research in favour of asking some questions and ignoring others.

Consider, also, the difficulty of figuring out what knowledge really matters and what does not. This isn't always obvious. Chris Grey points out that much pure mathematics only found a practical application once computing was invented. He argues that 'the production of useless knowledge is a public good because it is the price to pay for the possibility of producing useful knowledge'.[51]

Much that appears to be useful knowledge also turns out to be either useless or harmful. There can be few better examples than the extent to which academics working in finance contributed to the Great Recession of 2008. Until then, as Mark Learmonth, Andy Lockett and Kevin Dowd have pointed out, the work of finance academics was widely viewed by practitioners as a shining example of useful research.[52] Collateralised debt obligations (CDOs) were heavily influenced by finance research. A key turning point was an academic paper written by David Li in 2000, unpromisingly entitled 'On default correlation: a copula function approach'.[53] This proposed a 'Gaussian copula' that, in principle, enabled a much wider range of investments than before to be priced accurately. By using it, CDOs could be used to pool assets safely into discrete tranches that were then sold on to investors. In theory, this spread and reduced risk, while enabling people who might not otherwise be able to obtain credit to do so. Thus was born the market for sub-prime mortgages. This was fantastic – until suddenly it wasn't. Rather than inoculate markets against excessive risk, it injected them with a virus that caused immense destruction. Stubbornly, markets did not behave in the way that the formula predicted. This might not be surprising, since the Gaussian copula appears to have confused correlation with causation, and assumed that what had happened before would be a reliable guide to the future.[54] For all the model's mathematical elegance, perhaps it resembled astrology more than astronomy. So much for the marriage between rigour and relevance, at least in this case.

Of course, one paper and one academic can't shoulder all the blame for the crash in 2008. Li's ideas would have had no impact unless they resonated deeply with those working in finance. Pangloss was a character in Voltaire's satire, *Candide*, distinguished by his indiscriminate sense of optimism, even when he himself catches syphilis. His rationale for this goes as follows: 'It was a thing unavoidable, a necessary ingredient in the best of worlds; for if Columbus had not in an island of America caught this disease, which contaminates the source of life, frequently even hinders generation, and which is evidently opposed to the great end of nature, we should have neither chocolate nor cochineal.' More famously, he declared that 'All is for the best, in the best of all possible worlds.' Brendan McSweeney points out that Panglossian assumptions about the economy were widely held in the run up to 2008.[55] Many economists (and politicians) spoke of what they called the 'Great Moderation'. This assumed that the global economy had become so stable and sophisticated that it was now free of volatility. But Li's work certainly stands out for encouraging a cavalier attitude to risk, since it seemed to show that the astute packaging of financial products meant that risk management no longer mattered much, if at all. In that sense, he and others greatly assisted the mood of hubris that swept through those leading and managing the sector. 'The real world' is still reeling from its effects.

How Close to Business Should We Get?

One solution to many of these problems, particularly the lack of relevance, is that management researchers should spend more time in 'the real world'. For example, they should share their expertise with organisations by consulting. I recall a conversation that I had with one of our field's best-known US scholars who has many thousands of citations to his credit. We were discussing how to access organisations for data. He advised me to overcome this problem through consulting. 'Promise them a benefit', he counselled. 'Then use the data for papers.' In like mode, Michael Tushman and Charles O'Reilly extol the value of 'executive education', arguing that it offers a 'way for faculty and doctoral students to develop relationships with practitioners that can enhance the veridicality of our research and improve our field's ability to teach material that is both rigorous and relevant'.[56]

Of course, there are advantages to these ideas. But there are also disadvantages. Over-reliance on consulting skews the questions that we ask in directions that favour the short-term interests of management: they want a 'benefit', and the sooner the better. Bonds formed through executive education, which can lead to consulting, also change mind-sets. These problems are manifest in much research, including published case studies. For example, Ken Starkey and Nick Tiratsoo examined case studies that won prizes from the European Case Clearing House between 1995 and 2004. They identified one hundred and eighty-three direct quotations in the texts. One hundred and seven were from senior managers, fifty were from other managers, one was from an employee, two were from customers and twenty-three were from other voices. As Starkey and Tiratsoo remark, 'adopting such an unbalanced research approach sets a poor example to students, who might well be persuaded that interviewing the CEO is sufficient to understand an entire organization'.[57] It sets a poor example to researchers as well, since it tilts their data sources and interpretive frameworks firmly in one direction, and one that can only have a partial take on events.

Consistent with this, Michel Antebey's ethnographic account of teaching at Harvard Business School shows how case studies translate into teaching guides for faculty that stress the actions of heroic individuals engaged in 'warlike' activities in pursuit of organisational success.[58] Ultimately, any discussion of rigour and relevance 'cannot be separated from the contexts in which such judgments are shaped, made and enacted'.[59] Similar problems run through many of the dubious interpretations that we discussed above in relation to 'scientific' management and the human relations school of Elton Mayo.

Academics can all too easily become paid advocates for corporate causes – guns for hire – rather than disinterested searchers for truth. Consider Craig Pirrong, professor of finance at Bauer College of Business in Houston at the time of writing. An article in the *New York Times* in 2013 noted his defence of financial speculators.[60] This included the direct lobbying of federal agencies over an extended period and the convening of seminars with traders and regulators. Plaintiffs made much of his research when they mounted lawsuits in 2011 that delayed blocks on speculation for two years. Throughout this time, he was paid as a 'research consultant' by the Chicago Mercantile Exchange, the Royal Bank of Scotland and other companies that speculate in energy. A coincidence? I doubt it. The *New York Times* piece gives many other examples of academics in similar positions. All insisted that the payments they received didn't influence their opinions. If this were true, we would need to rewrite the psychology textbooks. This showcases a disturbing version of 'relevance', and of how some business academics see their role in society. It is suffused with relevance – if by relevance we mean that our research should serve only those with most power, the largest offices and the deepest pockets. I think we can do better.

CONCLUSION

I believe that our research can and must engage with the real problems facing the world without becoming beholden to one sectional interest. Such engagement requires a broader conception of 'relevance' than simply asserting the need to become 'close' to practitioners. It raises questions about how we should decide which issues are important and which aren't, who we should think of as the audience for and beneficiaries of our research, and how we should balance the joys of pure theoretical inquiry with the need to influence the world around us. John Mingers suggests that a specifically critical realist framework can assist us to do so, and I think his argument is persuasive. Among his many useful suggestions is that research needs to be transdisciplinary, recognising how physical, biological, social and political mechanisms, to name just some, interact to produce unpredictable outcomes. It also needs to be multimethodological. But research also needs to be

> Critical and committed in recognising the unavoidable ethical and moral dimensions to all our decisions and actions, not hiding behind technocratic, managerialist or positivist arguments that they are somehow 'value-free', and aiming towards improving the world for all.[61]

It is impossible to justify an academy in which management researchers ignore pressing problems, fail to reach a broad audience, write only for each other, and see relevance exclusively in terms of how it serves one organisational constituency. Can it be a coincidence that this version of relevance often benefits those who advocate it, including financially? In bowing to it, we risk producing knowledge that is relevant but fragmented, sometimes dangerous, often short-termist and which ignores many issues of primary importance. As Karl Weick wisely notes:

Practitioners who chide academics for their naiveté regarding the 'real world' are sometimes people who want their real world to be treated as it were the real world. That is not the academic's job. The academic's job is to understand how an idiosyncratic individual world comes to be seen as a universal world and how vested interests work to convey this definition of universality. Then the job is to convey these fundamentals in ways that encourage people to speak up when the vested interests produce blind spots and to enact alternative vested interests.[62]

Management research also takes place within universities, and in improving it we must remind ourselves of what these are, how they arose and what values they defend. John Gardner wrote in 1968 that the university 'stands for things that are forgotten in the heat of battle, for values that get pushed aside in the rough-and-tumble of everyday living, for the goals we ought to be thinking about and never do, for the facts we don't like to face, and the questions we lack the courage to ask'.[63] This is a vision of disinterested inquiry in the purest sense. It means the pursuit of truth wherever it takes us, a willingness to challenge power and a desire to see professional and institutional advancement as a means to an end rather than an end in itself. When we lose sight of these values we become complicit in their erosion, and also lose sight of ourselves. By reaffirming them we defend academic integrity in the face of those forces that seek to undermine it. We might even remember what drove most of us to embrace an academic career in the first place.

2 How Audit Damages Research and Academic Freedom

Concern about the quality and purpose of research in the social sciences in general and management studies in particular is now widespread. In an editorial in *Organization Studies* published in 2013, David Courpasson, the departing editor-in-chief, bemoaned 'the lack of political and social relevance of much research conducted in the field'.[1] He argued that a culture of productivity had become dominant in which publishing for its own sake was more important than what he called 'passionate scholarship'. More and more published research is nonsense, badly written, long-winded, and of little or no appeal to the public. The result of all this, Mats Alvesson, Yiannis Gabriel and Roland Paulsen assert, is

> a widespread cynicism among academics on the merits of academic research, sometimes including their own. Publishing comes to be seen as a game of hit and miss, of targets and rankings, crucial for the fashioning of academic careers and institutional prestige but devoid of intrinsic meaning and value, and of no wider social uses whatsoever.[2]

In this chapter I relate these problems to our growing obsession with measuring, monitoring, auditing and ranking universities, business schools, journals and individual papers. It sometimes seems as if there are almost as many league tables as there are universities. Each university struggles to find a table in which it is number one for something, and often succeeds. Opening my copy of *Times Higher Education* for 22 February 2018, almost the first thing I see is a two-page advertisement from Queen's University, Belfast, which proclaims that it is 'Number One in the UK for Knowledge Transfer Partnerships'. Who knew? And, frankly, why should anyone care?

Accountability is a perfectly reasonable expectation of academics and universities. But we have graduated to a stage where the systems designed to ensure accountability have overwhelmed what we are trying to do. A report published by the Higher Education Funding Council in the UK in 2015 is tellingly entitled *The Metric Tide*.[3] Under the watchful eye of the audit culture, academics have grown fearful of asking big questions that take time to answer. The beast of measurement is always hungry. Feeding it becomes more important than contributing to society.

Here, I look at how we have reached this sorry state – and throughout this book consider what we can do about it.

THE GROWTH OF THE AUDIT CULTURE

Michael Power published a book entitled *The Audit Society: Rituals of Verification* in 1997.[4] Something in it obviously chimed with his audience. It now has over 7,500 citations on Google Scholar and has been in print ever since. Power discusses what he terms 'the audit explosion', and the anxieties unleashed by ccaseless attempts to measure, evaluate and tabulate every activity in which people are engaged. Vast bureaucracies have emerged charged with conducting these activities. But:

> the values and practices which make auditing possible penetrate deep into the core of organizational operations, not just in terms of requiring energy and resources to conform to new reporting demands but in the creation over time of new mentalities, new incentives and perceptions of significance ... audit processes may contribute to the construction of a new organizational actor.

Auditing is not a neutral gaze trained on what we do. It *transforms* the subject of its inquiry. Reflecting some time later on his original book, Power argued that the growth of auditing can lead 'to a decline of organizational trust ... The audit explosion is associated with elaborate games of compliance (e.g. the construction of public "consultation"), and ... defensive strategies and blamism ... that stifle organizational innovation ... and lower employee morale.'[5]

Senia Kalfa, Adrian Wilkinson and Paul Gollan give us a vivid example of how this happened in a regional Australian university that introduced performance appraisals. In line with the all-encompassing audit imperative, the appraisals evaluated staff on teaching and learning, research and research training, community engagement and service. Complex grading systems were introduced, in which being 'satisfactory' came to be seen as a synonym for failure. Kalfa and colleagues report a paradox. Most staff were opposed to the changes, but nevertheless complied with them. They saw themselves as engaging in a 'game' that they needed to play in order to safeguard their jobs. Resistance was rare and exit commonplace. Those who remained fought to 'build their capital within the new order' by conforming to it, thereby undermining collegiality and any prospect of collective resistance.[6] Using Bourdieu's metaphor of 'games', Kalfa et al. conclude that people playing the game can forget that they are doing so, and allow themselves to be (re)defined by the new rules that they have initially opposed. Eventually, these rules become naturalised and then reproduce themselves in ever more intrusive forms.

In further exploring why and how this happens, consider Foucault's writings on Bentham's panopticon, a prison environment that is ideal at least from the standpoint of its guards and managers. He describes its operations thus:

> [T]o induce in the inmate a state of conscious and permanent
> visibility that assures the automatic functioning of power. So to
> arrange things that the surveillance is permanent in its effects, even
> if it is discontinuous in its action; that the perfection of power
> should tend to render its actual exercise unnecessary; that this
> architectural apparatus should be a machine for creating and
> sustaining a power relation independent of the person who
> exercises it; in short, that the inmates should be caught up in
> a power situation of which they are themselves the bearers.

To achieve this, it is at once too much and too little that the prisoner should be constantly observed by an inspector: too little, for what matters is that he knows himself to be observed; too much, because he has no need in fact of being so. In view of this, Bentham laid down the principle that power should be visible and unverifiable. Visible: the inmate will constantly have before his eyes the tall outline of the central tower from which he is spied upon. Unverifiable: the inmate must never know whether he is being looked at any one moment; but he must be sure that he may always be so ... [The panopticon] is an important mechanism, for it automatizes and disindividualizes power.[7]

At least some of this characterises the feelings that many academics now have of being under constant surveillance, with assessments and audits either pending, happening or being autopsied. Simon Head, in a 2011 article entitled 'The grim threat to British universities', traces much of this to the influence of ideas developed at institutions such as Harvard Business School.[8] He singles out the notion of a Balanced Scoreboard (BSC) and its associated lexicon of Key Performance Indicators (KPIs). Developed by Robert Kaplan and David Norton, the idea of a Balanced Scoreboard (an innocuous enough title) swept through the world of business practice like a tsunami and then engulfed higher education. Kaplan and Norton's original article in *Harvard Business Review* was published in 1992 and has become one of its most influential articles ever.[9] At the time of writing it has almost 23,000 citations on Google Scholar. Its first sentence sets the tone: 'What you measure is what you get.'

Hanne Nørreklit aptly characterises the BSC as a 'tool of strategic control'.[10] In line with the neoliberal zeitgeist of the past few decades it subordinates professional autonomy to the rituals of inspection and the demands of competition and commercialisation.[11] Lawrence Busch argues that a central assumption of neoliberalism is that 'all government agencies, research and educational institutions, private voluntary organizations, and other institutions must be reconfigured and reshaped as markets and quasi-markets'.[12] This requires ever more intrusive forms of audit and measurement. It is assumed that such measurement represents accountability and progress. But, as Jerry Muller notes, the target-chasing mind-set that it unleashes actually 'replicates many of the intrinsic faults of the Soviet system'.[13] It has consequences that bedevilled and eventually collapsed the Soviet economy, as people do whatever it takes to meet the numbers, regardless of quality, and ignore other important issues in order to focus on whatever it is that is being measured. Universities have become the peculiar offspring of a forced marriage between neoliberalism and the Soviet command economy. No wonder that whatever sense of purpose once drove them has become so hideously deformed.

Nor do Kaplan and Norton consider how the people being balanced, measured and scored might feel about all this. Rather, we are promised that their scoreboard provides a series of measures that 'gives top managers a fast but comprehensive view of the business'.[14] Embraced by universities, the peculiar vocabulary of KPIs has contaminated much of academic life. The result, as Mats Alvesson and Andre Spicer note, is that 'What was once thought to be an institution with its own logic, rituals and administrative tradition has come to increasingly resemble any other (over)managed organization.'[15] As managerial power has increased, so has the temptation to resort to crude, bullying and toxic forms of control.[16] Language also shifts. Books and papers have become outputs (Memo to self: Remember that you are *producing an output*, not *writing a book*). These are churned out in ever-increasing quantities, often with the sole purpose of being evaluated, graded and forgotten in time for the next round of research assessment.

I turn now to one of the strongest manifestations of these processes – namely, an increased reliance on journal rankings and journal impact factors in managing (that is, controlling) how academics conduct their research and where they publish.

HOW JOURNAL RANKINGS, CITATION METRICS AND
IMPACT FACTORS DAMAGE SCHOLARSHIP

Journal rankings list journals which are in some way approved. This is then viewed as a proxy measure of article or faculty quality. Happy are those acclaimed by such systems, and misery is the lot of those awarded a badge of shame. The *Financial Times* (*FT*) lists fifty journals, and considers faculty publication in them as an important measure of MBA quality.[17] This is like determining the quality of a movie by considering the publications in which it is advertised. In addition, the methods used by the *FT* to compile its rankings are as transparent as the deliberations of a conclave of cardinals. No-one knows what goes on, and the *FT* isn't telling. But the effects are severe. Business schools that want to inflate the ranking of their MBA programmes routinely 'encourage' their faculty to prioritise publication in journals listed in the *FT* top fifty, regardless of whether they are appropriate for the work in question. Inclusion in the list also confers prestige on journals. Journal editors lobby frantically to be included, celebrate when they succeed, and grieve when they are de-listed.

Other systems assign rankings to individual journals. In the UK, the influential Association of Business Schools (ABS) journal rankings listed 1,582 journals in 2018, up from 1,402 in 2015.[18] It mimicked the scoring system used in the government's Research Excellence Framework to give an overall rating to individual journals, with the added bonus of a 4* category for 'journals of distinction'.[19] A similar approach is followed in the rankings produced by the Australian Business Deans Council.[20] This was first published in 2007 and revised in 2009, 2013 and 2016, with another overhaul currently under way.

Ranking systems have also been developed in South Africa and Mexico.[21] Many French business schools place value on the list published by the Centre National de la Recherche Scientifique, whose judgements overlap significantly with those of the ABS.[22] Tribbles were an initially adorable furry creature in *Star Trek* that proceeded to breed exponentially, causing mayhem throughout the starship

Enterprise as they clogged up vital systems, spilled out of air vents and devoured more and more of the crew's time and energy. Journal rankings seem to have similar reproductive properties, so much so that I am tempted to suggest that we need a new system to rank them. In due course, this could be developed into a further system – to rank the rankings of journal rankings, and so on. A whole new industry awaits us. While this happy day is still some way off, existing systems are increasingly appropriated within universities as a performative tool that pushes people to prioritise publication in a select band of supposedly elite journals. They have entered the bloodstream of academia, and their effects and side-effects dominate countless academic conversations. Which journal is in? Which one is out? How can we improve the ranking of 'our' journal, so that it is better than *Journal X*? I can't help but wonder how much time is wasted by all this that could be devoted instead to conducting meaningful research.

This has serious consequences for scholarship.[23] Many valuable articles appear in what are not regarded as top journals, and many poorer-quality articles are published in top journals.[24] Interestingly, several contributors to a key text devoted to theory development, in which some of the best-known management scholars describe their theories and the processes by which they were developed, reveal that they struggled to publish their work in leading journals.[25]

Most academics have strong criticisms of these lists. A 2018 survey of 1,945 British academics, conducted by James Walker and a number of his colleagues, found 68.5 per cent agreeing or strongly agreeing that the ABS Guide shifts research efforts away from debates that researchers would like to contribute to, 68.4 per cent agreed that it fosters a research monoculture, 58 per cent were of the view that it promotes low-risk research, and so on. But we have a paradox. Despite their criticisms, 68.4 per cent thought that the Guide helps researchers to form judgements about the quality of people's work, while 67 per cent used the lists almost every time or always in deciding where they themselves should publish.[26] Such has been the Guide's performative impact that people seem to believe that its medicine does more harm than good, but feel obliged to keep taking it anyway. Meanwhile, the health of our research environment continues to deteriorate.

Another illustration is relevant. In the UK, the first run of the Research Excellence Framework (REF, completed in 2014) allowed business schools to decide which academics and therefore which publications should be entered for assessment. The then ABS list was central to a great many such decisions. If you had enough papers in journals that the list designated as four-star, champagne could be uncorked in the expectation of good times ahead. Some scholars who became known as 4 × 4 superstars were in high demand and could boost their salary by moving institutions just before census day. The assumption here, of course, is that any article published in an ABS four-star journal would receive the same score in the REF. It is a handy thought, since it enables university managers to evaluate the quality of a paper without having to undertake the tiresome job of reading it. Transactional relationships have become the norm. On all sides, it seems that long-term loyalty is an idea without a long-term future.

Alas, the illusion that a journal's ranking is a reliable guide to how a paper will fare in the REF has been spectacularly punctured. The chair and deputy chair of the 2014 REF exercise, Mike Pidd and Jane Broadbent, published their own analysis of its results.[27] Drawing on 1,000 randomly selected 'outputs', they showed that 239 papers were submitted which appeared in ABS four-star journals. Only ninety-four of these (39 per cent) received a rating of 4 in the REF. Ninety-five received a 3, forty-seven received a 2, and three received either a 1 or were unclassified. Similar fluctuations were found for papers published in ABS three-, two- and one-star journals. In short, many supposedly top journals had a wide variation in the scores attached to their papers, with many papers in supposedly lower-ranked journals doing better in the REF.

This is not surprising. Applying a single scale to diverse phenomena is akin to judging adults' and children's fiction, and books on history and science, by the same criteria. Of course, they have similarities. But their differences are often more important than what they have in common. When editors, particularly those from outside the UK, are deciding to accept or reject an article, they don't agonise over what score it will obtain in the REF, or any similar exercise. The data I have cited above strongly suggest that those involved in assessment exercises aren't worried about what the authors of the numerous journal-ranking lists think of various journals either. Both are trying to do different things. Those who conflate them are confusing their coccyx for their humerus.

Reflect a moment on the significance of this. Good papers were excluded from the REF, possibly damaging the careers of their authors, while many lesser papers were included, boosting the careers of their authors. I recall meeting a colleague who had written a paper on an important topic in my field, leadership studies, that I consider to be the best I have yet read on the issue concerned. It has been widely cited. Yet when I asked if it was being submitted to the then impending REF, I was told that since the paper only appeared in what was still a two-star journal it was being excluded.[28] The view seems to be that since we want to measure it, we will use a measure that takes no time at all, even though it is wildly inaccurate. It would be interesting to see this approach applied to the construction of nuclear power stations, bridges and skyscrapers. And what about healthcare?

PATIENT: Doctor, I'm having a heart attack.
DOCTOR: Nonsense. Only 39 per cent of people in your age group have a heart attack. You're fine.
PATIENT: But I think I'm dyin– … (slumps to the floor)
DOCTOR: Next!

The slavish devotion to the ABS rankings, and journal rankings more widely, encourages the view that the outlet in which one publishes is more important than the quality of the ideas contained in papers. In turn, this metric, when used by selection and promotion panels, is a performative tool that skews effort into outlets and sometimes subject areas that are often devoid of intrinsic interest to the academics concerned. Academic freedom is diminished. What Andrew Sparkes calls 'this audit frenzy' ensures that academics organise themselves 'as a response to targets, indicators, and evaluations'.[29] They must set aside their personal commitments to various topics and define themselves instead by the metrics that the system foists on them. Novel methods and theories are by definition more likely to be marginalised by such processes.

I offer testimony here from Ann Cunliffe, in describing her career on the tenure track at a US university:

> The 'track' meant conforming to the political game of publishing in the 'right' (the top 4 US) journals ... which, given the philosophical basis of my work and my obvious deficiencies in terms of being able to structure an article in an acceptable way, write a 'good' literature review, test propositions, construct a rigorous interview protocol, or develop generalizable theory (all comments from rejection letters) was never likely to happen. As one editor of a top journal noted upon rejecting my paper after a third revision, 'As I write these comments I realise that in essence there may be a difference in terms of our respective commitments and expectations in terms of what makes a theoretical contribution.' Yes, but even so we are still judged using the evaluation criteria of the mainstream paradigm![30]

She goes on to point out that her paper was later accepted in a top European journal and has been on the 'Most Read' list ever since it was published. The pressures she describes begin from the moment a student enters a PhD programme, particularly in elite US business schools where only a few journals are regarded as worth publishing in. Ajnesh Prasad reports that PhD students have changed their original topics when confronted with feedback that their original thought wasn't in favour with elite journals.[31] Maybe these changes are sometimes for the better. But I can't think of much worse criteria for selecting a PhD topic than what is flavour of the month with a handful of journals. The tyranny of favouring top journals now extends beyond the US or Europe. Emma Bell, Nivedita Kothiyal and Hugh Willmott have documented a growing preference on the part of Indian management scholars for positivist and quantitative methods, because they are seen as easier to publish in US-based journals.[32] Elke Schüßle describes a similar process in Germany, where doctoral management students are again encouraged to publish quantitative work in high-impact journals. She reports that books have become regarded as *Regalmüll* – that is, shelf trash. A further journal-ranking list has been created by the German business studies scholars' association and is used to create publication points for job applicants.[33] No wonder that so much of our research is formulaic, unimportant and dull.

All this has implications both for the impact of academic work and for the development of specialised journals. Such journals often speak more directly to the core academic audience in a given field. But they are often ignored by developing researchers since they may have a lower citation score and thus reside outside the top-tier categorisations in formal ranking systems.[34] Most ranking systems also place a great deal of weight on the journal impact factor (JIF) – on which subject, more below. This further constrains the possibility of new journals in emerging fields establishing themselves. Journals must wait for three years before being considered for inclusion in the Institute for Scientific Information's Social Science Citation Index. They then have a further three-year 'waiting period' before a score is awarded. This means a minimum period of six years from a journal's inception to when it receives its first JIF. The implications are stark. A journal's impact factor is one of the widely used criteria by journal-ranking systems. Given that emergent journals don't have one, they are severely disadvantaged. All this can become a self-fulfilling prophecy. People may avoid publishing in a journal because it does not yet have an impact factor or feature highly in journal-ranking lists. But this then ensures that it will ultimately receive only a modest impact factor and will struggle to establish itself in 'official' journal rankings. It is a perfect catch-22. A journal can only become highly ranked if it publishes excellent work, but it can only publish excellent work if it is highly ranked. Thankfully, some academics at least partially resist these pressures, ensuring that their effects are never complete.

Unlike the situation in the past, before journal ranking became so ubiquitous and iniquitous, they may now limit the scope for journals to move up and down the various lists, ceding a semi-permanent advantage to elite journals. While all such advantages can be squandered, the problem is that journals at the top of lists come to acquire a high desirability for authors because they are most prized by those who shape their careers. Authors are strongly encouraged and even materially incentivised to shape their work for submission to 'top' journals, regardless of their appropriateness for the paper's intended audience. These journals remain 'top' journals because they are viewed as publishing 'top' work, and they publish 'top' work because they are considered to be 'top' journals.[35] In terms of resource-based theory, their reputation becomes a valuable resource which attracts other resources – in this case, the preference of careerist academics to publish in them.[36] These advantages of incumbency impede competitors (i.e. other journals) from duplicating that resource and assuming an equitable or superior position. It is an illustration of the 'Matthew Effect', named after the Gospel of St Mark where it is written that 'For to everyone who has will more be given, and he will have abundance; but from him who has not, even what he has will be taken away.'[37] In this context, a high journal ranking becomes a self-fulfilling prophecy that can only really be lost if editors and publishers have an instinct for self-destruction.

Thus, while the ABS Guide of 2018 included 180 more journals than its previous edition, very little changed for those journals that had featured in previous editions. Four journals were upgraded to 4* and one was upgraded to 4.[38] In this instance at least, Jean-Baptiste Karr's famous aphorism is surely pertinent: *Plus ça change, plus c'est la même chose* ('The more things change, the more they remain the same'). Once a journal has achieved a top position in the ABS rankings, it may be easier for a camel to pass through the eye of a needle than it is for that journal to lose its position. A 'major review' is promised for 2021. We shall see.

This has grave consequences for original and ground-breaking scholarship. Journal-ranking lists, such as that of the ABS, routinely give star prizes to such 'elite' US journals as *Academy of Management Review*, *Academy of Management Journal*, *Administrative Science Quarterly* and *Organization Science*. There are major differences in approach between these journals and their counterparts elsewhere, and they remain hemmed in by a positivist and functionalist ortho-doxy. Work of a more critical and unorthodox disposition is rarely engaged with, let alone published. As Cynthia Hardy points out:

> Articles on power in these journals – which are few and far between – nearly always adopt a mainstream conceptualization of power as the use of financial and symbolic resources by actors to influence the behavior of others. In doing so, they view power dynamics as some kind of conscious strategy between protagonists who are fully aware of the political issues and who are able to exercise full agency in utilizing the power resources at their disposal in the event of conflict ... The profound and radical conceptual developments of the past 40 years are rarely mentioned, leaving the so-called elite U.S. journals significantly – and inexcusably – behind the times.[39]

She goes on to document how rarely the work of Michel Foucault, whose thinking has been so seminal to academic debates on power, is even cited in North American scholarship. When cited, it is usually by European scholars who smuggle in a few titbits, and when doing so sometimes display the furtive manner of students worried about being caught cheating in an examination.

Chris Grey astutely highlights the consequences for how we work:

> For the proponents of global journal rankings ... a single hierarchy of journals simply discriminates between 'excellent' or 'world class'

research and that which is of lesser quality. Such an analysis ignores the macro- and micro-politics through which this hierarchy has been constructed. It therefore fails to recognize that what is becoming marginalized is not research that is of poor quality, but research that is of particular types.[40]

To accept the hegemony of such journals means that we must accept their dominant intellectual, theoretical and methodological paradigms. Researchers can't simply pursue a publication agenda in supposedly 'top' journals without it being affected by the traditions, and biases, that dominate those journals. Thus, Grey points out, contributors to *Administrative Science Quarterly* are almost exclusively drawn from the US. The few non-US contributors that it publishes tend, of necessity, to embrace the positivist and functionalist orthodoxy of US scholarship in order to have their work included. There are, of course, exceptions, but they are not sufficient to disturb the general trend.

The Growth of Self-Citation

It is sometimes suggested that when universities make appointment and promotion decisions they should consider citation scores rather than, for example, where papers are published. This is well intentioned, and sounds both objective and harmless. Alas, the law of unintended consequences manifests itself here as well. In late 2010 Italy introduced a 'habilitation' system for professorial appointments. This included assessing people on the number of papers they produced, their overall level of citations and their *h*-index. A study of 886 Italian scientists has found, predictably, that these measures led to a significant increase in the number of self-citations in the scientists' publications.[41] Consider what this means for the scientific record. Papers that are less significant in a field end up being cited more frequently, and not only by the self-citing authors. Each such citation generates a further 3.65 citations beyond what would otherwise be expected.[42] In addition, more worthwhile papers are ignored, thereby skewing researchers' attention in inappropriate directions. Of course, there are worse practices than excessive self-citation. Nevertheless, it reflects the gradual erosion of academic integrity, driven by the conviction that audit and measurement must be applied to all things, with minimal consideration for the negative consequences.

THE SPECIAL HELL OF IMPACT FACTORS

Another approach much favoured by university managements is to emphasise the importance of a journal's impact factor (JIF). This is calculated by taking the total number of citations of papers in a journal over a two-year period, and dividing it by the number of papers that journal has published. The figure arrived at becomes a journal's impact factor, and is usually trumpeted on its webpages. Of course, two years is a preposterously short period of time to assess the impact of anything, let alone an academic paper. The work of writing a paper, submitting it and going through the process of revisions may itself take two years, with a further gap to publication. No wonder that 90 per cent of articles are not cited at all within this timeframe. Even after five years 84 per cent remain uncited, at least as counted by the Thomson Reuters Web of Science.[43] But, again, increases in the JIF lead to celebration and a decline results in mourning. The temptation is, of course, to take the JIF as a proxy measure of the quality of each article within it. To this end, academics are 'encouraged' to publish only in journals with a high impact factor. But, just as with a journal's standing in a ranking system, the JIF tells us absolutely nothing about the worth of individual articles.

The single most obvious problem here is skewness. A small number of papers garner high levels of citation while the majority do not. Vincent Larivière and Cassidy Sugimoto looked at citations in four biochemistry and molecular biology journals. They showed 'that, for all journals, most of the papers have a low number of citations and only a few obtain a high number of citations. Also striking is the similarity of the skewness: for all of these four journals, a nearly identical percentage of papers – 28.2%–28.7% – obtain a citation rate that is equal or greater to the JIF for that journal.'[44] Put differently, over 70 per cent of papers in the journals had fewer citations than the JIF would lead the unwary to expect. This is the norm rather than the exception.

It is easy to assume that journals with high impact factors publish better work, and of course they often do. But a study of work estimating the quality of publications in top science journals sounds a note of caution in assuming that we can make such inferences as a matter of course. In several fields, journals with high impact factors had lower levels of reliability than their lesser-ranked counterparts. For example, statistical power was negatively correlated with the ranking of journals in cognitive neuroscience and psychology.[45] It is not clear why this should be the case, but one obvious possibility is that academics respond to the pressure to publish in high impact journals by taking far more shortcuts in their work than they should. Nevertheless, journal editors and publishers are alert to the advantages of having a 'good' JIF. They therefore attempt to inflate it. 'Coercive citation' occurs when journal editors pressure authors to cite papers published in their journal to boost its impact factor. I once received such 'encouragement' myself, and meekly did as I was asked. As Boy Dylan sang in the 1960s, 'Ah, but I was so much older then, I'm younger than that now.'

Coercive citation distorts the research record by creating the impression that some papers and journals have a bigger influence on their fields than they do. It is also common. In a 2017 study, Eric Fong and Allen Wilhite obtained responses from 12,000 academics across eighteen disciplines, including business.[46] While over 90 per cent viewed coercion as inappropriate, 14.1 per cent still reported that that they had experienced it, and a great many went along with it. Fong and Wilhite's analysis also suggested that business journals are more likely to coerce citations than other disciplines. Moreover, the higher their impact factor the more likely they are to do so frequently. This is a creeping culture of corruption which feeds into research more widely and the behaviours of academic staff (see Chapter 4). If even journal editors bend the rules, individual academics may reason that they have nothing to lose by doing the same.

This is a problem with rankings of all kinds. Goodhart's Law, proposed by an eminent British economist in the 1970s, is commonly summarised as: 'When a measure becomes a target, it ceases to be a good measure.'[47] People game the system, and therefore change what the metric is attempting to measure. For example, many doctors working within the National Health Service in the UK have claimed that they have been pressured into falsifying patient records so that hospitals can report that they have met waiting-time targets.[48] Scottish police officers have reported charging suspects even when they have insufficient evidence against them, in order to meet targets for arrests and convictions.[49]

Universities are no different. Malcolm Gladwell has effectively skewered the influential *US News* College Rankings.[50] He points out that relatively slight changes in the weightings attached to various measures lead to huge shifts in an institution's position in the rankings. But it also encourages game playing of the most corrupt kind.[51] For example, the *Washington Post* reported in 2013 that five colleges had falsified data to *US News* so that they could rise in its rankings. These included Tulane University's Freeman School of Business. It had inflated the average GMAT scores of its full-time MBA students along with the number of applicants to its MBA during the previous two years.[52] This does not mean, of course, that the rest of the institutions produced valid data. It simply means that five were caught lying. The practices concerned are ongoing. In 2018, the dean of Temple University's business school was forced to resign for also falsifying data about its MBA programme. The school's online MBA programme was dropped from the *US News* rankings, having previously topped them for four consecutive years.[53]

A particularly notorious example of this phenomenon concerns the *Times Higher Education* ranking of universities in 2010. This placed Alexandria University in Egypt at 147 in the world.

Few had heard of it before, and few have heard of it since. It turned out that its meteoric rise was almost entirely due to the hefty number of citations accumulated by one of its academics, Mohamed El Naschie. He had published over 320 papers in an academic journal that he himself edited, and in which he cited himself numerous times.[54]

A reliance on journal rankings and JIFs, as we have seen, is part of a similar mind-set in which the only thing that counts is winning the publication game, and in which the status of the journals in which we publish, and that we edit and review for, matters more than what we have to say. It encourages highly questionable behaviour on the part of many who should be at the forefront of attempts to preserve the integrity of our research.

Of course, none of this matters – unless there are performative pressures within the higher education system to internalise journal-ranking systems and impact factors even more. It is this possibility that I now consider.

CLIMBING THE RANKINGS AND THE PRESSURES OF PERFORMATIVITY

I want to pay particular attention here to journal rankings, since these have become precisely such a performative tool. Moreover, academics themselves have become complicit in this process – including many of those who identify with the project of critical management studies (CMS), and who robustly critique performativity when it is manifest in non-academic settings.

Yiannis Gabriel has noted how journal editors have become imprisoned by the performative language of strategy, tactics and positioning that are often critiqued in corporate settings.[55] The aim becomes to improve the standing of 'their' journal in the face of competition from detested 'rivals' – rather than the advancement of a scholarly agenda for its own sake. Critically oriented journals, regardless of their mission statements, are also caught up in this game. There seems to be no escape.

One means of pursuing higher standing is to emulate the practices of those journals that have already secured top-dog status, which
generally means those based in the United States. Since rejection rates
of 90 per cent plus are common in such journals, this becomes a target
for others as well. It must be only a matter of time until a journal can
proudly boast a rejection rate of 100 per cent: its standards are so high
that nothing by anybody is considered good enough to grace its pages.
This requires an increasingly critical tone towards contributors.
Yiannis Gabriel's discussion of these issues highlights a trend which
many of us have experienced – a deterioration in the tone of reviewer
and editor comments, towards sharper, sometimes personal criticism,
and an increasingly pedantic approach that is often demoralising to
the recipient.

Reviewers, of course, approach the task of reviewing with an
abundant supply of biases in place. In particular, argue Eden King and
a number of his colleagues, they 'approach manuscripts, unconsciously or consciously, from the lens of criticism. One of their primary tasks is to identify problems. As such, a manuscript that has
several weaknesses as well as several strengths may be more likely to
get rejected than an article that has few weaknesses but also few
strengths.'[56] A study that is particularly relevant to problems with
peer review was conducted by Teresa Amabile in 1983.[57] She had 55
students read two book reviews from the *New York Times*. The same
person wrote the reviews, but Amabile altered them slightly to produce two versions of each review. One was predominantly negative
and the other positive. When the students were asked to rate the
author's intelligence, they viewed the negative reviewer as more
intelligent than the positive one. They were also rated as more competent and expert. Somehow aware of this, we tend to be more critical
when seeking to impress others with how smart we are. The resultant
tendency to 'accentuate the negative' results in what Bryan Gibson
and Elizabeth Oberlander describe as 'hypercriticism'.[58] Now imagine
the position that peer reviewers find themselves in. They certainly
don't want to appear amateurish, naïve, Pollyannish or incompetent

in the eyes of editors. The rational way forward is to be overly critical, even though this contributes to an environment in which the reviewer's own work will also someday be treated to hypercriticism. We end up complaining about the increased numbers of disparaging reviews that we receive, but then go on to write overly critical reviews of other people's work ourselves.

Increasingly, also, it seems to me that when reviewer opinion is divided the editor almost always sides with the critical review. This may be a display of excellent editorial judgement. Alternatively, it may be a reflection of the 'bad is stronger than good' effect, in which negative information or feedback about something seems to influence our judgements much more than what is positive.[59] Pressed for time and fearful for the reputation of their journal, it is easy to see why editors might be swayed in this direction. If they reject a potentially good paper no one will ever know. But if they publish a bad one it is out there for all to see. The reflex of criticism and rejection grows stronger. For authors, all this means endless rounds of painful revisions. As Yiannis Gabriel has also argued:

> Publishing is now a long process, involving numerous revisions, citing authors one does not care for, engaging with arguments one is not interested in and seeking to satisfy different harsh masters, often with conflicting or incompatible demands, while staying within a strict word limit. Most authors will go through these tribulations and the drudgery of copious revisions, accepting virtually any criticism and any recommendation with scarcely any complaint, all in the interest of getting published.[60]

Does this sound like overstatement? If so, consider the testimony of Scott Seibert, writing in 2006. Here he is discussing a paper that he co-authored in the *Academy of Management Journal*. It won the Outstanding Paper of the Year award for 2004. Seibert reports:

> the first set of editor-reviewer comments covered 13 pages of single-spaced text. The R&R was characterised by the action editor as

'high-risk'. Our reply consisted of 31 pages of single-spaced text. The second set of editor-reviewer comments covered 10 pages; our second reply was 13 pages. I can literally say that we invested as much work in the replies to reviewers as we did in writing the original manuscript.[61]

In one way, the dedication of Seibert and his co-author to the task in hand is admirable, and it is important to note that he framed his commentary on the process in wholly positive terms. The subtitle of his reflective piece says it all: 'reviewers are an author's best friends'. From another standpoint, it is insane, albeit a form of insanity that is clearly coerced. Submitting a paper to a top journal seems almost like becoming a hostage, with rejection (i.e. termination) the ultimate sanction for disobedience. Authors are desperate to escape this fate, but can only do so if they bow to each and every idiosyncratic reviewer request/demand, while expressing fulsome thanks for the pain that is being inflicted on them. They can either seethe in silence or fall victim to Stockholm syndrome, where the review process starts out badly but by the end they quite like it. I am not denying in the least that peer review can and does add value. But I am arguing that when it becomes this prolonged and ferocious there is a danger that it destroys all life, passion and individuality in a submission before it sees the light of day. Authors may feel that they have ended up writing what they don't want to write solely in order to satisfy reviewers, secure publication and build their careers.

Carl Cederström and Andre Spicer give a vivid account of how common this fate has become. They describe working on a paper that was submitted to several journals and underwent multiple revisions. It was eventually published – ten years after they began working on it. Rather than feeling satisfaction at this achievement they write as follows:

Was it better than our first version? We couldn't tell. All intellectual excitement had been beaten out of us. It no longer felt like our own words. It was now just an assemblage of what the reviewers wanted us to write, thinly disguised as an academic article . . . It felt like some form of double captivity. Authors feel as if they're trapped, destined to write things they don't find interesting. And reviewers and editors feel the same way, forced to comment on papers they find pointless. Hundreds of hours were spent writing, and dozens of hours in reviewing and editing. For what?[62]

Two colleagues recently told me of a saga that is becoming all too familiar. They submitted a paper to one of the best-known journals in our field. It went through three rounds of revision over a two-year period. Eventually, the reviewers and acting editor were in favour of acceptance. At that point, the chief editor stepped in and vetoed publication. I don't know who is supposed to benefit from such a lengthy procedure and such an arbitrary exercise of power. But I do know that it causes a great deal of wasted work, humiliation and despair. For what, indeed?

Research Grants and Academic Freedom

The audit mentality has also created an obsession with the need to secure externally funded competitive research grants. Income targets have been introduced at one in six UK universities, at either individual or departmental level.[63] The pointlessness of pursuing grant income for its own sake should be clear. Much of our work requires nothing more than time to think. It doesn't need a team of research assistants. As C. Wright Mills put it in *The Sociological Imagination*, published in 1959: 'I do not like to do empirical work if I can possibly avoid it. If one has no staff it is a great deal of trouble; if one does employ a staff, then the staff is often even more trouble.'[64] Grants can take away the most precious academic resource of all – time. Undaunted by such considerations, and making them worse, the audit process compels more academics to write more grant applications, in the pursuit of a diminishing pot of money, thereby further reducing their prospects of success. It is a zero-sum game. This is particularly problematic with management research. A report from the Chartered Association of Business Schools in 2018 showed that funding for business and management research from sources within the UK had fallen by 12 per cent in real terms over the previous six years.[65] Funding from research councils had fallen by 10 per cent and from industry by 20 per cent. Researchers had come to increasingly rely on European funding – just as Brexit unleashed further uncertainty about that. Yet academics are often 'performance managed' if they fail to meet the targets in question. Perversely, the audit culture sees problems created by *systems* as evidence of *individual* weaknesses that must be 'managed'.

This also has implications for academic freedom, defined by Terence Karran and Lucy Mallinson as 'freedom to determine what shall be researched; freedom to determine the method of research; freedom to determine the purpose of their research …; freedom to determine the avenues and modes … of disseminating research findings to one's peers, and the wider world'.[66] Grant targets and the requirement to publish in specific outlets are incompatible with such a definition, since grant-awarding bodies determine what research will be done, and specific journals prioritise particular approaches, methodologies and theories above others. We may be free to roam in any direction that we wish. But, increasingly, we can only roam within the limits of the leash to which we are tethered.

For example, the 2010 version of the ABS Guide declared that one of its purposes was to 'inform staffing decisions'.[67] It used to be said that the culture of academia was one of 'publish or perish'.[68] Now it is 'publish often (in an ABS four-star journal) or perish'. Look at how this performative intent is exercised. In late 2010, the University of Queensland in Australia, one of the country's leading research intensive universities, announced a 'Q index'. This measured individual research income, research publication (weighted by reference, of course, to journal-ranking lists), higher degree completions and research degree advisory loads. A Q index – down to two decimal points – was then produced for each faculty member, and compared to average scores at university, faculty, and school levels. It was also compared to all staff within an academic's faculty at the same appointment level, and was open to inspection by managers. Essentially, people became a number – I am a 9.22, you are a 10.33, she is a 12.34. A former colleague from UQ who first emailed me about this signed their email with doleful black humour: 'Yours, 8.22'. I can imagine few better methods of reducing intrinsic motivation, extending managerial oversight and demoralising people. It is a process of commodification and corporatisation that is poisoning the heart and soul of academic life. Whatever their original intent, it is this dismal trajectory that journal rankings have now placed us on.

The Plague of Predatory Journals

Yet there is another paradox here, and one that may be particularly irksome for inexperienced researchers finding it difficult to publish in well-established journals. This is the phenomenon of 'predatory' journals. These mimic the trappings of real ones, but publish anything by anybody on almost anything – for a fee. They lack any peer review or editorial process. Most academics regularly receive emails from them soliciting contributions – I receive several such 'invitations' each week. One insight into their 'standards' is offered by Katarzyna Pisanski and several colleagues.[69] They created a fictitious scientist named Anna O. Szust. 'Szust' is Polish for fraud. Various fronts, such as a spoof faculty webpage, were created on her behalf. A CV was crafted that listed no publications in academic journals, but which claimed various books and book chapters. None of these existed. They then applied for her to join 360 journals in an editorial capacity. Forty predatory journals and eight open-access ones appointed her to some editorial capacity, while others offered to do so if she paid a fee. Although she then withdrew her applications, Pisanski and her colleagues reported that she remained listed as a member of the editorial board on the websites of eleven 'journals'.

Such outlets snare the unwary and the desperate, and consume valuable time and resources. One study of 2,225 Italian scientists found that 5 per cent had published at least one paper in a predatory journal.[70] Some of these 'journals' are even included in citation indexes such as Scopus. Those without deep expertise in a field may evaluate people without being aware that publication in them is the equivalent of obtaining a degree from a mail-order firm. They are yet another manifestation of the unintended consequences that arise from the pressure to publish. However, important as it is that we deal with such problems, I very much doubt that official journal-ranking systems contribute much, and in any event I believe that they do more harm than good.

INSTRUMENTAL MOTIVATIONS AND MEANINGLESS RESEARCH

Increasingly, our writing is overwhelmed by the instrumental motivations that now attend to it, and which are sharpened by the tyranny of journal rankings. Here is an insight from Carl Cederström and Casper Hoedemaekers that resonates with me:

> You don't start with an idea that you work on and think through and then put into words. You start with the journal (did we mention a four-star, or at the very least a three-star?) and then think what might fly with the profile of that journal, or, more concretely, what might appeal to the editors and their idiosyncratic tastes, desires and fetishes. 'What's in vogue?' we ask ourselves. 'What might pass as a viable contribution?' ... to write something preconceived for a so-called four-starred journal, is something different altogether. Something in this process comes up against an unspoken assumption that this is somehow not what we signed up for. We seem to be doing something that is closer to tactical planning than putting thought on paper, and we are clearly not alone in the residual resentment we experience in this process. To cope with this disturbing fact, it seems all too easy and natural to resort to cynicism and a dash of self-loathing.[71]

Journal rankings embody the tensions within the university sector throughout the world between open-ended, scholarly inquiry on the one hand, and performative pressures that seek to corral our research and publication practices within tightly regulated spaces on the other. It is hard to see much that is good coming out of all this. Chris Grey describes well the debilitating effects on our scholarship:

> The result has been that both the elite US journals and those European journals that seek ... to join that elite have become increasingly formulaic and dull. A tiny research question is posed, followed by a compendious literature review (that might almost be computer generated) and perhaps a discussion of methodology (or, more commonly, method); then some findings are presented, some suggestions for further work are made, an acknowledgement of limitations is offered and a modest conclusion is given. Such writing requires a skill and dedication that I would not deny, any more than I would deny the skill and dedication of an expert cryptic crossword solver, an activity that seems to me to be very similar. But whatever its merits may be, the development of an exciting, vibrant, pluralistic, let alone radical, organization studies is not amongst them.[72]

It is increasingly clear that academic staff feel perplexed, debilitated and demoralised by the performative expectations now heaped on them and the audit regimes designed to check their compliance. Oddly, these feelings are omitted from the metrics that measure outputs, grant 'capture', impact, knowledge exchange and engagement – not to mention teaching, as if all these functions are pursued by immaterial objects rather than people. Yet the welfare of staff is central to any serious discussion of what universities are and where they are headed. The audit regime has exacted a fearsome human toll, and in the chapter that follows I attempt to bring at least some of these costs out from behind the curtain and into the open.

3 'When the Levee Breaks': Academic Life on the Brink

INTRODUCTION

It is, of course, impossible to separate the pressures on staff within business schools from the state of the universities in which they are based. I therefore start this chapter by paying tribute to the memory of an academic colleague in a different discipline, and who I never met. His name was Stefan Grimm and he died in 2014. The story of what happened to him is extreme, though perhaps less so than we would like to imagine. I think it serves as an illustration of university life at its worst and should alert us to the need for a change of direction.

Stefan Grimm was a professor of toxicology at London's 'world leading' Imperial College. His achievements in this role did not prevent the then head of the Division of Experimental Medicine at Imperial from emailing him in March 2014 to say:

> I am of the opinion that you are struggling to fulfil the metrics of a Professorial post at Imperial College which include maintaining established funding in a programme of research with an attributable share of research spend of £200 k p.a. and [I] must now start to give serious consideration as to whether you are performing at the expected level of a Professor at Imperial College.

There was no criticism of the quality of Grimm's work or the volume of his output. Rather, he was being criticised for doing work that was not expensive enough. Other emails made it clear that Grimm believed he was earmarked for dismissal. He may have been right. His line manager's email asserted that his communication was the 'start of informal action in relation to your performance'. It offered to 'help' him, if he wished to 'explore opportunities elsewhere'.

60

The stress was immense. In an email commenting on his treatment by Imperial College, Grimm wrote:

I have to say that it was a lovely situation to submit grant applications for your own survival with such a deadline. We all know what a lottery grant applications are ... Why does a Professor have to be treated like that?

He went on:

What these guys don't know is that they destroy lives. Well, they certainly destroyed mine. This is not a university anymore but a business, with a very few, up in the hierarchy, profiteering, and the rest of us milked for money.[1]

In September 2014, at a time when he faced further action by his managers, Stefan Grimm committed suicide at his home. His death attracted much media attention, including from the mainstream press. Imperial's treatment of Professor Grimm featured as a key issue in that coverage and at the inquest into his death. The coroner noted that the funding pressures on him were a major stressor, and described his death as 'needless'.[2] A fellow academic from Imperial was quoted in the press as follows:

Perhaps what is most shocking is that none of us are actually shocked this has happened. Higher education is like big business these days, and Imperial is absolutely focused on its position in the global rankings. Lots of us thought academia was about ideas and expanding the realms of science, not a business in which the people who do the research are treated as disposable commodities ... It is brutal and horrible and unfair. Everybody knows a story about someone who has been targeted because they no longer 'fit' or are deemed unproductive in some way.

This tragedy, though particularly horrific, is part of a broader process in which academic work is scrutinised more closely than ever before. For example, the *Times Higher Education* carried a report on

8 June 2018 headlined 'Cardiff plans review after suicide of "over-worked" lecturer'. It reported the death of Malcolm Anderson, an accounting lecturer, who had been given 418 exam scripts to mark within a 20-day period, in addition to his other duties.[3] In analysing how and why this has come to be, this chapter is my attempt to offer some answers to the agonising question Professor Grimm posed in his last communications: 'Why does a Professor have to be treated like that?'

When anyone writes about the pressures of modern academic life they are often accused of hankering after a lost Golden Age that never was. Their laments are viewed in the same light as those who pine for the return of steam engines and quill pens and for the un-invention of social media. But in criticising the present it isn't neces-sary to believe that everything before today was perfect. It is only necessary to argue that what we are now doing is diminishing the quality of academic life and that this is damaging the research which we produce. Stefan Grimm's memory, and those who have come after him, deserves better.

UNIVERSITIES AS HUMAN INSTITUTIONS

It is strange how much of the discussion of what universities do fails to consider the importance of the conditions under which staff work. Here is a typical example. David Willetts was at one time Minister for Universities and Science in the UK government. He is now a visiting professor at King's College London, an honorary fellow of Nuffield College, Oxford, chancellor of the University of Leicester and a member of the House of Lords. In 2017, he published a book entitled *A University Education*.[4] It is a passionate and eloquent defence of universities, of their value to society, and of how they enrich the lives of their students. When he declares that 'I love uni-versities' there is no reason to doubt his sincerity, even if one dis-agrees with some of his policy options. Yet there is a curious lacuna through its 439 pages. At no point does Willetts discuss the welfare of the staff who work within the system, or the impact on them of the various initiatives that he debates and often defends. Universities, he insists repeatedly, must 'do more' to improve the quality of their teaching, including providing students with more contact hours. But universities are not just buildings. They are people. When Willets says that 'universities must do more' in teaching, or anything else, he means that academic staff must do more. He doesn't say what we should stop doing in order to do more of whatever is currently in vogue with government. However, we are not – yet – an inexhaustible resource. Perhaps Willets thinks that our physics colleagues should work on bending the fabric of space-time, so that a 24-hour day becomes 48?

In line with this, he bullishly declares that research assessment 'has transformed the performance of British research by putting academic researchers under greater pressure to perform than in any other national system'.[5] Of course, those who work within Ivy League institutions in the USA, the Group of Eight in Australia or any other segment of a higher education system that regards itself as research-intensive could justly argue that they face similar pressures. Australia's research assessment exercise is grandly dubbed the 'Excellence in Research for Australia' (ERA) initiative. There is growing evidence there too that it has become an all-devouring preoccupation, distracting attention from teaching, and provoking alienation, stress and dissatisfaction on the part of staff.[6] In fairness to Willetts, he acknowledges problems with assessment in the UK, including its cost, its bureaucratic burdens and its stress on competition between institutions and individuals rather than collaboration. This leads to multiple absurdities. For example, many UK universities require those applying for promotion or jobs to specify the percentage contribution that they have made to joint publications. But no one keeps a detailed inventory of how many hours, and how much hope and sweat, they invest in a paper, whether it is co-authored or a solo run. This is a surreal and pointless requirement that compels people to invent figures (that is, lie) so that they can seem to comply with the request. It could be worse. The 'Handelsblatt' ranking is widely used in

Germany, and has rules and weightings designed to penalise co-authorship.[7]

But let us consider the implications of a system that is praised because it has put staff under 'greater pressure'. David Willetts seems to imply that academics will not be motivated to do their best work unless a blowtorch is held to their feet. This is implausible. There is also a difference between a research climate where more is produced, even when it is highly graded, and a climate that fosters the publication of work that makes a positive difference. No one can doubt that we have more management research than ever before, as is now true in all disciplines. Whether it is of genuinely better quality than work published before formal research assessments led to targets specifying how much of it we should publish, and where, is a different question. Nor does Willetts consider how individuals have been affected by the 'pressure' that he plainly thinks was needed to jolt us out of our natural state of lethargy. Let me try to help him out.

Working in the Twenty-First-Century University and Business School

The popular image of academic life remains one of a cloistered 'Ivory Tower', in which academics drink port and ponder great but useless ideas, before embarking on a three-month summer holiday. In reality, the audit culture I have discussed in the previous chapter has produced an environment of long hours, high stress and weakening commitment to an academic life. Maxamillian Fochler and Sarah de Rijcke argue that, as a result of audit pressures, we now have a situation where 'Higher education institutions fight for top positions in rankings, individual academics strive to be among the tiny top percentage funded by specific sources or published in selective outlets, and even scientific journals compete to be listed in the top percentage of their respective fields'.[8] Driven by these considerations, senior managers at the University of Exeter sought to improve their university's league table position in a truly fanatical fashion. They 'succeeded' – but at the cost of hugely increased levels of stress, intensified workloads, the creation of a top-down culture and 'alarming reports of bullying, [and] manipulative and unpleasant behaviour by particular senior managers when staff express views which contradict them'.[9] How far this takes us from what universities purport to be.

Thus, the pressure on individual academics is constantly ratcheted up, in a kind of arms race that always creates more losers than winners, and where the 'winners' are so shattered by their efforts that they often look in need of intensive care. There is only so much grant money to go around, only so many papers published in 'top' journals, and in any ranking system only ten universities can ever be in the top ten. People run at an ever more frantic pace, but mostly find that they are standing still.

The effects on morale are easily imagined. I recall a conversation with a senior colleague who has an international reputation and gazillions of citations, about a close relative who was considering studying for a PhD. My colleague said: 'But I think I've talked them out of it.' The data suggests why. A 2013 survey of University and College Union (UCU) members in the UK found that 73 per cent agreed with the statement 'I find my job stressful.'[10] Half felt that their general level of stress was high or very high. Nor is the UK unique. 'Burnout' measures the extent of people's emotional exhaustion, cynicism, inefficacy and reduced sense of personal accomplishment.[11] Across forty-two US universities, 1,439 faculty members were surveyed on the extent to which this applied to them.[12] Of these, 27 per cent experienced burnout often or very often, levels that are on a par with such high-risk groups as health-care workers. Speed, overwork and a feeling of always being 'on' have become endemic. Many junior and senior scholars in the US have now written about their experiences and why they have left academic life as a result of them – a genre that the *Chronicle of Higher Education* has termed 'QuitLit'. It has compiled links to many of these pieces, in which grief, pain and regret mingles with relief at the discovery that talented and educated people can find other worthwhile things to do with their lives.[13]

In 2018, *Times Higher Education* reported on a survey of 2,379 higher education staff.[14] Of its respondents, 61 per cent were from the UK, with 17 per cent based in the US and 5 per cent in Australia. A smattering of staff from 53 other countries also participated. Two-fifths reported working longer hours over the previous three years and 40 per cent said they worked ten or more hours a day. A social science professor in the US said that s/he hadn't taken 'a holiday of a full week in more than three years'. A lecturer at a prestigious UK university said that she had 'had to mark coursework every Christmas holiday for five years'. As Glaudo De Vita and Peter Case argue, increased bureaucratisation and auditing have 'transformed what was once one of the most rewarding professions into one that records increasing stress levels as a result of a feeling of loss of control in day-to-day working life'.[15] These seem unpropitious conditions under which to produce a great piece of research, or a great anything for that matter.

Undaunted, some Australian business schools now require academics to produce at least two papers in top journals in any two-year period. I know of one where professors are required to publish three A or A* papers over a rolling three-year period. At least one of these must be co-authored with a mentee/early career academic. They are also expected to submit a serious competitive grant application in the same period. The prospect of having such ongoing expectations is frankly nuts. Note that saying something meaningful is subordinated here to publishing frequently in the 'right' places. This is a Legoland model of scholarship, in which façades matter more than substance. Conditions in Australian universities have been dire for many years. Malcolm Saunders noted as far back as 2006 that 'a climate of fear pervades Australian universities; its most obvious product is what we might call conformist cynicism'.[16] This was certainly my impression during my brief tenure there, and all the indications are that this and many other problems have only grown worse. Australian higher education has certainly acquired an international reputation. Unfortunately, it is one for being at the cutting edge of bad ideas. But, throughout academia, it is fair to conclude that 'the numbers of journal articles published by a researcher and the level of the journal in which they appear has moved from a modest issue to a major concern. For some it has become almost the only concern.'[17]

Ben Martin has suggested that 'Amongst academics, one senses growing dissatisfaction, disillusion, even despair with life in universities.'[18] I do not think this is far-fetched. Consider Warwick Business School (WBS), one of the UK's leading business schools, and the crisis that befell it when an ambitious new dean, Mark Taylor, was appointed in 2010. He held the position until 2016. It was immediately clear that his top priority was moving the school up various league tables. In itself this is unobjectionable. Who would advocate that a school or a university should aim to move *down* the league tables? But his methods and his metrics were a different matter. Publishing articles in ABS four-star journals quickly emerged as the only criteria to be used for appointments and promotions. Teaching ability was unimportant. Those who failed to publish at the desired level found themselves being performance managed, and a great many – including internationally renowned academics – chose to leave.

When a number of administrative positions at WBS were then identified for possible redundancy, a discussion forum developed on the website of the University and College Union (UCU) where the anguish and despair of individual staff was clearly ventilated. I offer some samples in Table 3.1[19]

It is sobering to think of the ambition that drove this regime. The dean declared that his vision was to make WBS 'the leading business school in Europe'. What is striking is the absence of any serious justification for the vision in question or a sense of proportion. In what rational world is being in second, third or fourth place in a league table a cause for despair? Taylor of course had his defenders, some of whom participated in the UCU forum discussion. Positional games always create at least some winners. But, as Olan Alakavuklar, Andrew Dickson and Ralph Stablein have pointed out:

Table 3.1 *Comments from WBS staff*

1. 'There is now a growing sense of crisis at WBS. Since the appointment of the new Dean what used to be a very successful business school has been run into the ground, reflected in massive staff losses from amongst the best academic and non-academic staff and these losses far outstrip new hires. Those new hires are either semi-detached from the school or put immediately into the ever-changing so-called "senior management team" which as a result has no understanding of the institution. Some of these new staff have themselves left within months of joining so chaotic and unhappy has the School become.'
2. 'Crass, bullying attempts to achieve managerial aims have left WBS demoralised and disaffected. For example, new senior people (4 × 4*s) being hired for huge sums are, it transpires, frequently being told that they don't have to teach/mark … This is not what "research-led university" means.'
3. 'As a WBS member of staff who has recently left, I can honestly say that the decline of the school, in terms of collegiality and staff morale, has been shocking. Anyone employed at the school before the "Taylor era" will know that it was not always perfect but it was not a dictatorship and people were committed to their jobs. This is simply no longer the case.'
4. 'The 4 × 4* REF obsession clearly results in perverse consequences. As academics we have a choice: play the game and aim for the Magic 4 at any costs (i.e. sod students or collegiality or being human). Or we can trust our professional judgment that a more balanced portfolio of academic life is more suitable and rewarding both as a career and for student experience.'

when you frame accountability with a business discourse in line with a neoliberal agenda in terms of competition, efficiency, rankings, performance, and cost-benefit analyses, then it is very likely that institutional regimes intervene in, and transform, the nature of scholarship and its professionalism built up over the years.[20]

WBS is an excellent case study of this. Alas, it is not unique. A similar regime seems to have been installed at the UK's Swansea University in 2013, when Nigel Piercy took over as dean of the School of Management. He held this role for two tumultuous years. The tone of his leadership is best captured by his emails to staff, in which he explained that the school was 'not a rest home for refugees from the 1960s with their ponytails and tie-dyed T-shirts'. In another such communication, he described trade unionists as 'unpleasant and grubby little people ... usually distinguished only by their sad haircuts, grubby, chewed fingernails and failed careers'.[21] When he decided that the school's economics programme had to be closed, a position paper was circulated that described some of the staff as a 'poison' that is 'infecting and destroying the rest of the School of Management ... Certain senior individuals have created themselves into a cancer – that must now be removed to allow the rest of the school to survive.'[22] This is a model of academic management that sees staff as little more than recalcitrant cattle who must be rounded up, branded and herded West by their target-toting betters. It is not a formula for collegiate relationships.

In line with this top-down approach, Yiannis Gabriel describes a change process within another organisation that reads like a leading business school. Once more, improved positioning became the overriding aim, justifying all kinds of practices. Its effects on people were profound:

> criticism became internalized and part of the way many employees
> came to view themselves. Constantly measuring themselves
> against the idealized standards of the official story, the stars, the
> celebrities, the world leaders, it was not surprising that they found
> themselves lacking in some way or another. As a result, a widely felt
> depression afflicted many participants and was apparent but not
> generally discussed. People rarely smiled and rarely joked.
> Occasionally feeble black jokes surfaced, lacking the rebellious and
> original qualities of real humour. Even among the higher leadership

echelons, feelings of doom and gloom regularly prevailed, often associated with the futility of fighting the wider organizational bureaucracy or the competitors' ability to succeed in projects at which this organization was failing.[23]

All this demonstrates that attempting to perform at the level demanded by top schools over a prolonged period of time requires an obsessive commitment that precludes anything like living a normal life. Such Stakhanovite work norms provoke profound and debilitating identity crises. Nancy Day has published one of the few *outputs* that address the impact on authors when an output they have written is rejected. Given rejection rates at top journals, she points out that if 1,000 scholars submit their work to such an outlet, 900 of them will be rejected. If most of them then resubmit to a lower-tier journal with, say, a 20 per cent rejection rate, 720 will go on to experience a further rejection. If these scholars then submit to a still lower-tier journal with a 30 per cent rejection rate, 504 will remain rejected: 'Thus, unless they are consistently skilled or lucky, at least half of all scholars will experience rejection numerous times.'[24] The emotional effects include alienation, discouragement, disillusionment, damaged egos and threats to one's identity as a scholar. For those still on the tenure track at US universities, where six papers are normally expected within a six-year period, these pressures are particularly intense.

Nor are those who succeed in publishing exempt from anxiety about their overall worth. David Knights and Caroline Clarke conducted interviews with fifty-two academics.[25] Many reported that they suffered from what the authors called 'imposter syndrome'. This was the belief that they were not as secure and able as others, combined with a paralysing anxiety about their ability to meet the multiple competing demands on their time. Their worry is well founded, since past success is no guarantee of future success. Douglas Peters and Stephen Ceci demonstrated as much in an admittedly small but famous study published in 1982 where they resubmitted twelve psychology papers to journals that had previously accepted them.[26] While three of the papers were recognised, the rest went out to peer review. This time, sixteen out of eighteen reviewers recommended rejection. They provided devastating critiques of the methodological and theoretical shortcomings of the papers in question. The editors agreed, and rejected eight papers that their journals had already published.

Established scholars are evidently not immune from stress, rejection and the prospect of professional failure. Mats Alvesson has noted that

> increasingly also senior persons like myself may feel that one is only as good as one's latest journal article or book and increasingly aware of how much and in what journals we have published. This is certainly a drastic change over the past few decades.[27]

It seems likely that female academics face particularly heavy forms of stress. Here is just one example, from a comment on a *THE* discussion thread which looked at stress levels and why so many people are walking away from academic life:

> I was working on average 60 hours a week during term time – and spending another 30–40 hours running the household, cooking, childcare, etc. ... We are entitled to all of one research day a week, but that is always occupied with teaching prep and bureaucracy. The only time I found I could squeeze in any of my own research (much of which requires travel to a foreign country – and so is increasingly impossible to do) was after my child's bedtime, and I would work until 12–2 am 5 or so nights a week after being up and on the go non-stop since around 6. Not surprisingly, I became very ill. As I'm the family breadwinner I can't quit, but I also know that I simply can't keep this up. This is not a normal life – it isn't really any kind of life. Universities seem to think, dismayingly, that the problem in maintaining a home/life balance for people with children is to

ensure that they have adequate childcare – hence it's ok to ask me to do Saturday open days or, increasingly, evening teaching/ events ... The fact that I may actually want to spend time with my child rather than palming him off to others to care for doesn't seem to enter into it. I meet so many academic women who have avoided having kids because they can't imagine juggling life and work.[28]

I shared this quotation with a female colleague who is a professor in one of the UK's leading business schools. She immediately responded that she also knew of many women who had decided to have either only one child or none at all, such was the perceived impossibility of combining a normal family life with an academic career. What an indictment this is of the journey on which so many universities have embarked. As the eminent economist Andrew Oswald has argued: 'It is almost as though we have consciously designed a system to maximise stress and fear. That is dangerous, muddle-headed and against the spirit of universities.'[29]

But while the stress so valued by David Willetts may increase the quantity of what we produce, it is likely to have a negative effect on its quality. A meta-analysis of seventy-six experimental studies that examined the relationship between stress and creativity is telling. It found 'a curvilinear relationship between evaluative stress and creativity such that low evaluative contexts *increased* creative performance over control conditions, whereas highly evaluative contexts *decreased* creative performance'.[30] In short, the more intense the systems of evaluation the more damaging to creativity they are. This is why the data I have presented here on academic stress matter far beyond their implications for the well-being of individuals, important as that is. Exercises such as the REF in the UK and the ERA in Australia have intensified performance expectations and the process of evaluation to such an extent that they are now damaging the ability of academics to produce the kind of sustained, high-quality work that the system insists is necessary. With so many metrics in play it is always possible to find at least one where you can be judged a failure, by yourself and others. For many academics, feelings of shame, dejection and guilt have become constant companions.[31]

All of which begs the question: are we doomed to an endless process of decline, or is there anything that we can do individually and collectively to reclaim the primacy of disinterested academic inquiry?

RECLAIMING ACADEMIC INTEGRITY

Undoubtedly, there is a widespread sense of fatalism among academics about the depressing trajectory we seem to be on. University and journal rankings along with the tyranny of impact factors have rampaged through academia, and seem to have felled all opposition. Alexandra Bristow reports the following incident at one of her vice-chancellor's regular meetings with staff:

> I thought it my duty to raise my hand and point out that citation indices were misleading and journal lists and rankings were damaging ... 'Given these effects', I asked, 'should we not be collectively resisting journal rankings and citation indices rather than committing ourselves to becoming better at playing the game?' ... As everyone was leaving their seats at the end of the talk, I overheard (two unknown colleagues) discussing my question. 'What's the point of making a fuss about this?' said one of them: 'it's like arguing against the force of gravity'. 'Yeah,' echoed the other: 'it's like saying we don't like the force of gravity – let's resist it'.[32]

I think that this fundamentally underestimates our own agency. Despite how deeply they have become naturalised, academic rankings are a recent phenomenon. The influential academic ranking of world universities produced by Shanghai Jiao Tong University in conjunction with Shanghai Ranking Consultancy first appeared in 2003. The *Times Higher Education* university rankings were first published in 2004. (QS World Rankings was partnered with *THE* until 2009, and now stands on its own.) Recall also that the journal rankings produced by the Association of Business Deans Council in Australia was initially published as recently as 2007 while the infamous ABS Guide first inflicted its wisdom on us in 2009. Unlike gravity, these are human constructions, and what people make they can also unmake. Oppressive regimes seek to project the impression of permanence. But this is an illusion, as fallen despots throughout history could readily attest. In common with others, I urge a moratorium on journal rankings.[33] Whatever the initial intentions behind them, and these weren't all bad, we have certainly reached a stage where they now do more harm than good.

We can also help journal rankings and impact factors on their road to perdition by treating them with the contempt that they have worked so hard to deserve. This is certainly not a lost cause. Recall the evidence which strongly suggests that the 2014 REF panel set the ABS Guide aside when coming to its own judgements, rather than subcontract the task to the Guide's authors (see Chapter 2). The Australian Research Council has banned the use of journal ranking lists in its national research assessment exercise, and in the evaluation of grant applications. The influential San Francisco Declaration on Research Assessment urged universities to avoid using journal impact factors as a measure of scholarship. All seven of the UK's research councils signed the declaration in early 2018. Unlike the waters facing King Canute, this metric tide can be turned.

Our agency also extends to how we do our research. We can simply do more interesting work, despite the temptations to do otherwise. Mats Alvesson and Jorgen Sandberg offer many helpful suggestions to guide us on our way.[34] These include cultivating a greater curiosity about assumptions and theories outside whatever microtribe we may belong to, regular interaction with people who have different worldviews to ourselves, deliberate disloyalty to particular sub-fields (however popular they seem to be), and a willingness to make a radical contribution rather than filling unimportant gaps that no one has ever noticed before and that no one cares about anyway.

In addition, we can make better choices about how we live our lives. In a fascinating article, David Jones describes a 'slow swimming' club created by around a dozen academics, whose members met once a week to – yes, swim slowly – connect with each other, and just calm down. Jones described this as 'counter-spacing' – the conscious creation of a reflective, supportive and safe environment outside the hurly burly of 'normal' academic life. One member commented that the main effect of the Club was:

> to keep me sane as it provided a retreat from this daily grind and provided a freedom to think and feel about being truly a researcher again. I feel like my professional identity has been restored with what initially seemed like a deviant act – to have the audacity to get in touch with myself ... shocking I know.[35]

Maggie Berg and Barbara Seeber, authors of a manifesto for change entitled *The Slow Professor* published in 2016, would surely approve.[36]

Wiser choices can also be made by government and policy makers. The principle of accountability often seems to mean that researchers are required to guarantee success before they start their work. Consider how research grants are awarded. In line with the audit imperative, applications must offer precise theoretical frameworks, promise definite outputs (often termed 'deliverables') and minimise the risk of cutting-edge approaches that may fail. Otherwise, they are unlikely to win funding. We now seem to have a cottage industry of Nobel Prize winners complaining that they would be unable today to secure funding for the work that made their names. Sydney Brenner won the Nobel Prize in 2002 for work that led to key discoveries in organ development and programmed cell death. Interviewed by Elizabeth Dzeng in 2014 he was asked to reflect on the career of Fred Sanger, a two-time Nobel winner for his work on proteins and DNA sequencing methods. Brenner said:

A Fred Sanger would not survive in today's world of science. With continuous reporting and appraisals, some committee would note that he published little of import between insulin in 1952 and his first paper on RNA sequencing in 1967 with another long gap until DNA sequencing in 1977. He would be labelled as unproductive, and his modest personal support would be denied.[37]

Paradoxically, such an approach – designed to produce measurable outcomes and ensure value for money – diminishes the possibility of the major breakthroughs that have traditionally been a goal of university-based inquiry. Tim Harford illustrates this by reference to the awards of grants for medical research in the United States. There, the main source of government funding, the National Institutes of Health (NIH), follows careful protocols and encourages relatively safe research that is likely to produce incremental insights and auditable outputs. By contrast, the charitable Howard Hughes Medical Institute encourages researchers to take risks, invites highly speculative proposals, and provides generous funding with minimal interim reporting requirements. The latter's research results in more failures than the NIH, but the papers published from the research that it funds are twice as likely to be cited. Harford reports: 'They were also more original, producing research that introduced new "keywords" into the lexicon of their research field, changing research topics more often, and attracting more citations from outside their narrow field of expertise.'[38] Perhaps the approach of the Howard Hughes Medical Institute could be considered for at least some research council funding applications?

Other more radical options are also worth considering. As the success rate of applications has declined the costs of wasted effort have soared, as have levels of demoralisation. It has been estimated that the costs associated with failed applications amount to fully a quarter of the value of grants awarded by the EU's Horizon 2020 programme. The president of Science Europe, Marc Schiltz, is one of a growing number of influential voices who advocate instead that we experiment with a lottery scheme for those applications that meet basic criteria.[39] It has also been suggested that all researchers should receive the equivalent of a universal basic income that they could then combine with those of others to pursue more ambitious projects, if they so wish.[40] These ideas are well worth considering. They could rescue us from the safe and formulaic research that is now so commonplace and which ends up in our journals.

Lastly, governments need to consider whether the assessment exercises they initiate help or hinder the production of good-quality work. This is much more important than quantity. Unlike some, I don't advocate the abolition of the REF and similar exercises elsewhere. There must be some form of accountability for what we do, and some mechanism is needed to allocate research funds to universities. But we need a sense of proportion. The more layers of assessment that are added and the more bureaucratic the process becomes, the more game-playing ensues. I believe that much of this could be reduced in the next REF in the UK if the average number of publications required from each academic was reduced to two, and this was also made a maximum. At present, each academic must submit at least one publication and up to a maximum of five, with an average per submitting unit of 2.5. But a maximum of two would lower the burden of assessment on the relevant panels, and minimise the frantic and time-consuming evaluations of outputs internally to determine which ones should be submitted. By reducing people's feeling that they are labouring under oppressive systems of surveillance and never-ending evaluation, such a change would also improve their creativity and the quality of their work.

There are other benefits from this suggestion. A major review of the REF in 2016 was led by Lord Stern. It recognised that the REF 'could strongly influence academics in their choices about what problems they choose to tackle. This can drive them towards safe topics and short-termism, and a reluctance to engage in risky or multidisciplinary projects, in order to ensure reliable, high quality publication within the REF period, and may be discouraging innovative thinking and risk taking.'[41] Reducing the number of publications that researchers are required to submit would liberate them to pursue at least some projects for their own intrinsic interest rather than with the REF in mind. Systems elsewhere that mimic the REF should take note, and exercise some restraint. Not everything that can be measured should be, and doing so often does more harm than good. Would the world be any worse off if fewer management papers were published? I doubt it.

We have choices in how we respond to whatever performative pressures are thrown at us. In this chapter, I have lampooned Warwick Business School's ambition to be the leading business school in Europe: it is facile. But one can easily make similar criticisms of individual academics who feel that their self-esteem will wither unless they work at an institution garlanded with accreditation from the Association to Advance Collegiate Schools of Business, the European Quality Improvement System and the Association of MBAs, and which occupies a position at the top of this or that league table.[42] If the price of belonging to such an institution is a willingness to produce formulaic and empty research for its own sake, it is a price that may not be worth paying. These are choices that we can all still make, and which we should make with much greater thought for the consequences than we do at the moment.

CONCLUSION

Let us return to where we began – the suicide of Stefan Grimm. In its aftermath, Imperial College reviewed its processes for 'performance management'. This review did not revisit the grant income and other targets that Grimm was subject to. Rather, it concluded he had been under 'informal' review for too long, and had this advanced more quickly to the 'formal' stage, it 'would have provided more clarity to Professor Grimm on process and support through the written documentation, representation at meetings and HR involvement'. The suggestion seems to be that more pressure and an increased auditable 'process' would have reassured him. The review went on: 'It is further recommended that all performance management correspondence, both formal and informal, should be reviewed by a member of HR before dispatch by a line manager.'[43] Imperial

College's audit culture remains firmly in place, fortified by another layer of bureaucratic oversight. I am not reassured.

Really worthwhile work requires time, autonomy and the freedom to fail, often. I am tempted to suggest that research grants should only be awarded to people who can demonstrate that many of their previous projects have failed, since it at least shows that they dared to ask big questions with uncertain answers.

It is surely worth remembering what brought most of us into academic life in the first place. We do not write or seek research grants only to satisfy research assessment exercises. Nor do we do so to satisfy metrics whose sole purpose is to push an institution up various league tables, whatever the cost. The poet John Masefield, in a 1946 address at the University of Sheffield, described the university as

> a place where those who hate ignorance may strive to know, where those who perceive truth may strive to make others see; where seekers and learners alike, banded together in the search for knowledge, will honour thought in all its finer ways, will welcome thinkers in distress or in exile, will uphold ever the dignity of thought and learning and will exact standards in these things.[44]

These words are a rebuke to the performative practices now endemic in academic life. They did not appear in a top journal. But they express an enduring set of values that should guide each one of us in our publication practices and in the ambitions that we hold for our careers.

4 The Corruption of Academic Integrity

Management studies is not in a unique position. Unfortunately, 'questionable research practices' (QRPs) and outright fraud are attracting increased attention across the physical sciences and social sciences, and also within the humanities.[1] Ben Martin has concluded that

> the scale of research misconduct, whether in the form of plagiarism or the rather more ill-defined cases of redundant publication and self-plagiarism, is substantial, cross-national and growing. It is coming to occupy a large amount of time on the part of referees and particularly editors.[2]

In an interview, the former director of the Office of Research Integrity (ORI) in the US, David Wright, estimated that scientific misconduct occurs in nearly 3 per cent of all funded studies.[3] A government dossier in the UK suggested that one in twenty scientific papers contained errors or falsifications, and that scientists and journal editors remain reluctant to retract papers.[4] In line with this, Alison Abritis investigated final misconduct findings in 'hard science' research from the ORI: 43 per cent of individuals sanctioned for misconduct had at least one previous retraction.[5] They were serial offenders.

The issue of research integrity has been the focus of at least four major international conferences intended to promote good research practice. The Singapore Declaration on Research Integrity was endorsed at the second such conference. It offers a one-page guide to such issues as the preservation of research records, integrity, the reporting of irresponsible research practice, and authorship.[6] The San Francisco Declaration on Research Assessment (DORA) emerged from a meeting of the American Society for Cell Biology in 2012. DORA covers similar ground to the Singapore Declaration, although more comprehensively. Over 6,000 individuals have committed to upholding its principles in their research practice.[7] In addition, the Committee on Publication Ethics, originally established in 1997 by medical journal editors in the UK, now has approximately 10,000 members worldwide from all academic disciplines.[8] Numerous journal editors have committed to its code of conduct and to other guidelines, including how to manage retractions.

Recent scandals and high-profile retractions in academic journals have further fuelled concerns. The website Retraction Watch offers daily exposés, often gleefully, of research malpractice across academic disciplines.[9] These include the former Dutch psychologist, Diederik Stapel, who had fifty-eight papers retracted. I turn to examples from management studies in Chapter 5. But, for now, what do we mean by malpractice, and how widespread does it appear to be?

DO 'QRPS' DIFFER FROM RESEARCH FRAUD?

Research misconduct includes fabrication, falsification and plagiarism. Fabrication occurs when data are invented. Falsification is the inaccurate presentation of research, including the misrepresentation of processes, the omission of data or the deletion of inconvenient results that contradict the 'story' being told. Plagiarism is the unattributed use of someone else's work, and hence the claiming of undue credit. It is theft. Beyond these egregious examples, a range of other practices have been characterised generally as 'questionable' because they distort the record of research and damage trust in research findings. The Science Europe Working Group on Research Integrity[10] lists these as follows.

- **Research practice misconduct:** poor research designs that are incapable of adequately answering the research questions posed; the use of potentially harmful research methods; basic errors in analysis.
- **Data-related misconduct:** failure to preserve data; failure or reluctance to make data available for scrutiny by other researchers, particularly when its veracity is challenged.

- **Publication-related misconduct:** claiming authorship on papers to which one has not contributed; denying fair authorial credit to others; 'salami slicing' research into the maximum number of publications to boost a CV, thereby recycling existing knowledge.
- **Personal misconduct:** personal harassment, sexual or otherwise; insensitivity to important cultural norms.
- **Financial and other misconduct:** failing to disclose financial interests in research; misusing research funds; abusing the peer review process. Some management journals (e.g. *Organization Studies*) allow authors to suggest reviewers, although without necessarily committing to using them. Cat Ferguson, Adam Marcus and Ivan Oransky have identified approximately 110 papers in the hard sciences which were retracted in a two-year period because of manipulations of this system.[11] My own searches have found twelve papers retracted from an economics journal for the same violation. Some authors had suggested bogus reviewers who were the authors themselves or had nominated friends with whom they had formed 'mutual-reviewer' cartels. Others recommended genuine academics but provided fake email addresses that enabled authors to review their own papers.

Increasingly, criticisms are made of 'self-plagiarism' or 'text recycling': that is, authors recycling portions of their previous work without due acknowledgment. Serge Horbach and Willem Halffman give the example of a Dutch economist, Peter Nijkamp, who published about one-and-a-half papers *per week* over a number of years.[12] This truly astonishing rate of productivity was largely sustained by recycling portions of his earlier work. Unoriginal work is thereby presented as more novel than it is, again distorting the research record and further clogging publication outlets with unnecessary research. However, some journals encourage the reuse of 'methods' sections, arguing that changing them might make replication more difficult. A much less defensible practice is the wholesale reproduction of one's own ideas, data, and conclusions without recognising the original 'duplicated' source: for example, from a book chapter to a journal article, or from one journal article to another.

P-HACKING

I highlight two further practices that have been described generally as 'questionable'. These deserve more critical scrutiny than they have received. The first is '*p*-hacking' or 'data dredging'. It is worth pausing to reflect on exactly what a *p*-value is and the exaggerated claims that often surround it. David Colquhoun describes what a *p*-value can tell us as follows:

> If there were actually no effect (if the true difference between means were zero) then the probability of observing a value for the difference equal to, or greater than, that actually observed is called the *p* value. In other words the *p* value is the chance of seeing a difference at least as big as we have done, if, in fact, there were no real effect.[13]

In essence, the *p*-value tells us that the null hypothesis – that there is no real difference between two or more conditions – is unlikely to be true. Note: not impossible. Nor does it mean that a hypothesis advanced to explain a given effect is necessarily true.

Imagine that I design an experiment to determine whether a manager who bullies his or her employees increases their productivity. Drawing on human relations theory, I hypothesise that workers in the non-bullying conditions will be more productive than those who are bullied. I design an experiment that simulates bullying and non-bullying while the subjects in my experiment compete to make widgets. Every now and then a subject in the bullying condition who I appear to have randomly selected to play the role of a manager, but who is in fact a carefully trained stooge, shouts: 'You aren't doing very well. For God's sake take this more seriously.' In my non-bullying condition, my stooge says: 'You know, I think you are doing really well at this. We are making great progress.' I repeat my experiment multiple times, until I build an impressive data set capable of showing that some kind of difference is emerging between the groups. To my surprise, workers in the bullying condition are outperforming those in the non-bullying condition. The mean difference is 103 widgets for those in the bullying groups and 100 widgets for those in the non-bullying groups. I run my analysis of the results and find that $p < .05$. The result is statistically significant – that is, the null hypothesis (that there is no difference between performance in the two conditions) can be rejected. It seems likely that it has not arisen by chance. I get excited. The human relations school of management is out and sociopaths who work as managers can rejoice. Immediately, I think of variations in the experiment to produce yet more papers. What is the effect of the manager's gender on performance? Would the effect be enhanced or diminished by increasing the racial diversity of the subjects? What is the impact of age, sexual orientation, height and even hair loss when the manager is male? Moreover, I rewrite my hypothesis to suggest that these were the results I always predicted and redraft my literature review accordingly.

Now dig deeper. There are at least four problems with me getting so carried away about my results. The first and most important is that it tells me nothing about the size of the effect I have discovered. The word 'significant' here doesn't mean what it does in everyday language, where we associate it with importance. Recall that the difference in production between my two conditions is three widgets. This gives me a statistically significant result since my sample size is big. But the size of the effect is relatively small. As Dorothy Bishop has pointed out, 'Small samples are generally a bad thing, because they only allow us to reliably detect very large effects. But very large samples have the opposite problem: they allow us to detect as "significant" effects that are so small as to be trivial.'[14] After all, I have found a difference of only 3 per cent between my two conditions. As Stephen Ziliak and Deirdre McCloskey conclude:

> a finding of 'statistical' significance, or the lack of it, is on its own almost valueless, a meaningless parlor game. Statistical significance should be a tiny part of an inquiry concerned with the

size and importance of relationships. Unhappily it has become the central and standard error of many sciences.[15]

The second is the nagging worry of whether I have really found anything at all. David Colquhoun calculates that if I have a significance threshold of .05 I will be wrong at least 30 per cent of the time.[16] That is, I will be claiming that my result is significant when further work will show that is not. By now, you should be getting worried.

The third problem is that I can wrongly infer that my hypothesis has now been confirmed. All that has really happened is that the null hypothesis can be rejected. This absolutely does not prove that my hypothesis seeking to explain the productivity gap between two conditions are correct: there may be other much more robust explanations than what I have been able to devise. The American Statistical Association (2016) issued a strong statement about the misuse of probability tests. It pointed out that 'p-values do not measure the probability that the studied hypothesis is true, or the probability that the data were produced by random chance alone'. It also stressed that 'by itself a p-value does not provide a good measure of evidence regarding a model or hypothesis'.[17] Yet we routinely find claims in the literature that various propositions and hypotheses have been confirmed, as a result of significance testing.

My fourth and final problem is as follows. Imagine that, instead, I found no difference between my two conditions. This is potentially interesting, since it would suggest that whether people are treated well or badly at work makes no difference to their productivity. It may be even more interesting and certainly more surprising than the hypothesis I had advanced. However, my statistical tests have confirmed a null hypothesis. The results are not statistically significant. Since journals want to publish only positive results it is improbable that my findings will be viewed favourably by reviewers and editors. Thus, the paper is unlikely to be published in a so-called top journal: after all, I have found no difference between the conditions I have created. Moreover, I have only a tentative explanation for my findings rather than a fully formed theory to explain them. My results could therefore be described as uninteresting, they tell us nothing new, and they don't offer a strong and original contribution to theory. Again, this is what the so-called top journals are seeking – new theories which are clear-cut and linked to statistically significant results. I go down in flames. I have to dredge the data to ensure that I have statistically significant results that support my hypotheses so I can send the paper to another top journal; or, I am in the ignominious position of sending the paper to a lower-ranked journal and run the risk of being viewed as delinquent by my colleagues and boss.

P-hacking compounds these problems. It encompasses a variety of practices: failing to report all dependent measures in a study, selectively reporting only those studies that deliver the desired p-value, terminating a study when a desired p-level has been reached, dropping items from survey instruments that are preventing the attainment of a 'desirable' p-level; or rounding off a p-value by, for example, reporting that a lower one is actually .5. There are now a wide range of software packages which have been designed to help with this kind of data mining. Given the effort involved in conducting studies it is apparent that we are incentivised to engage in precisely these behaviours. As Leif Nelson, Joseph Simmons and Uri Simonsohn argue, it is unlikely that one failed test will lead researchers to give up on their analysis. Instead, they would 'explore the data further, examining, for example, whether outliers were interfering with the effect, whether the effect was significant within a subset of participants or trials, or whether it emerged when the dependent variable was coded differently'.[18] Note that no one suggests they would go to such pains if a result suggests statistical significance! These authors challenge the notion that the file drawers of researchers are stuffed with failed studies. They assert that researchers generally don't file failed studies but rather file failed attempts at p-hacking. It is the equivalent of asking several friends for advice on a marital problem, but only listening to the one who agrees with what you intend to do anyway.

Go back to my proposed experiment on bullying. I could do several things to obtain the statistically significant finding on which publication and my future career depends. I could perhaps delete the results of some of my experiments that went the wrong way from the analysis. Or I could stop gathering data at the point when the tests I am running (note, before I have completed my planned protocol) give me the result that I want. It is possible that if I persevered as I had originally planned the effect I have discovered would disappear. We will never know. Chris Chambers describes this as 'the sin of hidden flexibility', in that what researchers do is deliberately kept secret from editors, reviewers and ultimately readers.[19] This conduct is a form of 'data torture'. The data are interrogated mercilessly until they confess they support a given hypothesis.

Herman Aguines, Ravi Ramani and Nawaf Alabdyljader put it starkly:

> We simply do not know whether what we see is what we get. Most things seem just right: measures are valid and have good psychometric qualities, hypotheses described in the Introduction section are mostly supported by results, statistical assumptions are not violated (or not mentioned), the 'storyline' is usually neat and straightforward, and everything seems to be in place. But, unbeknownst to readers, many researchers have engaged in various trial-and-error practices (e.g., revising, dropping, and adding scale items), opaque choices (e.g., including or excluding different sets of control variables), and other decisions (e.g., removing outliers, retroactively creating hypotheses after the data were analyzed) that are not disclosed fully.[20]

The problem is that with enough determination and ingenuity, mixed in with few scruples, researchers can find a statistically significant relationship between almost any phenomena. For example, David Hendry was able to show a statistically significant relationship between levels of rainfall and inflation.[21] Joseph Simmons, Leif Nelson and Uri Simonsohn followed a similar course, this time looking at the effects of music on our feelings of age. They were able to show that when people listened to the Beatles singing 'When I'm Sixty-Four' rather than Kalimba (an instrumental song by Mr Scruff) they felt nearly eighteen months younger, with a p-level of .4. They then documented the statistical games they had played with their data to produce such an implausible finding.[22] An amusing website has emerged called 'Spurious Correlations'[23] which takes further advantage of this. There is a strong correlation between the number of people who die from falling into a pool and films released starring Nicolas Cage. Imad Moosa shows a high and obviously spurious correlation between the amount of money NASA spends and suicides by hanging, strangulation and suffocation, while the divorce rate in Maine is highly correlated with the per capita consumption of margarine.[24] If I ran enough tests I might even find that these connections are statistically significant.

These problems are rife within our discipline. We have become obsessed by finding p-values rather than exploring effect sizes. This risks saturating the literature with false positives known as Type 1 errors (the rejection of a null hypothesis that is in fact true). It sustains 'undead theories': that is, theories that are fervently believed but which are nevertheless unsound.[25] Quite incredibly, published management papers claim support for over 90 per cent of the hypotheses that are tested.[26] Kwok Leung reported that the hypotheses in 54 papers in the *Academy of Management Journal* were supported in 73 per cent of papers, and unsupported in 20 per cent of papers.[27] Russell Craig and I analysed fifty randomly selected papers in *Administrative Science Quarterly* that offered hypotheses: 90 per cent of the hypotheses proposed were either partially or fully confirmed. In line with this, an analysis of approximately 250 psychology papers found that more than 10 per cent reported incorrect p-values.[28] Over 90 per cent of the errors favoured the researchers' expectations and led to non-significant findings being reported as significant. Raymond Hubbard concludes that this has resulted in 'an empirical literature consisting almost entirely of unverified, fragile results whose role in the development of cumulative knowledge is of the shakiest kind'.[29] A detailed review published in 2018 summarised the evidence as showing that '25 to 50 per cent of published articles in management have inconsistences or errors ... Overall, there is a proliferation of evidence indicating substantial reasons to doubt the veracity and, justifiably, the conclusions and implications of scholarly work.'[30] Nor do meta-analyses overcome these problems. Despite the injunction that they should consider publication biases, 60 to 90 per cent of meta-analyses don't do so, and between a quarter and half don't include any unpublished results.[31] The bias towards publishing only positive results pervades and undermines research in management studies at every level.

The social science community's obsession with statistical significance may generate all sorts of other problems with research. Balazs Aczel, Bence Palfi and Barnabas Szaszi analysed over 35,000 articles in 293 psychology journals using Bayes factor analysis techniques. They found that 55 per cent of all analysed results provided evidence for the alternative hypothesis, and more than half did not pass the Bayes factor level threshold for being no better than anecdotal evidence.[32] The emphasis within the discipline on 'statistical significance', even if the tests are applied properly, may set the evidence bar for hypotheses too low, again reinforcing rogue findings and hindering reproducibility. In what may be a harbinger of things to come, at least one journal, *Basic and Applied Psychology*, has now banned null hypothesis significance testing. Of course, it is possible that research in management studies may be more robust than psychology research in its statistical practices and less in need of such remedies. Somehow, this seems unlikely.

HARKING

The other outstanding QRP that is now attracting increased critical attention is HARKing – that is, Hypothesising After the Results are Known, but presenting the hypothesis as *a priori* rather than *ex post*. Look again at my experiment on workplace bullying. My original theory has fallen apart so I come up with new hypotheses to show that my experimental design actually found what I had intended, and that the theory I used was more able to predict particular outcomes than was actually the case. This approach increases the adoption of practices that are erroneously assumed to have obtained reliable scientific support and theoretical justification. Norbert Kerr argues that it 'violates a fundamental ethical principle of science: the obligation to communicate one's work honestly and completely'.[33] In my view, it transforms the methods sections of papers into works of creative fiction, rather than rigorous accounts of actual practice and how theory development takes place. Yet honesty in all aspects of research, including methods, is one of the core elements found in any definition of research integrity.[34] A failure to be transparent about our methods mis-educates the next generation of researchers. Perhaps more importantly, it hinders the falsification of theories by reinforcing the already strong bias of journals to publish only positive findings. Note that I am not criticising the practice of developing new hypotheses after empirical research has been conducted. I am criticising the pretence that they were in place beforehand.

Other pressures are highlighted by the Levelt Committee's report into the Stapel fraud. The committee interviewed his co-authors, many of whom reported

> that reviewers encouraged irregular (journal) practices. For instance, a co-author stated that editors and reviewers would sometimes request certain variables to be omitted, because doing so would be more consistent with the reasoning and flow of the narrative, thereby also omitting unwelcome results. Reviewers have also requested that not all executed analyses be reported, for example by simply leaving unmentioned any conditions for which no effects had been found, although effects were originally expected. Sometimes reviewers insisted on retrospective pilot studies, which were then reported as having been performed in advance. In this way

the experiments and choices of items are justified with the benefit of hindsight.[35]

A Crisis of Replication and Reproducibility?

Another indicator of the extent of problematic practices can be gleaned from a crisis of replication. The infrequency of replication allows poorly supported or rogue findings to remain undetected. The problem is compounded by the bias in favour of publishing only positive results, a lack of accountability, and the minimal sharing of data.[36] A study by Donald Bergh and several of his colleagues reported their attempt to reproduce the results from 88 papers published in *Strategic Management Journal* using data reported in the studies themselves. They found that 'about 70% of the studies did not disclose enough data to permit independent tests of reproducibility of their findings. Of those that could be retested, almost one-third reported hypotheses as statistically significant when they were no longer so and far more significant results were found to be non-significant in the reproduction than in the opposite direction.'[37] Their understated conclusion is that 'the strategic management literature appears vulnerable to credibility problems ... If we cannot reproduce a study using its own data, then can we have confidence in its findings?' I think this is a rhetorical question.

Of course, these issues are not unique to management studies. A study of 100 psychology journals with very high five-year impact factors concluded that the overall rate of replication in psychology is only 1.07 per cent.[38] *Replications in Social Psychology* began publishing in 1979 to address the problem. It issued only three volumes before collapsing. The likelihood of replication in psychology is therefore low. The exception is where researchers make claims that are 'too good to be true', inviting replication. Such was the case with the physicist Jan Hendrick Schon, who worked with eight collaborators to produce, on average, one research paper every eight days. The quantity of his output, and the potential importance of his findings, encouraged other scientists to replicate his research. They uncovered one of the most audacious frauds in the physical sciences.[39] When researchers offer more modest findings by filling in 'gaps' in existing theory, or findings that seem logically consistent with previous research, their work is less likely to be replicated.

Yet replications of previously published studies are important in helping to preserve the integrity of the cumulative empirical foundation of knowledge. Failure to replicate, alongside the absence of sufficiently detailed enabling research protocols, are among the reasons offered by John Ioannidis in support of his celebrated claim that most published research findings are false.[40] Nevertheless, a study of eighteen leading business journals from 1970 to 1991 found that replication papers constituted 'less than 10% of published empirical work in the accounting, economics, and finance areas, and 5% or less in the management and marketing fields ... [which] ... raises the prospect that empirical results in these areas may be of limited value for guiding the development of business theory and practice'.[41]

The problem is compounded in our field by the prioritisation of theory development over theory testing, and the associated preference for 'novelty' over incremental contributions. I discuss this very serious problem in detail in Chapter 6. Here, I simply note that while most major management journals insist on theory development as a condition of publication, I know of none that regularly publish replications. Developments in cognate disciplines suggest that testing and replication identifies problems with research findings more readily and helps to correct the scientific record. The Open Science Collaboration published the results of an attempt to replicate 100 studies in psychology in 2015. Although 97 per cent of the original papers reported statistically significant results, these could only be obtained in 36 per cent of the replications. Effect sizes were also much lower.[42]

One area of social psychology seems, at the moment, to be particularly problematic. Much of Diederik Stapel's research fell into the category of 'social priming'. This is concerned with the notion that 'the mere exposure to socially relevant stimuli can facilitate, or *prime*, a host of impressions, judgments, goals, and actions, often even outside of people's intention or awareness'.[43] In one typical study, participants were asked to either recall the Ten Commandments (a moral reminder) or ten books they had read in high school (a neutral task). Those who had been the moral reminder were subsequently less likely to cheat when given a problem-solving task.[44] However, a major study that involved twenty-five direct replications of this experiment found only a small effect, and that was in the opposite direction to what the original study had suggested.[45] Other social priming replications have also either failed or found much smaller effects than were initially claimed. Of course, the Stapel fraud ensured that this field would attract particularly close scrutiny. In a widely publicised letter written in 2012, the Nobel Prize winning psychologist Daniel Kahneman gloomily predicted 'I see a train wreck looming. I expect the first victims to be young people on the job market. Being associated with a controversial and suspicious field will put them at a severe disadvantage in the competition for positions. Because of the high visibility of the issue, you may already expect the coming crop of graduates to encounter problems.'[46] While some psychologists are frankly in denial about the extent of these problems,[47] others have responded more thoughtfully. They have launched the *Society for the Improvement of Psychological Science*.[48] Maybe management studies should follow suit. A new journal, *Advances in Methods and Practices in Psychological Science*, began publication in 2018. It is doing sterling work in publishing both replications and discussions of how research in general can be improved.

My own view at this stage is that any area of the social sciences at the receiving end of the kind of attention that psychology has attracted would be equally likely to reveal problems. Consistent with this expectation, problems with replication have now been identified in many other disciplines. An attempt to replicate sixty-seven pre-clinical studies dealing with cancer only managed to do so for between 20 and 25 per cent of them.[49] Nearly 72 per cent of 869 members of the American Society for Cell Biology reported problems in replicating the work of other laboratories.[50] John Ioannidis and a large number of his colleagues were able to replicate only two out of eighteen microarray-based gene expression studies.[51] This doesn't in the least minimise the importance of the issue within management studies, or psychology for that matter.

While the Open Science Collaboration is careful to point out many possible reasons for failure other than false positives, I think that these findings can only be described as disturbing. Some responses to this outcome have been unconvincing. For example, Wolfgang Stroebe and Miles Hewstone stress that statistical power in many of the original studies was likely to be low, and suggested that this was likely to be the main reason for the failure to establish replications.[52] But if the power of a study is so low that the claim of statistical significance cannot be replicated then studies that prioritise significance should be more suspect in the first place.[53] I am also not convinced that growing recognition of the problems caused by such practices as p-hacking means that we are now entering a 'renaissance' in psychology – a view articulated by Leif Nelson, Joseph Simmons and Uri Simonsohn.[54] Progress is certainly being made. Whether it is sufficient to merit being called a 'renaissance' surely remains to be seen.

How Common Are QRPs and Fraud?

A crucial question at this point is 'How widespread are these practices?' To explore this, Table 4.1 summarises data from studies that have explored these issues in business and management studies.[55]

The research summarised in Table 4.1 suggests that levels of retraction reflect problems of reporting and detection, rather than actual levels of misconduct. There seems to be a strong belief that QRPs are common. Much of the self-reported data in Table 4.1 also shows widespread approval (or at least tolerance) of p-hacking and HARKing. For example, about 90 per cent of US management faculty respondents admitted to HARKing and 24 per cent reported engaging in

Table 4.1 *Reported frequencies of fraud and questionable research practices in business and management studies*

QRP	Sources	Method, sample, location (survey unless specified otherwise)	Results
General	Bedeian et al. 2010	438 mgmt faculty, 104 colleges: US	73% reported knowledge of QRPs in previous year
Data fraud	Hoover & Hopp 2017	1,215 mgmt faculty: Int	9.18% of editors (18 respondents) sometimes, often or very often encountered falsified data; 3.8% of reviewers (29 respondents) reported same
	Bailey et al. 2001	107 highly published accounting researchers: Int	3.7% reported engaging in data fraud
	Banks et al. 2016	344 mgmt researchers, 126 PhD students: US	1% of researchers self-reported fraud; 7% of PhD students reported witnessing fraud
Plagiarism	Honig & Bedi 2012	Reading of 279 AOM conference papers: Int	35% of papers had some plagiarism
Self-plagiarism	Bedeian et al. 2010	438 mgmt faculty, 104 colleges: US	85% reported knowing colleagues who had self-plagiarised
P-hacking	Hoover & Hopp 2017	1,215 mgmt faculty: Int	19.9% of editors (39 respondents) sometimes, often or very often encountered data deleted unjustifiably; 9.1% of reviewers (69

Table 4.1 (*cont.*)

QRP	Sources	Method, sample, location (survey unless specified otherwise)	Results
			respondents) reported same; 25% reported selectively deleting or reporting data after analysis, at least once; 60% admitted knowing colleagues who had dropped data points
	Bedeian et al. 2010	438 mgmt faculty, 104 colleges: US	13% of mgmt faculty agreed 'rounding off' was appropriate; 50% said they had selectively reported hypotheses depending on significance
	Banks et al. 2016	344 mgmt researchers, 126 PhD students: US	21% approved of excluding data after viewing the effect on significance tests
HARKing	Banks et al. 2016	344 mgmt researchers, 126 PhD students: US	25% of researchers agreed this was appropriate; 50% reported HARKing; 58% of PhD students had observed HARKing
	Bedeian et al. 2010	438 mgmt faculty, 104 colleges: US	About 90% reported HARKing

Key: AOM = Academy of Management; Int = international; mgmt = management; QRP = questionable research practices; U = undeterminable self-plagiarism. In one of these studies, 25 per cent of respondents disagreed that HARKing was inappropriate; 23 per cent disagreed it was inappropriate to selectively report hypotheses depending on their statistical significance; and 13 per cent disagreed it was inappropriate to round down p-levels. A reasonable inference is that these respondents are likely to engage in practices they see as relatively unproblematic. In some cases, the very practices that so many see as acceptable have constituted grounds for retraction. Overall, our scholarly record has been sorely compromised, and many academic reputations surely rest on dodgy foundations. Although the bulk of the data cited in Table 4.1 was sourced in Europe and the USA, more investigation of research integrity appears warranted in other countries (such as Brazil, Russia, India and China) since they are the source of much of the growth in journal publications. Yet little is known about how their researchers view research ethics. However, there has been a wave of retractions by Chinese scholars because of fake reviewers. Of 31 Chinese researchers who had papers retracted for this, 29 admitted to using a 'broker', and to paying them fees that in some cases reached US$5,500: fraud has become a business.[56]

Table 4.2 summarises data from studies of fraud and QRPs in other disciplines.[57] Awareness of research misconduct engaged in by others (reaching 51 per cent in a survey of biostatisticians) tends to be higher than self-reports. Generally, the incidence of self-reports of research fraud and misconduct is much lower. Nonetheless, a survey of 215 UK researchers across several disciplines found that 17.9 per cent admitted to using entirely invented data. Self-reports of p-hacking are disturbing. In a study of psychologists, 63.4 per cent of respondents admitted they did not report all dependent measures and 22 per cent admitted to 'rounding off'. This reflects the pressure to publish only positive results. A study of graduate students and postdoctoral research fellows involved in cancer research found that 39.2 per cent of them had been pressurised by a collaborator or principal investigator to produce 'positive' data, and 62.8 per cent conceded that publishing pressures influenced how they reported

Table 4.2 *Reported frequencies of fraud and questionable research practices across disciplines*

QRP	Sources	Method, sample, location (survey unless specified otherwise)	Results
General	Necker 2014	631 economists: Europe	94% reported engaging in at least one QRP
	Cossette 2004	134 academic admin staff: Canada	56% reported witnessing misconduct
	Kalichman & Friedman 1992	549 biomedical trainees: US	36% reported observing some form of scientific misconduct
Data fraud/ data falsification	Boulbes et al. 2018	467 graduate students & postdoctoral fellows in cancer bench research: US	27.1% had witnessed data falsification/ fabrication
	Fraser et al. 2018	494 ecologists, 313 evolutionary biologists: Int	4.5% of ecologists and 2% of evolutionary biologists admitted filling in missing data points without identifying those data as simulated
	Williams & Roberts 2016	215 researchers: UK	17.9% reported having entirely invented data
	Titus 2014	5,100 medical school researchers: US	5.6% could distinguish seven or more of nine scenarios depicting fraud
	Swazey et al. 1993	2,000 PhD students, 2,000 faculty: US	10% knew of people committing fraud

Table 4.2 (*cont.*)

QRP	Sources	Method, sample, location (survey unless specified otherwise)	Results
	Ranstam et al. 2000	166 biostatisticians: US	51% were aware of fraud by others in the prior decade
	Kalichman & Friedman 1992	549 biomedical trainees: US	15% were willing to select, omit or fabricate data to publish a paper or secure a grant
	Titus et al. 2008	212 National Institute of Health researchers: US	8.7% had observed (or had direct evidence of) fabrication, falsification or plagiarism
	Fanelli 2009	Review of 21 surveys, with 18 included in meta-analysis: Int	1–2% of scientists had fabricated, falsified or modified data or results at least once
	Martinson et al. 2005	1,768 scientists: US	0.3% reported they had falsified or 'cooked' data
Plagiarism	Williams & Roberts 2016	215 researchers: UK	13.6% self-reported engaging in plagiarism
	Pupovac & Fanelli 2015	Meta-analysis of surveys: Int	30% reported plagiarism by colleagues
Self-plagiarism	Williams & Roberts 2016	215 researchers: UK	36% reported they had self-plagiarised
	Necker 2014	631 economists: Europe	24% reported they had self-plagiarised
	Martinson et al. 2005	768 scientists: US	4.7% reported they had self-plagiarised

Table 4.2 (*cont.*)

QRP	Sources	Method, sample, location (survey unless specified otherwise)	Results
P-hacking	Boulbes et al. 2018	467 graduate students & postdoctoral fellows in cancer bench research: US	24.2% omitted results that did not favour their working hypotheses
	Fraser et al. 2018	494 ecologists, 313 evolutionary biologists: Int	27.3% of ecologists and 17.5% of evolutionary biologists admitted 'rounding off'
	Agnoli et al. 2017	277 psychologists: Italy	47.9% admitted not reporting all of a study's measures; 22.2% admitted to 'rounding off'
	Tijdink et al. 2016	535 biomedical scientists: Europe	25% reported selectively deleting or reporting data after analysis, at least once; 60% reported knowing colleagues who dropped data points
	Eastwood et al. 1996	331 postdoctoral fellows: U	27% reported willingness to select data to 'improve' results
	John et al. 2012	2,155 psychologists: US	63.4% failed to report all dependent measures; 55.9% collected more data after seeing if results

Table 4.2 (*cont.*)

QRP	Sources	Method, sample, location (survey unless specified otherwise)	Results
			were significant; 27.7% failed to report all conditions; 22% rounded off *p*-values; 45.8% selectively reported studies that 'worked'; 38.2% excluded data after looking at the impact of doing so
	Martinson et al. 2005	1,768 scientists, 126 PhD students: US	15.3% reported dropping observations or data points
HARKing	Fraser et al. 2018	494 ecologists, 313 evolutionary biologists: Int	48.5% of ecologists and 54.2% of evolutionary biologists admitted reporting unexpected findings as having been expected from start
	Agnoli et al. 2017	277 psychologists: Italy	37.4% admitted to reporting an unexpected finding as having been predicted from the start
	Necker 2014	631 economists: Europe	79% reported HARKing
	John et al. 2012	2,155 psychologists: US	27% reported unexpected findings as if they had been predicted from the start

Table 4.2 (cont.)

QRP	Sources	Method, sample, location (survey unless specified otherwise)	Results
	Kerr 1998	156 behavioural scientists: U	30% reported they knew colleagues who engaged in HARKing
	Tijdink et al. 2016	535 biomedical scientists: Europe	63% reported HARKing once; 39% did so more than once

Key: Int = international; QRP = questionable research practices; U = undeterminable

their data. Astonishingly, given the virtual impossibility of achieving any such thing, 56 per cent felt that it was necessary to publish in such journals as *Cell, Nature* or *Science*, as a first author, to land an academic position. One can readily imagine how this might translate into shortcuts and worse, accompanied by the rationalisation that once the goal of securing a permanent job is achieved there will be more room for ethics later. Some researchers seem to be channelling the spirit of St Augustine, who once wrote: 'As a youth I prayed, give me chastity and continence, but not yet.'[58]

A study of 789 scientific papers in science and medical journals, with 1,105 co-authors, found that at least one author in 34 per cent of papers had an undeclared financial interest in the reported outcome.[59] These findings are a worrying indicator of the incidence of research fraud and misconduct across disciplines. If we assume that business and management studies is no purer than other disciplines in terms of QRPs, this suggests that the poor practices highlighted above are much more common than the level of retractions would suggest.

Ghost authorship is a particular problem in the medical literature. Pharmaceutical companies sometimes hire professionals to write the results of clinical trials for publication, thereby disguising possible conflicts of interest.[60] I have no data regarding the prevalence of such practice in business and management. There is also the associated habit of gifting authorship to friends or influential scholars. Moreover, anecdotal evidence suggests that some scholars have formed publishing cartels to 'beat the system': friends give each other credit for papers on which they have provided little or no input, enabling them to artificially inflate their publication 'score'. While this is less serious than fraud, I nevertheless concur with the view of Xavier Bosch and Joseph Ross that these 'are acts of research misconduct ... because they entail maintaining secrecy, falsifying credentials, and fabricating the attribution of writing to another'.[61] The fact that 1.88 per cent of respondents to a survey of economists listed in Table 4.1 reported accepting or offering sex for authorship credit shows the scope for misbehaviour it sometimes unleashes. Scholars who engage in such practices also seem prone to graduate to other forms of research misconduct.[62]

The Corruption of Research

I view research fraud and malpractice as a form of corruption. I realise that corruption is a strong word here. But I can't think of another that does justice to what is involved. After all, we are discussing the progressive erosion of scholarly integrity, and the prioritising of publication above seeking truth. Publication, in this environment, is widely seen as just a game that we play in pursuit of career-building. In many cases, the rewards from such publication are immediate and tangible. On average, Chinese universities offer first authors more than $43,000 for publishing a paper in *Science* or *Nature*. At Qatar University, authors share up to $13,700 when they publish a paper in *Nature* or *Science*. At the Miller College of Business in Muncie, Indiana, those who publish in a list of business journals earn $2,000. They can take this as cash, or use the money for personal research funds.[63] The University of New South Wales in Australia offers cash to academics for publishing in highly ranked journals, which is paid into their individual research accounts. The university also provides training in how to 'get into' such journals.[64] Management scholars least of all should be surprised that this may further incentivise people to cut corners, invent results or exaggerate the importance of their work.[65]

Moreover, universities throughout the world now often proclaim their commitment to 'excellence'. As part of this they express the wish to rise up the various league tables that seem to be proliferating at an exponential rate. Such single-minded pursuit of 'excellence' gives rise to a paradox: it provides incentives for forms of misconduct that may become normalised and embraced by wider groups or whole organisations.[66] Researchers seem likely to rationalise their actions by drawing on what I term the 'Lance Armstrong defence'. Armstrong, who finally admitted to routinely using prohibited performance-enhancing substances throughout his cycling career, explained that at the time he didn't think he was cheating, since 'everyone else was doing it'. He was therefore only levelling the playing field.[67] If researchers who engage in any type of QRPs imagine they are widespread (and the survey evidence reviewed in this chapter suggests that many of them do) it is easy to see how these rationalisations could be developed. Corruption, fraud and QRPs are routinised: they become an ongoing and habitual process that no longer attracts much critical thought by individuals or groups. Essentially, corruption becomes *normalised*. Herbert Kelman describes the outcome as *mindlessness* – a state obviously useful to the conduct of research malpractice, since it subdues any inner voice disturbed by what is occurring.[68]

A sense of 'bounded ethicality' may emerge, in which people are led astray, irrespective of how well-intentioned they initially are.[69] The more people develop a single-minded focus on instrumental goals (such as securing 'hits' in top journals) the more likely this is. 'Bad apples' (malpracticing individuals) can then lead to 'bad barrels', where more members of an organisation follow their example. Ultimately, this may produce 'bad orchards', in which unethical practices have become normalised throughout an industry or sector. These processes can be facilitated by what Marc Edwards and Siddhartha Roy describe as a 'perversion of natural selection' that may occur within academia.[70] Younger academics have no experience of an alternative academic environment to that of the present. Those of them that respond positively to perverse incentives prosper. As they acquire power and influence, the status quo seems completely natural to them – why should they change it? Our social field is not static. This dystopian scenario is, at least, one possible outcome.

Under these conditions, we might well follow Richard Smith who, in addressing the question 'Why does research misconduct happen?', responded that his preferred answer is: 'Why wouldn't it happen?'[71] There has been insufficient consideration of the extent to which the contextual processes discussed here undermine academic integrity. As I will now seek to show in Chapter 5, this process is well under way in management studies.

In short: *Houston, we have a problem.*

5 Paradise Lost but Not Regained: Retractions and Management Studies

In Chapter 4, I discussed the nature of questionable research practices (QRPs) and fraud within academia generally. Now it is time to turn attention closer to home. To do so I look at retractions within management studies, analyse the reasons provided for them, and consider what they imply about the overall state of our research. I also draw on interview data from four editors who had retracted papers, and two co-authors of papers retracted because of fraud perpetrated by another author. To encourage candour, the confidentiality of the editors and co-authors has been maintained. This was important because if the editors' identities were known, so would the retractions they discuss, and authors' identities would then be revealed.[1] This could raise legal issues, and would certainly have inhibited the interviewees. Co-authors had similar concerns. In addition, I interviewed a former academic guilty of research fraud. He is Diederik Stapel, mentioned briefly in Chapter 4.[2] His fifty-eight retractions include three in management journals. Given the intense scrutiny of Stapel's activities, and his authorship of a freely-available online book detailing his actions, issues of confidentiality do not arise.[3]

In conjunction with Russell Craig, I compiled a database of retracted journal articles in business and management by searching the Business Source Complete listing of peer-reviewed journals, using the key search terms 'retraction' and 'retracted'. This resulted in a final total of 129 retracted papers. Retractions are ongoing, particularly for some prolific offenders. Thus, two retractions after this search have been included in the analysis, bringing the total to 131.

All retracted articles were profiled in terms of year of retraction, author(s) and year published, number of Google Scholar citations, journal involved, journal impact factor (JIF), journal Scimago quartile classification (Q1, Q2, Q3, Q4), and the principal reason for retraction.

Fifty-eight of the retractions that we examined took place within two years of publication. However, eighteen papers were in the public domain for ten years or more before retraction. The retracted article with the most citations (593) was sole-authored by Ulrich Lichtenthaler. This was published in the *Academy of Management Journal* – a journal with the second highest JIF (7.417) of any in the database. Eighty-five papers were retracted by Scimago Q1 journals. There are at least two plausible explanations for this large proportion of retractions in highly ranked journals. The first is that 'top' journals usually have more stringent submission and review procedures, and a larger and more attentive readership, enabling them to detect problems more efficiently. The second explanation is that their prestige tempts authors to take shortcuts that enhance their prospects of successfully publishing in them.

Seven authors co-authored seventy-seven retracted papers (with ninety-six co-authors) in thirty-six separate journals. These data reveal the potential for a few scholars who engage in sustained fraud, or who have made serious mistakes with data analysis, or who have engaged in other unethical practices, to have a damaging long-term impact. Delays in retracting highly flawed research compounds this problem, since defective work continues to be cited. The pressures on co-authors that flow from this are enormous. They have to devote significant time to dealing with the fallout from them. The pressure on editors who have to manage the process is also considerable, and the tension sometimes spills over to the wider community associated with a journal. For example, the decision by *Leadership Quarterly* to retract five papers led to prolonged and anguished email debates among members of its editorial board. Several resigned in protest while others expressed their full support. This signifies a grievous waste of time by the wider academic community in reading, being influenced by and citing defective work, and in debating how to deal with it.

It is worth pausing to consider two individual authors in more detail. The case of James Hunton is undoubtedly the most striking. His thirty-seven retractions are more than anyone else, and his work also clearly had considerable impact. Between 1986 and 2010 Hunton was the most cited author in the *Journal of Information Systems*.[4] He certainly had a stellar career until his disgrace. Hunton served as president and vice-president of the IS Accounting Association, worked at a prestigious university and published regularly in top accountancy journals. Ironically enough, his specialisms included ethics in accountancy. One of his co-authors, Dan Stone, reflected at length on his experiences with Hunton, his impact on accountancy and the lessons that can be drawn from his fraud. He describes him as 'charming, engaging, likeable, friendly, persuasive, intelligent, hardworking, and dedicated to his craft'.[5] Hunton gave no one any reason to suspect that he was anything other than an excellent academic. I have spoken to others who either worked with Hunton or published with him, and they use similar terms to describe his character. Evidently, fraudsters do not go around clanking chains and reeking of sulphur. Rather, they are plausible individuals who appear to be successful and with whom people are keen to work.

Bentley University, where Hunton last worked, published a five-page report addressing his misconduct, written by its ethics officer Judith Malone.[6] It makes it abundantly clear that Hunton committed extensive fraud by inventing data and by exaggerating sample sizes. He repeatedly created fictitious organisations from where his data were allegedly obtained. Bentley's investigation could not find *any* raw data: it is entirely possible that all the claims in his extensive body of work rest on fraud. Hunton's modus operandi involved inventing 'confidentiality agreements' with the organisations allegedly participating in his research which prevented him from sharing his raw data with co-workers. He invoked the same justification for not sharing it with those who eventually investigated his activities.

Of course, he is not alone in pursuing this stratagem: it is an obvious method to justify data concealment, and one of my co-author

PARADISE LOST BUT NOT REGAINED 109

interviewees reports a similar case. In addition, when Bentley began investigating him he refused to cooperate, claiming that he had a serious medical condition. Bentley's model of openness has not been matched by others. Stone reports that a previous employer, the University of South Florida, had also investigated accusations against Hunton but did not find sufficient evidence to pursue them. As Stone notes, however, the detailed charges that were investigated and how the investigation was conducted remain confidential. It is not obvious quite whose interests this is supposed serve. Hunton's motivations are also not clear. He was widely regarded as a brilliant scholar, and could have made a major impact without engaging in fraud. Perhaps this wasn't enough. He may have burned with the kind of intense ambition that could only be satisfied by building a reputation as the top scholar in his field, like an actor who feels that his career has been a failure without an Oscar to adorn his mantelpiece. In pursuit of this, anything could be sacrificed.

Coming up behind him is Ulrich Lichtenthaler with sixteen retractions. He was widely feted as an upcoming superstar within his field. The leading German business newspaper *Handelsblatt* ranked him first among German business and economic researchers under forty. One can imagine the boost that this gave his career, but also the pressure he must have felt to maintain this rocket-propelled trajectory. Lichtenthaler was prolific. A post by Joel West on the Open Innovation Blog reported that Lichtenthaler had published forty-five articles, many of them in 'top' journals such as the *IEEE Transactions on Engineering Management, California Management Review* and *MIT Sloan Management Review*.[7] Forty-two were published between 2007 and 2012. West identifies a common problem in such situations: 'Some of his work is highly cited, leaving many researchers in a quandary: if there is a relevant article, how would I know if it will be retracted in the future?' West's analysis identified several papers that have not been retracted but which drew on data that overlapped with some of his retractions. Lichtenthaler's university,

Mannheim, tersely announced in March 2015 that it had accepted his 'resignation'. This was almost three years after his first retraction in June 2012. His unretracted papers continue to be cited and influence the work of others. Without a mandatory review of all work published by someone guilty of fraud, researchers are essentially left to make their own choices about how to treat those that remain in the public domain.

But, in an amazing coda, Lichtenthaler's story does not end there. A German business school, the International School of Management, announced in May 2018 that it had appointed him as a professor of business management, and later acknowledged that it knew of his retractions when it did so.[8] Presumably, he may soon be submitting papers to academic journals once again. There are, it seems, second lives in academia after all. Whether this sends a strong enough signal to discourage others from committing fraud is an issue that may be open to debate.

REASONS FOR RETRACTION

Table 5.1 lists common reasons for retraction among the cases we examined. Classifying these reasons was not straightforward. As Patricia Woolf observes: 'for masterful obfuscation, it's hard to beat the wording of some retractions'.[9] Statements that failed to provide any clear reason for retraction were designated as 'unclassified'. Some papers were retracted for more than one reason. Hence, there is a higher total of reasons in the table ($n = 154$) than there were total retraction statements.

The most frequent reason for retraction was data fraud ($n = 51$). Typically, retraction statements for fraud are terse, as these brief examples illustrate:

- 'Based on the pattern of misconduct identified in the investigation summary ... and the co-authors' inability to produce data or other information supporting the existence of primary data or how the study was conducted ... the AAA is retracting this article.' *Journal of Information Systems*, 2015.[10]

Table 5.1 *Reasons for retraction*

Reason	No.
Data fraud	51
Self-plagiarism	23
Plagiarism	16
Data analysis errors	16
Dispute over authorship	11
Inappropriate manipulation of citations	11
Reviewers with conflicts of interest	9
Data-reporting/presentation irregularities	1
Data-gathering ethics	2
Administrative error	1
Incorrect conclusion	1
Unclassified	12
Total	154

- 'This article contained evidence of fraud.' *Organizational Behavior & Human Decision Processes*, 2015.[11]
- 'The institution of the first-named author ... has conducted investigations that find compelling evidence that Dr. Hunton fabricated data in two other studies without the knowledge of his co-authors ... the validity of the data cannot be confirmed.' *Journal of Management Studies*, 2015.[12]

The last quotation draws attention to the reluctance by journals to explicitly identify fraud as a reason for retraction. They tend only to do so when an institutional investigation has reached the conclusion that fraud has been committed.

Plagiarism was cited as the reason for retraction on sixteen occasions. The non-detection of plagiarism prior to publication is initially surprising, given the availability of plagiarism detection software. However, a survey of journal editors who had retracted papers in business, management and economics found that 54 per cent did not use any form of plagiarism detection software.[13] This may have changed by now, given greater awareness of how prevalent plagiarism is. In any event, software has limited effectiveness because it tends to raise concerns only when a written text exceeds a minimum threshold. Furthermore, it does not necessarily detect the plagiarism of data, ideas or interpretations. Despite this, editors and reviewers often miss instances of plagiarism until these are exposed by attentive readers – by which time the paper has been published.

Self-plagiarism (n = 23) is a more frequent cause of retraction than plagiarism.

Data Analysis Problems

Problems with data analysis warrant scrutiny because some papers retracted for this reason appear to have greater problems than is acknowledged formally in retraction statements. A consistent policy in dealing with them would be helpful. As Table 5.1 shows, sixteen papers were retracted for this reason. I explore some retraction notices in this category before focusing on retractions from the prestigious journal *Leadership Quarterly*. The cause of retraction in this journal is stated in much more depth than is usual. Typical formulations in retraction statements attributable to this cause include:

- 'The retraction has been agreed before print publication based on discussions about the presentation of the empirical results.' *Entrepreneurship Theory & Practice*, 2014.[14]
- 'The article is retracted at the authors' request due to material technical errors ... (the regression coefficients and standard errors do not fit with the significance levels of some of the controls and some of the independent variables in a number of the paper's models) which have rendered many of the article's conclusions incorrect.' *Strategic Management Journal*, 2012.[15]
- 'The article is retracted due to data errors in the reported empirical results, which form part of the basis for the conclusions drawn.' *Journal of Management Studies*, 2012.[16]

These sample statements are vague. They rarely explain the nature of the 'errors' involved. Detection of data analysis problems requires diligent scrutiny and an ample investment of time by reviewers and editors. This is difficult in an era when there is less time to spend on editing and reviewing papers – and the time that is spent has a high opportunity cost. To emphasise the problem of inadequate scrutiny, John Bohannon sent a fabricated manuscript containing unacceptable errors to 304 journals where poor review practices were suspected.[17] 157 of them accepted the manuscript even where reviewers identified problems. While some of these were predatory open access journals, others were under the auspices of such reputable publishers as Sage and Elsevier. We should be alert to the fact that no journal, however prestigious, is immune to accepting papers with major analytical errors. Several top-tier journals have done so, including the *Journal of Organizational Behavior, Strategic Management Journal* and the *Journal of Management Studies*. Close inspection is needed to identify what often appears, in retrospect, to be obvious problems.

However, I turn here to an exception. *Leadership Quarterly (LQ)* retracted five papers in 2014, all co-authored by Fred Walumbwa of Florida State University. He has been a prominent researcher on ethical and authentic leadership. I return to his work, and that of others, on authentic leadership in Chapter 7. Data analysis errors were the cited reason for all the retractions of his papers in *LQ*. Walumbwa's work has since attracted further retractions for similar reasons, together with an 'expression of concern' and a mega-correction – that is, a particularly long statement that acknowledges and corrects data analysis problems. The *LQ* retraction statements were unusually detailed and accompanied by an editorial in the journal.[18]

The retraction statements ranged from 194 to 747 words, with a mean of 589. Their terms are almost identical. Each notes that 'concerns were raised', and that a methodologist was engaged to initially determine whether suggested problems with data analysis justified an investigation. A second methodologist was then involved to conduct a further study. At this point, the authors were informed that 'allegations' had been raised and invited to respond. A repeated observation is that 'the authors did not provide the original data, but rather sent a letter replying to the methodology report, along with new analytic results'. Nevertheless, the ultimate conclusion in each case was that findings had been misrepresented and so 'compromised the scientific review process' or that 'the model stated in the published paper was not tested, thus compromising the scientific review process'. Each retraction statement concludes: 'As a consequence of the processes above, the scientific trustworthiness of this work cannot be established. However, intentional wrong doing should not be inferred.' According to Google Scholar, at the time of writing, the number of citations of each paper ranged from 46 to 513, with a mean of 201 citations. Clearly, this flawed work had considerable impact on the field of leadership studies before being retracted. Some papers even continue to attract citations after their retraction – a common problem. There are many reasons for this.[19] One is that journals do not always mark retracted papers accordingly. For example, as of 22 January 2016, a retracted 2011 paper by Ulrich Lichtenthaler remained accessible on the website of the *Journal of Product Innovation Management*. There was no indication of its retracted status. Another reason is that when researchers search such databases as Scopus they will often find that the papers identified are only labelled as retracted when they retrieve the full text.[20] Once again, they risk citing papers without being aware that they have been retracted. Yet another factor is that many authors cut and paste references from other papers without actually reading the originals, and may therefore be unaware that some of their citations have been retracted.

LQ's editorial on retractions does not discuss these papers in detail. However, it offers a robust discussion of the meaning of retraction and a detailed account of how journals should approach the matter. The frequent inability or unwillingness of authors to provide their original data for reanalysis is notable. This has been a recurrent issue with Walumbwa's work. His previous university, Arizona State, carried out its own investigation when the problems with *LQ* and other publications were first raised. This investigation drew attention to defects in the maintenance of data records, noted that Walumbwa was unable to provide the raw data requested, and described this as an example of 'poor research practice'.

As with the *LQ* retractions, the report is critical. However, it carefully avoids statements of intentional misconduct, noting that: 'The investigation was severely hindered by the near total unavailability of raw data files and statistical output files for the seven papers under study.' It goes on to conclude 'that the preponderance of evidence does not support the charge of research misconduct by Dr. Walumbwa in relation to the seven papers that were the focus of the investigation'.[21]

This example points to the importance of maintaining accurate data records, and therefore being able and willing to share data for purposes of re-analysis. A failure to do so is inexcusable in today's digital world, and hinders any investigations that journals may wish to undertake.

RETRACTIONS OF QUANTITATIVE AND QUALITATIVE
PAPERS

To explore the extent to which retractions afflict quantitative studies and qualitative studies, the 101 retracted papers from the database that remained publicly available were downloaded. Of these, eighty-seven were classified broadly as quantitative, rather than qualitative, given the methodologies they employed. Despite this high proportion of quantitative papers, I see no reason to suppose that qualitative researchers are any less disposed to invent data, exaggerate sample sizes, or 'cherry pick' data than their quantitatively oriented colleagues. Rather, it seems likely that the extent of research misconduct is under-represented in qualitative research. Two organisations participating in research may become six; twelve interviews become twenty-four; and interview transcripts obtained from only one interviewee could easily be reported as coming from several. The fact that fewer qualitative papers are retracted is possibly due to the continued dominance of positivist and quantitative methods in business and management journals and to the greater ease of detecting problems in quantitative papers because they usually follow precise analytical procedures.

That said, it is undoubtedly true that null hypothesis signifi-cance testing lends itself to all kinds of distortions. Yet it dominates quantitative research in our field. I discussed some of the poor prac-tices associated with it in the previous chapter, including p-hacking and outright fraud. Andy Lockett, Abagail McWilliams and David Van Fleet argue that it dominates research because it is convenient (that is, easy), rewards large data collection efforts, values novelty rather than replication and provides an illusion of scientific rigour.[22] It also enables researchers to present findings as clear-cut when they aren't.[23] Note that none of these reasons has much to do with exploring issues in the most effective manner possible. More creative and pluralist approaches to research design may well create a more questioning culture that undermines the abuses discussed in this book.

EDITORS' PERSPECTIVES

The editors I interviewed raised a number of issues, including the time involved in dealing with allegations of misconduct, the threat of legal action and the stress that this created. They also addressed the pro-blem of how to explain the reasons for retraction in retraction state-ments. For example, Editor A retracted papers for 'data analysis errors', but avoided describing this as research fraud. When asked about this, s/he responded:

> it's almost impossible to prove ... [that] people have actually just
> made up data. ... But to say that data and analysis problems were
> intentional as opposed to just errors or sloppiness – I can't prove that
> ... my job is to protect the integrity of the journal. ... Typically
> [their university's] integrity officers get involved in this, conduct an
> investigation, and then they can determine whether or not an
> employee ... engaged in misconduct. But that's not my job. My job
> as the editor is only to say whether or not this work merits
> publication in the journal.

Research fraud is particularly difficult to prove when the research claims seem plausible. In the case of Stapel, '[he] could have ... gotten away with it, had he not claimed that that these data had been collected by his contacts in schools. When the rector wanted to contact these schools, Stapel admitted that they did not exist.'[24] Editor B also spoke of an important institutional impediment to the detection of research fraud and misconduct – the reluctance of universities to pursue allegations of misconduct:

> We have had some authors, guilty of various forms of misconduct, of such severity that we have informed superiors at those institutions, whether it was supervisors, head of department, or higher. And in a distressingly large number, we've had no response, which might suggest they haven't taken it any further because they're embarrassed.

This reluctance creates problems. As Joanna Thielen notes, 'Without evidence from [such] investigations, the editor [of a journal] may lack conclusive proof to support a retraction.'[25] Thielen also goes on to point out: 'Even if an institution finds that an article violates professional ethics the journal publisher or editor may not retract it due to fear of legal action or other forms of retribution.' Of course, management studies is not alone in facing institutional reluctance to take action. The world renowned Karolinska Institute in Sweden was disgracefully slow to respond to allegations against a so-called superstar surgeon, Paolo Macchiarini, until TV documentaries exposed his activities. These showed that proper ethical approval for his studies were never obtained, and many of his patients had died, even as Macchiarini maintained in a number of prominent publications that their treatment had been a success.[26] Internal whistle-blowers came under intense pressure to drop their allegations and were threatened with dismissal.[27] A reluctance to act often runs deep.

But stress comes from multiple pressures. Editor A commented that:

These were not just random people ... they were friends. ... I had to take this on, knowing that three or four or five of the people involved were personal friends of mine. And in hindsight, I wish I would have recused myself and said, I can't do this. But who was I then going to dump this glorious deed on, of investigating these papers? Because ... these were a very well known, powerful group of people. And no one, including the statisticians that I enlisted, wanted to be identified as going against them ...

The personal toll was clearly immense:

the authors ... tried to appeal to my sense of friendship, my sense of ... You know, this is going to be bad for the journal ... bad for you, ... bad for the authors. Can't we find another way around this that doesn't require retraction? ... Then when the personal appeals didn't work, they started pulling out every other trick in the book. They sent me letters from lawyers, they personally attacked me ... The best was ... when it started getting really clear that these papers ... were going to be retracted. An author ... emailed my dean and my provost and said that I needed to be investigated ... I dreaded waking up in the morning ... Every day for over a year.

When asked about the threat of legal action, Editor B said:

s/he only did that later on in the process. We knew there was a possibility that s/he was going to do it, s/he's ... very smart ... very well organised. And s/he did start doing this, but at a later point, with later journals. And I know from speaking to an editor of one of those other journals, that the threat by them was pretty substantial. S/he had got, you know, quite a good lawyer, fighting her/his case ... and that editor did hesitate for some while, while making a decision as to whether or not to retract another of the papers .... Yes, there are still some editors and some journals who prefer to cross by on the other side of the road. It may be because they are aware how much work and hassle can be involved, and most academics, probably 99.9%, are overloaded and chronically overstretched at any point. So, the last thing they want is extra work. Some of them maybe feeling that, well, if they do this and show that their journal has been victim of this sort of crime, in some way that reflects adversely on the journal. Others, perhaps, don't see this as quite such a serious thing as I, and a number of others, do.

The possibility of legal action also adds to the time demands on editors, as Editor C reported:

(This took) probably six months. It would be as long as that, because I had to go to X, and then I'd wait for a response from X, and then I'd have to work on it and send a response back to X. Then his/her lawyers got involved, and I worded the retraction a certain way, and then s/he'd wanted to change the retraction, the wording of the retraction ... You know it's not a matter of whether s/he accepted it or not, but I mean I just had to be careful for legal reasons.

Editor B provided insights into another problem: the danger of assuming that each instance of malpractice is a one-off, and that the offender therefore deserves to be treated lightly. As s/he reported:

It was drawn to our attention that we had published a paper by X that turned out to be based, 80%, on plagiarism of another article in a different field. We investigated; found that this guy had basically been engaging in blatant plagiarism throughout his career ... he'd been found out half a dozen times. On each occasion, people assumed it was a one-off moment of madness; gave him a slap across the wrist; assumed that he'd stopped; and he went on his merry ways. We also discovered there were others who were aware of what he was doing, but couldn't be bothered to put in the effort to bring him to justice, as it were. Or, there were one or two cases where institutions quietly got rid of him, but did so in such a way that they did not reveal to the wider world that he was guilty of serious misconduct. So this was part of the reason why he got away with it so long.

Earlier in this chapter, I discussed the inadequate scrutiny that many papers receive until after they are published, when readers sometimes highlight their flaws. My interview with Editor D touched on this issue. The editor reported that investigation into an article that s/he had retracted uncovered problems that were 'obvious'. How then had it survived the editorial and peer review process intact? My interviewee offered the following observation that may explain many of the retractions discussed in this book, and also how other papers remain in circulation despite often suffering from similar problems:

> I think a lot of reviewers take the stats at face value. If a coefficient is statistically significant ... if it's got two or three asterisks behind it, they don't ask any questions. If you find huge correlation coefficients, you'll immediately think this is a bit weird, there's something wrong here. (But) I think when you look at something like a regression table, if a coefficient appears to be statistically significant, you tend to accept that. I think part of the reason for that is that, fundamentally, publishing is based on trust.
> Notwithstanding the amount of misconduct that there seems to be out there, I think it's still a trust based business.

This adds weight to the view that the current level of retractions understates the actual frequency of research fraud and misconduct. Trust and the pressure of time lead reviewers and editors alike to take much on face value and neglect to ask probing questions. This is understandable. Nevertheless, it contributes to the publication of papers that contain fabricated data, and others based on invented or sloppy statistical analyses. Given the pressures of academic life that I discussed in Chapter 3 it is hard to see this changing for the better any time soon.

CO-AUTHORS' PERSPECTIVES

While retraction statements often exonerate co-authors, exoneration does not occur until the end of what is usually an arduous and traumatic process. Co-authors experience high levels of stress, combined with a personal sense of betrayal and reputational harm arising from dealing with investigations to determine whether they are implicated. Even those not directly involved may experience reputational damage. For example, a study of the impact of retractions for fraudulent work by scientists found that prior collaborators, wholly uninvolved with the papers in question, subsequently saw a 8–9 per cent drop in their level of citations. It is, as Katrin Hussinger and Maikel Pelklens put it, a case of 'stigmatization by mere association'.[28] The pressures on direct co-authors are, of course, even more intense, as Co-author A discussed:

> So the initial allegations, which turned out to be true, were that X's sample-size for [a] paper was larger than the available population. And so those were posted anonymously on [Y] website ... My initial reaction was: there's no way these could be true. Because this is [someone] I've hung out with for years. We're friends. We've talked about all aspects of our careers. There's just no way this could be true. And I publicly posted ... to that effect ... it was horrifying. Yes, it was horrifying. I mean, certainly one of the low points of my career. Probably *the* [emphasis of interviewee] low point of my career ... at that point ... I go talk to my dean. He says you've got to go talk to the university attorney. And so I'm spending time at the attorney's office assembling documents, and assembling emails about the projects that I have had with X that describe my role and what I understand about the data source; all that sort of thing.

Co-author B shared similar experiences and highlighted a warning sign of developing research fraud:

> S/he basically invited me to become his/her co-author on this great data and I thought, wow, this is so great, how can I say no? ... But s/he told me, 'you have to realise this is of course highly confidential, I will not even be able to share the name of the [contact] firm even with you and so we have to be very careful. I am signing all these confidentiality agreements here.' I thought, yes, I'm fine with that ... as long as we can get access to this fantastic data.

But the problem was that Co-author B never actually saw any raw data:

> I would basically write up the introduction, theory, development, and methodology and then s/he would get back to me basically with the whole results section ready. So, I do have the data but not the raw data, but I do have the Excel sheet with the data that s/he used to run (the) analyses and I at some point ... because I actually had a student who replicated this study ... so I had her kind of compare her statistics to his/ hers ... the data that s/he provided me with was completely consistent with the paper that we eventually wrote, but I never saw the raw data ... and I never saw any proof that the experiment actually took place.

Clearly, prospective co-authors need to cultivate a modicum of scepticism when presented with unusually convenient access to (almost unbelievably) good data sets, particularly if the access is shrouded in 'confidentiality'. If it looks too good to be true, then it may well be too good to be true. The problem is intensified in an environment of low scrutiny of data inputs by journals. Co-author B spoke of the high stress engendered by suspicion and investigation, and the career damage caused when exoneration is delayed:

> I was panicking. I was ... this was very uncomfortable and I slowly started realising that s/he might not be telling me the whole truth. So ... very early on I started involving close colleagues of mine; so, the head of my department and some other professors at my school. So, they've been supporting me all along. Without their help ... I probably would have had some kind of nervous breakdown. It was very stressful ... This also had great impact on my career because just a few months before this I had been contacted by a different university ... to move there and become a full professor and so just before this happened I had just disclosed this to my school and they had promised me, then we'll, you know, start the process of getting you to become a full professor here, because they wanted to keep

me. Of course, when this started we put everything on ice, which I wouldn't have wanted in any other way, but this was very stressful ... in the end it's all good, but ... yes. It took about three or four years longer than it otherwise would have.

Co-author A also alluded to the reluctance of journals to thoroughly investigate the possibility of research fraud. The author had papers that had been retracted because of fraud by the lead author. But others remained unretracted. Discussing these, the author commented as follows:

CO-AUTHOR A: I've heard nothing about them, but certainly if there's a request to retract them, I'm going to agree that they should be retracted.

DT: Well why haven't they been retracted yet?

CO-AUTHOR A: You would have to ask that journal.

In a further coda, I exchanged emails with my interviewee as I finished writing this book. S/he wrote as follows: 'Over a year ago ... I wrote to (the journal) and requested that the papers that we co-authored with X be retracted. And the result has been ... Nothing.' This is both remarkable and appalling. The journal identified by Co-author A is highly ranked and has a prestigious publisher. As with this case, it suggests that many papers containing fraudulent data remain in circulation, are cited, and so influence the direction of other people's research work. It seems that some journals and publishers have a cavalier attitude to ethical research standards, whatever formal commitments they make in public.

The International Committee of Medical Journal Editors' policy on 'Scientific misconduct, expressions of concern, and retraction' is unambiguous in respect of this matter. It suggests three options, as follows:

The validity of previous work by the author of a fraudulent paper cannot be assumed. Editors may ask the author's institution to assure them of the validity of other work published in their journals, or they may retract it. If this is not done, editors may choose to publish an announcement expressing concern that the validity of previously published work is uncertain.[29]

But even after a decision is made to retract, several years may elapse before a retraction notice is posted, while, as I have already noted, many retracted papers remain available without any indication of their retracted status. Eighteen of the retracted papers I analysed were not marked as retracted. Posting retraction notices years after publication is far from sufficient to warn readers against injudicious citation.

These problems are compounded when fraudsters deny that they have committed fraud. This was the case with Co-author A. The burden on the academic community is therefore intensified:

CO-AUTHOR A: So, in my last call with him/her ... I heard the charges. S/he said: 'These charges are all false. You were doing the right thing by defending me, and I really appreciate your support. And in the end it will come out that all these charges are false.'
DT: So his/her initial response was complete denial.
CO-AUTHOR A: No. ... Not his/her initial response. His/her response to this day is complete denial.

As a senior scholar, my interviewee stressed that the career consequences in his/her case were minimal. But s/he made the following pertinent point:

> I was lucky ... other people got hurt worse. I mean, there are people, I can't name names here, but there are people who very clearly failed to get tenure and had to change jobs because of these, because of the retractions.

My interviewee regards this experience as career-transforming. Among other conclusions, s/he offered the following *mea culpa*, which is worth reflecting on:

When I was a Psych. student many years ago, there was … this expression: Always handle your own rat. And originally that used to mean: You have to be involved enough in the data collection analysis to know that it's legitimate. But when I've now said this to people, they think I'm referring to my co-authors! And I guess it kind of works both ways. You have to have sufficient engagement, and … my failing here was: I wanted the publications, and I didn't say to X … show me proof that these data really exist. I never said that. And I should have. And we all should have. And we all should.

A research environment in which there is low scrutiny of data inputs is a problem for editors, reviewers and co-authors. While it is not suggested that all authors should be involved in data collection, it seems imperative that all authors and all editors and reviewers show greater interest in the authenticity of data and its alleged sources.

A FRAUDSTER'S PERSPECTIVE

Stapel is unique among research fraudsters because of his willingness to discuss his actions. He described his *modus operandi* as follows:

The beginning … is where you have a theory or you have read the literature. You have an idea what the next step in a particular field or domain should be. You do the experiment, you collect the data. But not everything fits with the theory. Many things fit, but several things don't fit. So you leave out the things that don't fit. So say you did five experiments and four 'worked', which is an interesting linguistic idea, the idea that scientific experiments 'work' or 'do not work'. An experiment that 'worked' means that it verified the hypothesis … What I did is that I left out the experiment that didn't work. Apparently I did something wrong, so I just only reported the four experiments that did work. Or I just asked many questions, say I ask 20 questions … 20 dependent measures and I only report the ones that worked.

Stapel clearly availed himself of the obstacles to the detection of research fraud that persist in the research environment (e.g., the practice of not making research inputs available prevented close inspection of his findings). He is describing *p*-hacking, and offers a self-description that is consistent with the interpretations others have made of his actions. William Stroebe, Tom Postmes and Russell Spears commented that

> people like Stapel probably start by slightly altering their data to make them statistically significant or to make them fit their hypotheses even better ... Once they score early successes and become known as highly promising researchers they have to keep on publishing at a high rate in top journals to meet these high expectations. If studies do not work out at all, they have to make greater and greater changes to their data, until they decide to abandon data collection and to invent the total data set.[30]

There are many biases in favour of publishing only positive findings. This is what Nuzzo describes as 'hypothesis myopia'[31] and John Antonakis calls a 'disease' that he terms 'significosis'.[32] Under such conditions, research fraud may be a tempting 'solution' to the implacable demand for positive results.

Stapel also suggested that his activities were prompted partly by the systems, culture and performance expectations within which academics work – that is, by institutional factors driving universities to reward success while penalising failure:

> You start as a curious, enthusiastic, smart researcher. You enter the field and you try to do your best and things work out. You are talented and you are working in a big, nice group so things work. Then you become aware of the culture in the group or that things are left out and it's very selective. And you see that only positive results are published and you see how science works basically. It's not only about science in the old fashioned way. It's also about communication, marketing, publishing, getting grants or making

money to make a living. And there's this process of disenchantment where you say 'wow'. This is just business . . . that idea basically got hold of me. Okay, I just need to do this. I need to do my best. I want to be part of this. I better publish more papers, I better. So it becomes sort of detachment from my scientific or curious self and . . . you're becoming a robot or a marketing person. That's a description . . . of a process of disenchantment that completely wipes everything out. It's not one particular point in time.

Stapel's account, and the accounts of editors and co-authors, broach the subject of a range of institutional, environmental and behavioural factors that prompted research fraud. These factors merit closer consideration. My interview with Stapel led to a sobering point near the end, as we discussed how widespread fraud had become. He made the point that it would appear he was a very poor fraudster, since he had been caught and his career destroyed. As he said, there may be 'many others, or several others are still out there, who are much better because you don't know they're there'. Some may even study his example to avoid the mistakes that led to his exposure rather than to become more ethical.

FRAUD, QRPS AND STRENGTHENING RESEARCH INTEGRITY

Should we do anything about all of this? I am not merely asking a rhetorical question. I argue throughout this book that most management research isn't really read by anyone outside a small coterie, least of all by practising managers. Defective medical research causes real harm. But, as Jeremy Hall and Ben Martin point out, 'it is rare for companies to blame their failure or poor performance on following the advice of a fraudulent academic publication'.[33] They note that some perpetrators may even rationalise their actions on precisely these lines: no-one really suffers from what we do, so where is the harm? But harm there is. Countless research hours are wasted writing, editing, reviewing, reading and following up on drivel. Moreover, the prevalence of such nonsense is itself one of the reasons why managers and others have turned their backs on much management research. They often distrust its empirical and theoretical claims: is this *really* true? When theories are taken up and findings implemented they are often bogus or flawed and cause real damage (see Chapter 8). We can only perform a socially useful role when we do meaningful and ethical research that addresses genuinely important issues.

But how? The San Francisco Declaration on Research Assessment (DORA) and the guidelines produced by the Committee on Public Ethics (COPE) are well-known starting points for addressing these issues. I will not reiterate them here. Rather, I suggest additional steps to strengthen research integrity, as follows.

- **Maintain proper data collection records, and share data.** The International Committee of Medical Journal Editors has proposed that all de-identified patient data should be available to others no later than six months from publication.[34] This is controversial. However, in the era of digital information storage there is no reason why journal publishers cannot require and accommodate the submission of de-identified raw data with all article submissions. Publishers have an opportunity to add value to the academic effort by providing appropriate administrative support and absorbing the costs. Undoubtedly, academics often have a proprietary attitude to data. A survey of over 1,200 management faculty found that 57.69 per cent of editors (120 respondents) and 48 per cent of authors (406 respondents) strongly disagreed or disagreed with the suggestion that journals should require authors to make their data publicly available.[35] Another study of 141 psychologists who had published empirical articles revealed that 73 per cent didn't respond to requests to share their data over a six-month period.[36] Others have argued that companies may be unwilling to permit researchers to obtain data, fearing that it could enter the public domain.[37]

In my view, we have reached a stage where such concerns are outweighed by the need to demonstrate ethical research practices. Firstly, to suggest otherwise is to argue that all researchers are ethical and their word should be taken at face value. It is akin to abolishing the mandatory inspection of new buildings on the basis that all builders are trustworthy professionals. We can't hide much longer from the fact that data need to be open for inspection, re-analysis and replication. This would remove the frequently offered excuse that the data have become corrupted or 'lost', a defence that reduces them to the status of misplaced sunglasses. It would form a further obstacle to the perpetration of fraud, and enable clearer retraction statements to be made when these are necessary. Secondly, I suspect that sufficient assurances about anonymising data would alleviate the concerns of all but the most paranoid company. If they don't, losing access in some cases may be a small price to pay for reassuring everyone about the integrity of our data sets. Sometimes what are presented as good reasons for not doing something are actually excuses.

- **Clarify responsibility for data collection on submission**. Usually, expertise is unevenly distributed among research teams. It would be debilitating to require each research team member to be fully responsible for every aspect of the work, including data collection. However, the *Journal of Accounting Research* now requires clear statements identifying the authors responsible for the data, describing how they were obtained, and stating who can confirm their authenticity. I think that this should become standard practice, and be incorporated into COPE guidelines. It would compel co-authors to show more interest in the authenticity of data, and enable investigations of data fraud to focus more closely and more quickly on the sources of any suspected problems.

- **Redefine *p*-hacking as a deceptive research practice**. *P*-hacking contributes to the bias in favour of publishing only positive results, favours the prior interpretations of authors, produces unreliable knowledge, and contributes to a 'reproducibility crisis' in academic research. There needs to be greater recognition that it constitutes a fundamental distortion of data, often amounts to outright misrepresentation, and is tantamount to misconduct. Relabelling it as a 'deceptive research practice' rather than one that is merely 'questionable' would encourage a shift in mind-sets away from condoning its use.

- **Substitute the term 'deceptive research practices' for 'questionable research practices'**. Language matters in framing how social situations are perceived. As Nachman Ben-Yehuda and Amalya Oliver-Lumerman point out, phrases like *mismanagement* or *misconduct* 'are terms that clearly minimise and soften the implied stigma and negativity associated with terms such as "deviance" or "fraud" or even "criminal"'.[38] This spares the feelings of offenders, and in encouraging minimal sanctions allows then to repeat poor research practices. I think it is unjustifiable. The term 'deceptive research practice' is a stronger way of communicating the unacceptability of the practices concerned.

- **Require journals to make clearer statements of reasons for retraction.** To announce that papers are 'withdrawn', but fail to give a reason, serves no obvious academic interest. It obscures the prevalence of malpractice and prevents other scholars learning from what has gone wrong. I appreciate that there are legal issues to be faced. Yet journals in general could afford to be more transparent about the rationales for their decisions.

- **Investigate the whole body of work of authors who have more than one paper retracted for fraud.** Consider again the example of James Hunton. He authored approximately 133 papers, of which at least 37 have been retracted for fraud. It is unclear how many of the remainder are under investigation. Nor is he alone. A mandatory review would help to cleanse the research record of other papers that have a better-than-evens chance of containing fraudulent data.

- **Review the primacy accorded to significance testing.** I subscribe to the view that 'statistical significance should be a tiny part of an inquiry concerned with the size and importance of relationships'.[39] There should be greater focus on effect sizes and much less on statistical significance. This approach has been recommended to psychologists, and has much to offer management scholars.[40] Its adoption would help undo the prevalence of p-hacking and reduce the bias in favour of publishing only positive results.

- **Differentiate between HARKing and post-study theorising.** The former is damaging but the latter is helpful. Andreas Schwab and Bill Starbuck suggest that when 'researchers discover new hypotheses after or during data analysis, they should report such observations as inferences, conjectures or discoveries. Likewise, researchers should identify hypotheses and proposed models that originated with editors or reviewers as having come from these people after submission to the journal. Honest reporting enables readers to recognize and account for the exploratory nature of these observations.'[41] This, of course presumes that editors and reviewers will support such practices. Unfortunately, the evidence at present suggests that many of them encourage the opposite.

- **Develop research misconduct policies in more countries**. Writing in 2015, David Resnik, Lisa Rasmussen and Grace Kissling found that twenty-two of the top forty research and research funding countries had such policies in place.[42] Encouragingly, others are following suit. While US universities generally have research integrity officers, this is not standard in other educational systems. It should be. Such a step would provide a point of access for whistle-blowers and diminish institutional reluctance to investigate allegations of misconduct. Greater support for national initiatives by individual institutions is also required. In the UK, the House of Commons Science and Technology Committee reported in 2018 that at least seventy-one universities, more than half, did not subscribe to the UK Research Integrity Office (UKRIO).[43] This was created in 2006 as an advisory body on research integrity. The annual subscription fee is £2,600. Either our universities have taken financial rectitude to new heights, or they have failed to recognise the importance of these issues. More serious engagement with such bodies as UKRIO seems a minimal step in the present climate.
- **Develop clearer rules for disclosure**. Sources of funding can distort research. For example, studies funded by drinks companies are five times more likely than studies not funded by them to deny the link between sugary drinks and obesity.[44] A great deal of management research has its origins in consulting relationships between faculty and business, most undisclosed. Much of this consulting is useful. But I also suspect that it often enhances the bias in favour of publishing only positive results. I am not suggesting that we should prohibit data obtained through consulting, but only that we should be open about it. This has become an issue in economics, a field adjacent to business and management, after the 2008 financial crash. Jessica Carrick-Hagenbarth and Gerald Epstein studied the outside interests of nineteen prominent US economists.[45] In a four-year period that included the crash, fifteen of them had worked for private financial institutions and three even had their own firms. The American Economic Association now stipulates that 'Each author of a submitted article should identify each interested party from whom he or she has received significant financial support, summing to at least $10,000 in the past three years, in the form of consultant fees, retainers, grants and the like.'[46] I urge business and management journals to adopt a similar approach.

CONCLUSION

Research malpractice is not a new phenomenon. Many of the most important names in the history of science, including Ptolemy, Galileo and Newton, are alleged to have on occasion 'improved' results to confirm their theories.[47] If even the great and the good were not paragons of virtue this suggests that the problems discussed can never be fully eliminated. Nevertheless, greater awareness of the disastrous effects of malpractice, and stronger steps to discourage it, would help.

In addressing this challenge, we should focus afresh on what drives our research. When our only purpose is career advancement we are complicit in the erosion of those scholarly values that stress the primacy of disinterested inquiry for its own sake. Ultimately, this ethos is our strongest safeguard against fraud and research malpractice. I endorse Nancy Adler and Hans Hansen's injunction that we should dare to care, and embrace passionate commitment to research that matters.[48] We should remember that we are (or used to be) driven primarily by curiosity, by a desire to address important issues, and by an urge to improve the world. We need to refrain from describing publishing as a 'game', and reorient our conversations away from an obsession with league tables, journal rankings and publication 'hits'. This would strengthen our collective commitment to research integrity. I return to this issue in the final chapter of this book. For now, I conclude that research malpractice and research fraud are evil twins who have taken up residence within the academic tent. With a more concerted effort, they can be expelled into the night.

6   The Triumph of Nonsense in Management Studies

Look at the guidelines for authors provided by any of our top journals, and the odds are that you will see an explicit call for 'theory development' in the papers that it publishes. There is no equivalent demand that authors should develop guidelines for practice, describe an interesting phenomenon for which no theory is yet available or address important issues. Rather, as the *Academy of Management Journal* (*AMJ*) puts it:

> Meaningful new implications or insights for theory must be present in all *AMJ* articles, although such insights may be developed in a variety of ways (e.g., falsification of conventional understanding, theory building through inductive or qualitative research, first empirical testing of a theory, meta-analysis with theoretical implications, constructive replication that clarifies the boundaries or range of a theory).[1]

I am not disputing that good theory is important. Without it, we would be left with a series of disconnected observations but lack explanations for what they mean. However, I am arguing that theory development has become an unhealthy obsession in our discipline. It is rare to find a convincing rationale for this. Journals take it as self-evidently important that 'developing theory' should take pride of place in the long list of things that a paper can do. The result is a great deal of pretentious gibberish. Trivial insights are converted into theoretical statements that read like English translated into Esperanto and then back again, in both cases by a malfunctioning software program. It often seems that the objective is to baffle readers rather than enlighten them, while inflicting as much pain as possible. Management studies suffers from an infestation of such writing that, through mimicry, reproduces itself at an exponential rate. No one reads a management journal for pleasure, and on the occasions that a delightful piece of writing catches our attention it feels as rare as the sight of a pink unicorn unicycling across a campus quadrangle.

My purpose here is to examine how this has come about, outline its effects and suggest what we can do about it. I begin by looking at what theory is, show what a fetish we have made of it in our discipline and then explore the effect of this on our writing. We have turned something that is inherently positive (that is, building theory) into a painful obstacle course that prevents effective communication with each other, never mind the rest of the world. It is time for change.

WHAT IS THEORY ANYWAY?

You might imagine that this is a straightforward question. After all, journals place such a strong emphasis on theory building that it seems reasonable to expect some standard definitions that tell us what theory is in fine detail. I haven't found this to be the case. Rather, there are plentiful definitions that are characterised by their *vagueness*. This is problematic. It means that, like beauty, what constitutes good theory is in the eye of the beholder. The final judgement on whether a paper is making a theoretical contribution is often reduced to subjective opinion. For example, John Sutherland has described theory as 'an ordered set of assertions about a generic behavior or structure assumed to hold throughout a significantly broad range of specific instances'.[2] Each of these terms is, of course, open to different understandings. How do we know what constitutes 'an ordered set of assertions'? What counts as 'a significantly broad range of specific instances'? There is no weighing machine for ideas that can tell us the answer.

Perhaps fuzziness is unavoidable in defining theory and in making judgements about whether a paper develops it. Samuel Bacharach defines theory as 'a statement of relations among concepts within a boundary set of assumptions and constraints. It is no more than a linguistic device used to organize a complex empirical world ... the purpose of a theoretical statement is twofold: to organize (parsimoniously) and to communicate (clearly).[3] *Boundaries* are hard to define (where do you draw the line?), and *linguistic devices* are plainly always open to multiple interpretations. In some ways, this quite open definition is attractive, since it frees us from narrow conceptions of what constitutes theory and allows us to play constructively with data and meanings. On the other hand, it makes it easier to reject any paper on the grounds that it 'doesn't develop theory', for in many cases there is no clear criteria on which such judgements can be made.

Other definitions seek to be more prescriptive. In a famous article entitled 'What theory is not', Bob Sutton and Barry Staw suggest that

> Theory is the answer to queries of why. Theory is about the connections among phenomena, a story about why acts, events, structure, and thoughts occur. Theory emphasizes the nature of causal relationships, identifying what comes first as well as the timing of such events. Strong theory, in our view, delves into the underlying processes so as to understand the systematic reasons for a particular occurrence or non-occurrence.[4]

This is not a definition that I for one would fully buy into. Social science does indeed explore 'connections among phenomena', but not all social science explores causal relationships in the manner that is suggested here. There are many phenomena where the mapping of causality is pretty impossible. Consider, for example, the processes whereby leadership emerges. These consist of complex interactions between multiple organisational actors where causality and prediction are notoriously difficult to establish. Reflecting these constraints, studies often limit themselves to modelling the causal relationships between piddling variables (first A, then B), and in doing so grossly simplify the relationships involved. For example, attempts by leaders to influence others involve multiple variables in numerous feedback loops between all sides. It surely follows that theory must not just explain causal relationships, but also explain their *absence* and their *indeterminacy*.

John Campbell defined theory as 'a collection of assertions, both verbal and symbolic, that identifies what variables are important and for what reasons, specifies how they are interrelated and why, and identifies the conditions under which they should be related or not related'.[5] Key words here include 'specifies' and 'identifies'. Theory, in this view, seems to be something that facilitates precise and definite knowledge claims about the world. Once again, this might be desirable, but is often impossible. It is hardly surprising, as I shall discuss later in this chapter, that theorists are tempted either into making grand generalisations that are hard to relate to the world around us, or into the study of micro-variables that few find of much interest.

Others are more circumspect in their definitions and in their views of what theory should seek to accomplish. Kevin Corley and Dennis Gioia describe theory as 'a statement of concepts and their interrelationships that shows how and/or why a phenomenon occurs'.[6] An editorial in *Academy of Management Review* considers theory to be 'explanations for why some sort of relationship exists between variables or why some phenomenon occurs'.[7] Theory, here, can be descriptive as well as, or instead of, predictive. For my purposes, however, the key point is that, again, these definitions leave much to the subjective opinions of editors and reviewers. Does my theory do enough to clearly explain the concepts I am using? Does it show with sufficient precision how they relate? Does it help others to understand how a phenomenon is occurring? There is no cookbook of theory development that can tell me how to go about ensuring that the answers to these questions are positive. Authors are tempted to make simple concepts unnecessarily complex, in the hope that if they can't convince the reviewers that they are making a theoretical contribution by the power of their ideas they might at least bamboozle them into submission.

Here is an example. Andras Tilcsik published a paper in the prestigious journal *Administrative Science Quarterly* in 2014. It was entitled 'Imprint-environment fit and performance: how organizational munificence at the time of hire affects subsequent job performance'. 'Munificence' is not a word that I encounter every day. It simply means largesse, benevolence or generosity, among a variety of other synonyms. Why didn't our author use words with which people would be more familiar? Now read the abstract:

> The core hypothesis, supported by the results, is that the more similar the initially experienced level of organizational munificence is to the level of munificence in a subsequent period, the higher an individual's job performance. This relationship between what I call 'imprint–environment fit' and performance is contingent on the individual's career stage when entering the organization and the influence of secondhand imprinting resulting from the social transmission of others' imprints. A possible implication of the core hypothesis may be a 'curse of extremes', whereby both very high and very low levels of initial munificence are associated with lower average performance during a person's subsequent tenure. One mechanism underlying these patterns is that employees socialized in different resource environments develop distinct approaches to problem solving and client interactions, which then lead to varying levels of imprint–environment fit in subsequent resource environments.[8]

I would translate this as follows: 'When managers behave well with new employees, and continue to do so, they work better, and when they behave badly the opposite happens. This is partly because already existing employees also behave either well or badly and so role model attitudes and behaviour for others.' 'Imprinting' seems to mean the impact on us of our experiences with others. But since this doesn't sound sufficiently theoretical, we read instead of 'imprint–environment fit'. As Michael Billig observes, sometimes big words are used 'not to identify a discovery, but to cover over a lack of discovery'.[9] Note also the reference to 'supported by the results'. This means that some hypotheses which stated the blindingly obvious were developed, and, in the manner of someone hypothesising that alcohol can be bought in a bar, they were duly confirmed. The paper strives for enigma, and I suppose achieves it, since without the help of a dictionary it is hard to know what point is being made. There is a skill to this kind of writing, just as there is in playing scrabble. Whether it really advances the sum of human knowledge is a different matter.

It is hard not to agree with John Van Maanen, who wrote in 1995 as follows: 'I am appalled at much of organization theory for its technocratic unimaginativeness. Our generalizations often display a mind-numbing banality and an inexplicable readiness to reduce the field to a set of unexamined, turgid, hypothetical thrusts designed to render organizations systematic and organization theory safe for science.'[10] This is still the state of theory in our field today. It might even be worse than when Van Maanen reached the dismal conclusion that I have just quoted.

Consider also the words of Karl Weick. He has suggested that 'Theorists often write trivial theories because their process of theory construction is hemmed in by methodological strictures that favour validation rather than usefulness ... These strictures weaken theorizing because they de-emphasize the contribution that imagination, representation, and selection make to the process, and they diminish the importance of alternative theorising activities such as mapping, conceptual development, and speculative thought.'[11] Weick is highlighting how the norms of writing a journal article for publication often violate the actual processes whereby valuable insights are really generated. Most papers follow what is now a very tired formula – introduction, literature review, methods, results and discussion, written to fairly standard lengths. There is little room for the reporting of inspiration, luck, happy accidents or the exercise of what Weick calls 'disciplined imagination'. An impersonal writing style is adopted, in which we find expressions such as 'this paper argues' rather than 'I think'. One might imagine that they are written by a computer rather than a human being. Come to think of it, when you consider how much of quantitative papers consist of tables auto-generated by SPSS, and how many 'critical' papers seem to just cut and paste obligatory sets of references, this might not be so far from the truth. This helps authors achieve their primary goal – publication. What it doesn't do is produce meaningful theories that offer useful insights into the world of organisations. The question is: why and how this has come about?

THE FETISH OF THEORISING IN MANAGEMENT STUDIES

Donald Hambrick is a distinguished management academic who, among other duties, served as president of the Academy of Management in 1992–93. In 2007, he published a paper in *AMJ* entitled 'The field of management's devotion to theory: too much of a good thing?' With well over 600 citations to its credit, it has been widely read, even though the problems it complains about remain substantially intact. In it, Hambrick writes: 'Our field's theory fetish, for instance, prevents the reporting of rich detail about interesting phenomena for which no theory yet exists. And it bans the reporting of facts – no matter how important or competently generated – that lack explanation, but that, once reported, might stimulate the search for an explanation.'[12] It is hard to think of other fields that share our obsession.

Gerald Davis gives the counter-example of financial economics. He co-authored a paper dealing with conflicts of interest in proxy voting by mutual funds. The paper's starting point was the identification of a problem: anecdotal evidence to the effect that fund companies tended to support management rather than their fellow shareholders when they ran the pension funds of the firms concerned. This led to a straightforward question: 'Do mutual funds vote differently in clients than they do in non-clients?' As Davis wrote:

> Once the basic premise was established, no particular 'theory' was required – just a careful description of the data and analyses required to answer the question and subsidiary analyses to rule out alternative interpretations. The analyses did not particularly

contribute to theory, but they did answer the question, and that was enough to count as a contribution to finance.[13]

But management studies is another country, and we do things differently here. Donald Hambrick offers the following illustrative example of the problems that it causes us:

> Imagine it's the 1930s, and you are an epidemiologist who has a hunch that cigarette smoking does bad things to people. Smoking is stylish and has even been portrayed as healthful, so your nagging suspicions to the contrary make you a bit of a crackpot. But you persevere, and in a series of matched-sample studies, you find recurring evidence that smoking is associated with an array of serious maladies. As an epidemiologist, rather than a biologist, you have no clear insights about the central mechanisms at work ... But you feel a strong need to get your findings reported, so you send your manuscript to a prominent journal ... You see where I'm going. If the epidemiologist's paper went to a journal like one of ours, it would be rejected. No matter how important the topic or persuasive the analysis, the message would be: Go away and don't come back until you have a theory.[14]

It also seems that serious minds in management studies are too busy developing theories to test them. As Keith Leavitt, Terence Mitchell and Jeff Peterson put it: 'Researchers often make their names by developing a theory and showing support for their ideas. Theories are attached to authors and it is one route to professional recognition. Many of the best techniques available to test or disconfirm a theory, while still focusing on one theory, are infrequently conducted, often hard to publish, and may not be career enhancing.'[15] A study of papers in the *Academy of Management Journal* over five decades highlights a growing focus on theory development, and hence construct proliferation, even when such constructs differ little from what existed before.[16] This hinders the accumulation of empirical information about issues for which no theory yet exists, however pressing a problem may be in the real world of management practice. One study has concluded that no more than 9 per cent of the theoretical presentations published in *Academy of Management Review* articles are ever tested.[17] Actually testing theories has come to be seen as an eccentric hobby pursued by the maladjusted. This is truly bizarre. It is the hallmark of an immature field that is striving too hard to impress, and so has placed far too high a premium on novelty rather than the painstaking work of checking factual claims, theoretical formulations and causal predictions.

Even assuming that we wanted to test our profusion of theories, would we be able to do so? I acknowledge that this issue is raised in a different form for a great deal of qualitatively based theorising, particularly that which takes the form of thick description. It is at the very least questionable whether it is useful to couch such research in the format of quantitative research, designed to formulate and test hypotheses. It may even be harmful, despite the fact that many people try.[18] But it seems that quantitative and positivist research itself often falls short of testability. A fascinating study by Jeffrey Edwards and James Berry tried to assess how precise management theories are. They examined papers published in the *Academy of Management Review* over the twenty-five year period between 1985 and 2009. Ultimately, they settled on twenty theories that offered 183 propositions. In terms of the magnitude of relationships that the propositions predicted, they report that:

> 19 (10.4%) simply stated that a relationship would exist, 164 (89.6%) described the direction of the relationship, and none of the propositions predicted a point value or range of values. With respect to the form of the relationship, 177 (96.7%) of the propositions were silent on this issue ... For the most part, the theories in our sample developed propositions that predicted the direction of a relationship but said little about the form of the relationship or conditions that might influence the relationship. Rather, the majority of the propositions essentially stated that, if one variable increases,

another variable will increase or decrease. It follows that, as the methodological rigor of studies designed to test these propositions increases, the likelihood of finding support for the propositions and their associated theories will likewise increase, putting the theories at progressively lower risk.[19]

This is a polite way of saying that the theories they studied had little real predictive value. It also means that that they are hard to falsify, a common problem in organisational studies. Such theorising is ultimately vacuous, even if it appears in so-called top journals. The truth is: *we know much less than we think we do, and much of what we think we know is plain wrong.*

An example is helpful. Geert Hofstede, beginning in 1980 and then developed in numerous other publications, asserted that he had identified four and subsequently six main dimensions of national culture that explained variations in work behaviour and attitudes within different countries.[20] His data were obtained from employee attitude surveys in sixty-six countries, although data from only forty countries were used in his analysis. But, and it is a big but, all *were derived from IBM employees.* The national cultures he described are causal in their effects, widely shared, implicit to people's understanding of themselves and territorially bounded. These are huge claims, and have had a huge impact. As his most trenchant critic, Brendan McSweeney, puts it: 'Essentially, he endorses national cultural determinism.'[21] Hofstede has frequently claimed that his work represents a 'paradigm shift' in the field.[22] At the time of writing he has over 161,000 citations on Google Scholar and a h-index of 97.[23]

While the details of Hofstede's work are beyond the scope of this chapter, some points are not. It simultaneously makes weak and strong predictions. The weak prediction flows from the view that national cultures are a statistical average of the given population. It is a central tendency rather than an absolute characteristic, such that individual behaviours will inevitably vary widely in many directions from the norm. Since divergences from the putative norm are to be expected, then precise predictions of how national cultures impact on individuals are hard to make. If I behave according to what Hofstede says is the national culture that I come from, his theory stands. If I don't, then I am outlier, and the theory still stands. Thus, Hofstede offers weak predictions. Hofstede's work is also unfalsifiable. Whatever happens, or does not happen, his theory is somehow confirmed. Despite this, he also draws strong causal explanations for individual behaviour from the notion of national cultural differences. For example, Freud's development of psychoanalysis is explained as a result of the fact that he was Austrian, and 'the Austrian culture is characterised by the combination of a very low power distance with a fairly high uncertainly avoidance ... The low PDI ... means that there is no powerful superior who will take away one's uncertainties: One has to carry these oneself.'[24] Yet, as Brendan McSweeney points out, another Austrian, Adolf Hitler, argued precisely for subordination to a powerful superior, and persuaded a great many other Austrians that he was right.[25] How useful can a theory of national culture be when it is held to explain one person's behaviour in fine detail but fails to account for the opposite behaviour of someone else?

As with many attempts at theory development, we have an example here of strong claims based on weak data. Fewer than one hundred respondents were surveyed in several of the countries from which Hofstede drew his data, including Hong Kong, Singapore and Pakistan (where the figure was thirty-seven). This is a poor base from which to extrapolate to national populations. Moreover, why should IBM employees be representative of the national group from which they come? If I were to survey, say, farm workers, miners or the unemployed instead, and found something different, would that be equally valid?

How then can we account for the extraordinary impact of Hofstede's work? I suggest that management theories often have an impact, despite their weak empirical basis, if they fulfil the following conditions:

1. *They offer a strong narrative that makes bold claims.* Certainty is more appealing than uncertainty, and we shouldn't underestimate the appeal of grand theories that seem to explain the world to us. They answer a need.
2. *They seem intuitively to have something going for them.* In this case, it is easy to believe that there are differences between national cultures, but it is also easy to exaggerate these differences and the extent to which they explain individual behaviour. Moreover, once we buy into the theory it can frame our perceptions such that we interpret the behaviour of others in the light of the theory, and so find it 'confirmed' by our own experience.
3. *They can fit readily into pedagogy.* Business schools have to teach students something, and intercultural communication is an important issue. University teachers don't always have the time to study the details of Hofstede's methodology, or ponder the contradictions in his conclusions. A class awaits.

This leads us to yet another damaging paradox. On the one hand, academics are constantly urged to develop innovative new theories, and spend a great deal of effort at least pretending that they have done so. Scholars are socialised into this expectation at an early stage of their careers, and often come to see developing theory as much more important than tackling real problems or having an impact outside academia.[26] Yet there is a pervasive feeling that all this work is often for nought, and that genuinely insightful, breakthrough theories continue to elude us. Based on their six years (2003–2008) editing the prestigious *Journal of Management Studies* Tim Clark and Mike Wright published a parting editorial in which they write in terms that are becoming familiar:

> While we, along with many other journals have witnessed
> a proliferation of articles submitted, it is hard to conclude that this
> has been accompanied by a corresponding increase in papers that
> add significantly to the discipline. More is being produced but the
> big impact papers remain elusive . . . The emphasis on improving the
> rigour of theorizing and of empirical method . . . may have led to
> more incremental research questions being addressed . . . [And] the
> impact of the audit culture and incentive system is likely to affect

the extent to which both junior faculty and, somewhat surprisingly, highly competent senior faculty ... engage in consensus-challenging research. The emphasis on 'gap filling' seems to assume that we know what the boundaries of a field look like and tends to dissuade examination of new areas outside this matrix.[27]

True as this is, the demand for novelty means that we are increasingly bombarded with papers that claim not just to make incremental advances on theory but ones that impulsively claim to be revelatory – that is, they purport to offer a radically new way of thinking on some issue within our field.[28] Dirk Lindebaum offers the example of neuroscience in management research, and concludes that 'accelerating *demands* for novel theories in management studies imply that new methodologies and data are sometimes accepted prematurely as *supply* of these novel theories'.[29] The rush to comply with the imperative to 'develop theory' populates our landscape with theoretical bandwagons that, on close inspection, are often built of tinsel, and held together by little more than hope and hype.

The 'Anxiety of Influence'

This leads us to some unhappy conclusions. Back in 1973 the critic Harold Bloom published a book called *The Anxiety of Influence: a Theory of Poetry*.[30] I think its central point is relevant here. Bloom pointed out that poets are inevitably inspired by reading the works of others, but argued that the more such work influences them the more likely it is that their own will be derivative. In our field, beginning researchers face similar anxieties. They are confronted with a mountain of existing theories, but are still encouraged to create new ones. There is, simultaneously, the need to do something new, but a sometimes paralysing fear that this is impossible. In our field, some seek to cover up their fear by writing overblown nonsense, often in the style of some dead philosopher whose work is held up as a master lens that can be used to understand all the world's problems.

Still others resort to what Mats Alvesson and Jorgen Sandberg have astutely identified as 'gap-spotting'.[31] With this approach, a compendious literature review is compiled and an associated theoretical framework identified. Instead of challenging – what Alvesson and Sandberg call 'problematizing' – the framework in question, the researcher identifies some tiny gaps in the knowledge claims that it makes and then proceeds to fill them, like a plasterer obsessed with miniscule cracks in a wall. Often, no one has ever noticed these gaps before because they aren't that important, and no one really cares anyway if they are filled or not – including the authors of such papers themselves. After all, the real goal is publication rather than advancing knowledge. Mark De Rond and Alan Miller are among many who argue that the pressure to publish, including as part of the tenure review process in the US, discourages people from addressing difficult and complex issues and encourages instead the pursuit of projects that are more likely to yield quick publication.[32] From this standpoint, gap filling is attractive because it is relatively easy. Often, all you need is a forensic eye for minutiae and an immunity from embarrassment. Since most journals require authors to situate their work in the context of what others have already done there is even an institutional bias towards the publication of this kind of work. Once more, however, it is written as a 'contribution to theory' and further clogs and befuddles our senses with waffle. Yet, as Jay Barney points out, 'it is important to know the major theoretical issues in the literature, how they are related, and *especially what is missing in the literature* ... If all one does is answer questions defined by the received literature, it will rarely be possible to go beyond that literature. Only by ignoring parts of the received literature is it possible to set aside its blinders to do theoretically creative work' (my italics).[33]

Again, I'm not denying that a great deal of skill is involved in gap spotting. As Mats Alvesson and Yiannis Gabriel point out, it is associated with researchers becoming 'experts' in a sub-field so that they understand all its conventions and typical modes of expression and come to know its key players.[34] They define themselves as researchers in identity, diversity, discourse, leadership, change or whatever, and rarely venture beyond the comfort zone afforded by their expertise. This is one reason why reference lists in papers have become ever longer. Desperate to avoid offending a possible reviewer, authors cite all and sundry in a pre-emptive strike against rejection. Readers, meanwhile, feel that they are being clubbed over the head with an endless series of names and dates. But there are also costs for the authors. Ever tinier gaps in the literature are identified, such that 'one is left with the impression that certain authors are rewriting the same paper any number of times'.[35] Careers may be built by these means, despite the boredom that I imagine must eventually settle in. Whether it is a worthwhile use of anyone's time or of benefit to society is a different matter. What it does produce is some dreadful writing, always in the name of 'building theory'.

NONSENSE WRITING DISGUISED AS BUILDING THEORY

The famous American sociologist C. Wright Mills published one of his most important books, *The Sociological Imagination*, in 1959. It included a chapter that was highly critical of what he called 'grand theory'. Mills characterised this as 'the associating and disassociating of concepts', and wrote of it as follows:

> The basic cause of grand theory is the initial choice of a level of thinking so general that its practitioners cannot logically get down to observation. They never, as grand theorists, get down from the higher generalities to problems in their historical and structural contexts. This absence of a firm sense of genuine problems, in turn, makes for the unreality so noticeable in their pages. One resulting characteristic is a seemingly arbitrary and certainly endless elaboration of distinctions, which neither enlarge our understanding nor make our experience more sensible. This in turn is revealed as a partially organized abdication of the effort to describe and explain human conduct and society plainly.[36]

To illustrate his case, Mills took various passages from the influential work of Talcott Parsons, then the doyen of American sociology, and translated them into plain English. He suggested that the 555 pages of his book *The Social System* could be turned into about 150 pages of straightforward prose. The effect was like watching a hot air balloon slowly deflate. In Mills's view, the faults he highlighted weren't just a personal peccadillo. Rather, they were a means of avoiding having to deal with such issues as power, since it was more comfortable to retreat into a world of arcane abstractions that created the impression of intellectual substance precisely because few understood it.

The quality of much academic writing is equally terrible today. Most papers in mainstream journals are formulaic, cautious, dull and unreadable. Many are evidently composed to the following formula:

$$\frac{\text{big claims} + \text{jargon} \times \text{gaps} - \text{humour}}{\text{humungous list of references}} = \text{contribution to theory}$$

Writing by critical management scholars is little better, and indeed is often worse. As Chris Grey and Amanda Sinclair put it:

> Much of the writing in our field is tendentious, jargon-ridden, laboured. Partially, this seems to us to stem from attempts to make our writing academically legitimate, as if describing and explaining organizational lives must invest itself with a language quite different to those lives. As if, in rejecting positivism, we feel obliged to adopt an equally abstracted vocabulary so as to show that we are, after all, still serious scholars.[37]

In such work, bonus points are awarded if you can find a French philosopher that no one has ever heard of, the deader the better, and fashion a claim that the implications of their writings for management studies has been 'unjustly neglected'. Jackpot.

Again, an example is helpful. A personal favourite, written by Robert Chia and Robin Holt, is entitled 'Strategy as practical coping: a Heideggerian perspective'. It was published by *Organization Studies* in 2006.[38] The paper must have its fans, since it has now been cited over 500 times. Its abstract reads thus:

Specifically, we argue that the dominant 'building' mode of strategizing that configures actors (whether individual or organizational) as distinct entities deliberately engaging in purposeful strategic activities derives from a more basic 'dwelling' mode in which strategy emerges non-deliberately through everyday practical coping. Whereas, from the building perspective, strategy is predicated upon the prior conception of plans that are then orchestrated to realize desired outcome, from a dwelling perspective strategy does not require, nor does it presuppose, intention and purposeful goal-orientation: strategic 'intent' is viewed as immanent in every adaptive action.

So far as I can figure, this means that instead of sticking to rigid plans managers often wing it. The authors make a valiant attempt to show that Heidegger is relevant to their view of strategy as practice, and in doing so segue into Bourdieu's notion of habitus:

By introducing Heidegger's distinction between the building and dwelling modes of engagement to the strategy-as-practice literature, we are able to begin to explore further why it is that individual and organizational practices may exhibit sufficient consistency for constituting identities and strategies without recourse to *intentionality* and the presumption of the existence of conscious mental states. Yet, in emphasizing the primacy of dwelling, we do not imply a blind obedience to orthodoxy, or conformity to internalized structural forces; actors have more than adequate room for manoeuvre, because what the dwelling mode of engagement precipitates are unconscious *predispositions* to act in a manner congruent with past experiences but to do so in a manner that ensures the smooth and uninterrupted adjustment to local situations. It was this question of how to account for a kind of 'absorbed intentionality' from within practices that led the French

> sociologist Pierre Bourdieu to extend Heidegger's work to the study
> of the material structuring of human action within socio-cultural
> contexts. Bourdieu's work must therefore be understood within the
> context of Heidegger's insights.

Have you got that? With all due respect to our eminent authors, I still don't think this really adds anything to the notion that managers are often forced to improvise rather than stick to rigid plans.

There seems to be four golden rules for academic writing these days. Firstly, never use a short and familiar word where a long and unfamiliar one will do. This prevents anyone understanding what you mean, so they can't criticise it. Secondly, never use one word when you can stretch to four. This wears your readers out, and bores them to boot. Thirdly, bamboozle people with jargon, big words and plenty of well-known names. This further paralyses their critical senses: if Bourdieu or Heidegger says it, then it must be right, right? Fourthly, fresh metaphors, humour and irony wake people up, and are therefore your enemy. They should be shot on sight.

It is difficult to believe that people who write like this have any motive other than publication. They are not interested, at least not primarily, in shaping public discourse or addressing important issues and certainly not in changing the world. They have internalised the performative norms of research assessment, and are numb to the stupefying effects their prose has on others.

These effects seem to become stronger the more that researchers draw on grand theory taken from the likes of Jacques Lacan, a deceased French psychoanalyst. Michael Billig is among many critics of Lacan's famously impenetrable style of writing, arguing that he 'was an obscure writer, who seemed to delight in making things difficult to grasp, offering few examples to illustrate his allusive points'.[39] Noam Chomsky described him as 'a total charlatan, just posturing before the television cameras the way many Paris intellectuals do. Why this is influential I haven't the slightest idea.'[40] But influential he is, including among management and organisation scholars. I have found forty-four papers in the journal *Organization Studies* and seventy-four in its more critically oriented counterpart, *Organization*, that favourably cite his ideas. The latter felt that Lacan's influence was important enough to justify a special issue devoted to his impact on organisation studies. Its introductory editorial begins thus:

> Lacan, of course, does not exist. By this we do not mean to say that he died, in 1981, but rather to say that when we say 'Lacan', we are using a language, or more precisely a signifier, and that signifier is caught up in a chain of other signifiers. This might be obvious to us now, but this has not always been so.

Obvious? This is not an adjective I would use at this stage. Ploughing on we read:

> This is perhaps only obvious to us *because* of Lacan, or because of the things that we here condense by the name Lacan. This calling into being of a single signifier that stands in the place of a subject is one of the key illusions that Lacan shows us, again and again. It is also the kind of stupidity that we have started to sense, throughout the 20th century, that results from any effort to say 'I'.[41]

It is initially baffling that people choose to write this way. One possible explanation is given by Paul Gross and Norman Levitt. Describing the arcane mysteries of postmodernism, they suggest that such writing offers 'the possibility of becoming an initiate, part of an elect whose mastery of a certain style of discourse confers an insight unobtainable elsewhere and authorises a knowing (and often smug) attitude'.[42] Nor is the editorial from which I have just quoted the worst example to be found. I picked a Lacan-themed paper at random from *Organization Studies*, and almost the first sentence that catches my eye is this:

> According to him, one of the key functions of fantasy (belonging to the imaginary) is to veil the lack constituted by the failure of symbolization (in the symbolic) in order to sustain the illusion of

wholeness and to avoid the anxiety resulting from the emergence of the real. Fantasy is a narrative structure whose content can greatly vary, but which rests on the imaginary promise of recapturing what has been lost.[43]

This is a shame, since the paper deals with an important issue – how employees in a factory responded to the threat of closure. It contains many pieces of brilliant writing and has fascinating data. But the good writing appears when Lacan isn't on stage. When invoking The Master, his disciples seem prone to mimic his writing style, thereby showcasing the 'anxiety of influence' at work in our own field. In the interests of sanity one example from Lacan's oeuvre must stand in here for the rest:

> The question of the two is for us the question of the subject, and here we reach a fact of psychoanalytical experience in as much as the two does not complete the one to make two, but must repeat the one to permit the one to exist. The first repetition is the only one necessary to explain the genesis of the number, and only one repetition is necessary to constitute the status of the subject. The unconscious subject is something that tends to repeat itself, but only one such repetition is necessary to constitute it … In simple terms, this only means that in a universe of discourse nothing contains everything, and here you find again the gap that constitutes the subject.
> The subject is the introduction of a loss in reality, yet nothing can introduce that, since by status reality is as full as possible.[44]

I greatly admire how Lacan says 'In simple terms', after which, as Alan Sokal and Jean Bricmont observe, 'everything becomes obscure'.[45] Inescapably, this style calls to mind George Orwell's famous essay *Politics and the English Language*, published in 1946. He pointed out that

> The whole tendency of modern prose is away from concreteness … modern writing at its worst does not consist in picking out words for the sake of their meaning and inventing images in order to make the

meaning clearer. It consists in gumming together long strips of words which have already been set in order by someone else, and making the results presentable by sheer humbug. The attraction of this way of writing is that it is easy. It is easier – even quicker, once you have the habit – to say *In my opinion it is not an unjustifiable assumption that* than to say *I think*.[46]

It seems unlikely that Jacques Lacan ever read this essay. Nor is he alone in sinning against clarity. Judith Butler is an American philosopher and gender theorist whose work, including her ideas on performativity, is also having some impact on organisation studies. Unfortunately, her style of writing does her important topics a disservice. The journal *Philosophy and Literature* used to run an annual Bad Writing Contest, and Butler won first prize in 1998 for the following sentence:

> The move from a structuralist account in which capital is understood to structure social relations in relatively homologous ways to a view of hegemony in which power relations are subject to repetition, convergence, and rearticulation brought the question of temporality into the thinking of structure, and marked a shift from a form of Althusserian theory that takes structural totalities as theoretical objects to one in which the insights into the contingent possibility of structure inaugurate a renewed conception of hegemony as bound up with the contingent sites and strategies of the rearticulation of power.[47]

This is mind-boggling stuff, but perhaps less mind-boggling than Butler's subsequent comment: 'I don't see what's so hard about that.'[48] She took to the pages of the *New York Times* to defend her writing style – without, however, explaining what the sentence in question actually meant.[49] Butler justified the obscurity of her prose on the basis that her difficult subject matter requires a specialist vocabulary to express it. This is a well-worn defence. She repeated it in a preface to the second edition of one of her most famous books,

Gender Trouble, where she also suggested that 'The demand for lucidity forgets the ruses that motor the ostensibly "clear" view.' Butler then seems to suggest that since politicians, among others, sometimes use plain language to lie, unpretentious writing itself is most likely a trick used by powerful elites to befuddle the masses. She urges us to 'deploy a certain critical suspicion when the arrival of lucidity is announced'.[50] This turns reality upside down, and inside out. In my opinion, it prostrates reason before power, patriarchy and homophobia instead of subverting and resisting them.

So what does her award-winning sentence mean? Steven Pinker is a braver man than me, and has had a go at understanding it: 'Insofar as the passage has a meaning at all, it seems to be that some scholars have come to realize that power can change over time.' He also comments: 'A reader of this intimidating passage can marvel at Butler's ability to juggle abstract propositions about still more abstract propositions, with no real-world referent in sight ... What the reader cannot do is understand it – to see with her own eyes what Butler is seeing.'[51] Language is used as a barricade to keep readers out rather than an open door to invite them in. It is a style that is adopted, as Martha Nussbaum suggests, to quite spuriously create 'an aura of importance'.[52]

We need to call time on this kind of nonsense. Staying with Steven Pinker, he argues, in an article appropriately entitled 'Why academics stink at writing', that 'Our indifference to how we share the fruits of our intellectual labours is a betrayal of our calling to enhance the spread of knowledge. In writing badly, we are wasting each other's time, sowing confusion and error, and turning our profession into a laughing stock.'[53] I agree. But there are other approaches that we can adopt, if we so wish, and I discuss two examples here, drawn from papers that I particularly admire. Both are highly accessible and beautifully crafted. Anyone can understand them, without needing a dictionary at their elbow or some analgesic substance to dull their pain.

Writing Differently

Karl Weick is always worth reading. His 1993 paper 'The collapse of sensemaking in organizations: the Mann Gulch disaster' is a scintillating analysis of how thirteen smokejumpers perished in a fire disaster in 1949.[54] Weick addresses key questions: how role structures, sensemaking and resilience collapsed and led to the disaster, and what sources of resilience could have enabled a better outcome. His paper begins by reviewing the incident itself, in spare prose. Note that it does not start with a literature review, but with an account of the disaster. Nor does Weick draw on original empirical data. He derives his facts from Norman Maclean's book *Young Men and Fire*.[55] Weick then describes the difficulties Maclean had in assembling material for his book, since he didn't start working in it until many years after the events in question, when most key sources were dead and he himself had become elderly. Obliquely, we are being reminded that this study of sensemaking is itself an exercise in sensemaking, and a fraught one at that. It isn't until five pages in that Weick turns to why he thinks that the smokejumpers who perished and those who survived can be regarded as 'an organization', and extrapolates from this incident to suggest that it highlights 'an unsuspected source of vulnerability in organizations'.[56] It is this which constitutes the paper's significance. Weick then revisits the events in detail to explore the collapse in sensemaking that occurred and the panic that led to fatal decisions, and develops the idea that promoting positive interdependence on the part of team members could have averted the disaster.

Does the paper offer 'new theory?' I don't think so. Weick's abstract concludes that 'The analysis is then embedded in the organizational literature to show that we need to reexamine our thinking about temporary systems, structuration, nondisclosive intimacy, intergroup dynamics, and team building.'[57] We have recursive loops throughout the paper, where Weick moves from briefly outlining some relevant theory (e.g. on sensemaking) to the deadly fire, and back again. He uses existing theory in a novel way to transform how we think about organisations in the context of crisis. There is no mention of an overarching metatheoretical framework. Generations of students have benefitted from Weick's paper. It can still be read by practising managers, students or even the public, and they will find something of human interest and value in it, as well as enjoying the prose.

Fascinating as this is, I am not suggesting it is the only way to write an accessible and memorable paper. In 1992, Bill Starbuck published 'Learning by knowledge-intensive firms' in the *Journal of Management Studies*.[58] *JMS* republished it in a booklet of *JMS* Classic Articles some years later. It made a key contribution to our understanding of what knowledge-intensive firms are, how they are organised, and how they are manged. Starbuck starts with a story: 'The General Manager of the Garden Company (a pseudonym) invited John Dutton and me to advise him about what he called their "lot-size problem". He was wondering, he said, whether Garden was making products in economically efficient quantities.' We then move to a new paragraph consisting of one sentence: 'We had no idea what a strange but memorable experience this would be!'[59] Starbuck develops the 'story' of how he and Dutton had a guided tour of the plant. It is a rich, detailed account of the manufacturing process, the attitudes of the workers, and the inefficiencies that were observed. Then, like many good stories, there is a twist. Despite all the inefficiencies that were plain to see, it turned out that the company was in fact highly profitable. Starbuck writes: 'John and I had received several lessons in business ... and the General Manager had not even charged us tuition!'[60] The narrative has been inverted: the client turns out to be the teacher, and the teacher the client. From there they identify the major factor in the Garden Company's success – the expertise of its workers: 'It was a knowledge-intensive firm (KIF)'.[61]

Now notice what is missing in my summary so far. There are no research objectives, no methods, no details of interview protocols – and so far no literature review. What could be called a literature review only begins some three pages into the paper, under the heading 'What is a KIF?' It could have begun like this, but look at the advantages of not doing so. The real experiences described now anchors the literature in a concrete way that would normally be impossible. Starbuck also places himself as a central character in the story: 'Debates about how KIFs differ from other firms persuaded me to focus on firms that would be knowledge-intensive by almost anyone's definition. As a starting point, I defined an expert as someone with a formal education and experience equivalent to a doctoral degree, and a KIF as a firm in which such experts are at least one-third of the personnel.'[62] Eschewing any pretence of omniscience, he frequently says things like 'To my surprise' and 'To our amazement'. The paper then builds to what I think is a beautifully written conclusion:

> To appreciate such currents' beauty and intricacy, social scientists need to stop averaging across large, diverse categories … In the social sciences, broad patterns over-simplify and capture only small fractions of what is happening. They leave scientists in worlds that look random. Broad patterns also tend to emphasize what is consistent with the past and to overlook subtle changes. There is also a world of bright colours, sizzling days, exceptional firms, rare experts, and peculiar KIFs.[63]

It is a paper that is both intellectually stimulating and aesthetically pleasing, and I have absolutely no doubt that it would be desk rejected by *JMS* if it were submitted to the journal today.

WHAT CAN WE DO?

For a start, and in line with a major theme of this book, we need to free ourselves from the belief that great ideas can only be found in 'top' journals. These beliefs die hard. James Walsh delivered a 2010 presidential address to the Academy of Management, subsequently published in *Academy of Management Review*. He tells us that 'I once asked a very distinguished colleague in a well-known business school why he never wrote a book that pulled together his many years of research into a single powerful statement. I will never forget his quick answer: "If I don't write for our top journals, I might as well be writing a letter to my mother."[64] I am tempted to suggest that writing to our mothers, even those that have passed away, would be a better use of our time than writing many of the papers that appear in our hallowed journals. Nevertheless, consider some evidence that runs contrary to the belief this quotation expresses.

Jay Barney published a paper entitled 'Firm resources and sustained competitive advantage' in the *Journal of Management* in 1991.[65] It now has over 60,000 citations on Google Scholar, an impressive tally by any measure. Yet Barney reported, in a retrospective commentary on his work published in 2005, that his paper was rejected multiple times by leading journals, until he himself accepted it for a Special Issue of *JOM* that he was editing.[66] Writing in 2007, Jeffrey Pfeffer listed many other examples of key management ideas that 'were all published either first in books or chapters or, if in articles, in journals that were not top-rated'.[67] These include transaction cost theory, the relationship between agency theory and corporate governance, stakeholder theory, and resource dependence theory. In short, we need to pay more attention to the quality of our ideas rather than cowering before the forums in which some of them are published.

We also need to rethink our approach to both theory development and how we conduct empirical work. Henry Mintzberg has wisely commented: 'We are altogether too hung up on fancy methods in our field, and in much of the social sciences in general. All too often they lead to banal results, significant only in the statistical sense of the word . . . What, for example, is the problem with a sample of one, at least for induction?'[68] It seems that we feel compelled to make our methods and our theories more complex than they need to be as a form of intellectual exhibitionism, designed to show off how clever we are. We might just be achieving the opposite.

We need much more variety in how we write. The standard approach to papers in our journals works well for much of our

work. It doesn't suit it all. I have given examples in this chapter of
work from Karl Weick and Bill Starbuck that triumphantly violates
these norms. I encourage authors, editors and reviewers to be much
more open to different ways of structuring papers, and different
styles of writing them. As Mintzberg has written, 'The world is
so rich and varied, that if you see it as it is, you are bound to appear
creative.' It is also surely too rich and varied to fit into the straitjacket of one format, and a prose style that accommodates only
shades of grey rather than the full spectrum of the rainbow. We can
do better.

CONCLUSION

In 1859, Charles Darwin concluded *The Origin of Species* with one of
the most famous passages in all of the scientific literature:

> It is interesting to contemplate a tangled bank, clothed with
> many plants of many kinds, with birds singing on the bushes,
> with various insects flitting about, and with worms crawling
> through the damp earth, and to reflect that these elaborately
> constructed forms, so different from each other, and dependent
> upon each other in so complex a manner, have all been produced
> by laws acting around us ... from the war of nature, from famine
> and death, the most exalted object which we are capable of
> conceiving, namely, the production of the higher animals,
> directly follows. There is grandeur in this view of life, with its
> several powers, having been originally breathed into a few forms
> or into one; and that, whilst this planet has gone cycling on
> according to the fixed law of gravity, from so simple a beginning
> endless forms most beautiful and most wonderful have been, and
> are being, evolved.[69]

This was the first time, incidentally, that any variant of the word
'evolution' appeared in his book. How vivid, inspiring and memorable
this is. I can't immediately think of an equivalent in our writings
about organisations. Yet organisations are teeming with as much life

as any rural field or hedgerow. They contain tribes and micro-tribes, outbreaks of insanity, struggles for existence, mass extinctions and the flourishing of new forms of organisational life. They are full of love and hatred, optimism and despair, and all the emotions in between these extremes. Organisations are maddening to study, absorbing, often funny and rarely boring. Our line of work gives us the privilege of writing about the human beings who inhabit them, the endless mistakes and triumphs that we all experience, and countless opportunities to discuss how they could be improved. Seemingly unimpressed, most of our writing has drained all life and colour out of the fantastic spectacle in front of us. It is not an approach that will win a wide audience for our ideas, nor does it deserve to.

Perhaps it is time to write about management and organisations with less obscure theorising, with more variety, and with a little more humour, curiosity, and passion.

**Flawed Theorising, Dodgy
Statistics and (In)Authentic
Leadership Theory**

There are at least ninety-three academic journals devoted exclusively to 'leadership', in one context or another. At the time of writing, Google Scholar lists 244,000 articles and Amazon identifies over 100,000 books with 'leadership' in their titles – figures that must have been obsolete as soon as I typed them. Clearly, there is a fascination with the subject, fuelled by airport-bookshop business books and outlets such as *Harvard Business Review*, which seem convinced that all our problems can be solved if only the right leader is in place. Leaders are often depicted as some version of Superman – strong, confident, bold, decisive, empathic and visionary. Researchers identify an ever greater range of attributes and skills that all leaders should aspire to develop and which a select few are deemed to possess. Nor does there seem to be any cap on the number of consultants who promise to teach the skills that are said to be needed. CEOs and wannabe CEOs find much of this appealing. After all, it is more satisfying to believe that you are transforming the world rather than simply manipulating figures on a spreadsheet.

Business journalists have also found that such models of leadership help them craft appealing accounts of business success and failure. If a business does well, credit goes to its CEO, whose vision is said to have inspired an enthusiastic army of devoted followers. And if a business fails, all the blame can be dumped on the shoulders of a CEO whose vision – so the story usually goes – has become outdated, and whose leadership style, praised to high heaven in good times, now inspires only apathy and inaction. This is a world of great triumphs and crushing failures, of thwarted ambitions and improbable comebacks, and of regicide, patricide and matricide that fans of *Game of Thrones* would surely appreciate.

But any appearance of success with leadership research is a façade. In this chapter I support this argument by looking at an area of leadership research that has gained much ground in recent years – authentic leadership theory (henceforth ALT). The growing interest in this approach reflects a wider preoccupation in our society with the whole idea of 'authenticity', often defined in terms of how consistent our internal values are with how we express ourselves to others.[1] However, as I will show, ALT exemplifies many of the themes that run through this book – feeble theorising, shoddy empirical work, questionable research practices, a bias for positive results and dubious statistical analysis. Its glossy surface conceals dry rot, crumbling foundations and more than a whiff of scandal.

In Chapter 5, I discussed 131 retractions in our field, seven of which have Fred Walumbwa as a co-author. Three of these are (or were) key papers in the development of ALT.[2] Another paper that he co-authored, published in the prestigious *Journal of Management* (*JOM*), purported to validate an Authentic Leadership Questionnaire (ALQ).[3] Although freely available to researchers, the ALQ is paywalled for commercial purposes on the website www.mindgarden.com. But almost immediately after its publication it was obvious that the statistical analyses which sought to validate the ALQ rested were flawed, and many academics publicly posted their concerns. Critics alleged that some of the claimed results were impossible, given the nature of the data.[4] However, the *JOM* declined to retract it. Instead, they published a new paper by the original's authors in 2018 (minus Walumbwa) that claimed, this time definitively, to support the ALQ.[5] It seems that it is a valid and reliable instrument after all. This is as though builders who continually confused centimetres with inches still managed to construct a house with pin-point precision – possible, but unlikely.

What has gone wrong, and what can we do about it?

WHAT IS AUTHENTIC LEADERSHIP, AND WHY DOES IT MATTER?

Some limited background is necessary. Leadership research entered the 1970s in the doldrums. Fad after fad had resulted in a great pile of research that established – well, not much really. It was often said that there were as many definitions of leadership as there were people writing about it. Rescue arrived in the form of 'transformational leadership'. Back in 1978, James McGregor Burns proposed that leadership could be viewed as either transactional or transformational.[6] With the former, goods, services and other rewards are exchanged so that the various parties achieve their independent goals. Burns observed that the object of this transactional approach 'is not a joint effort for persons with common aims acting for the collective interests of followers but a bargain to aid the individual interests of persons or groups going their separate ways'.

He presented transformational leadership in an altogether more favourable light. Here, the leader transforms the goals, motivations, aspirations, values and feelings of followers. The new mind-sets were assumed to be of a higher level since they would represent the 'collective good or pooled interests of leaders and followers'. Implicitly and often explicitly, this view also suggests that most power should be concentrated in the hands of leaders. But it was quickly obvious that such power could just as well be used to advance the interests of the leader at the expense of any collective to which they belonged. Astonishingly, managers and employees did not always behave as if they played for the same team. Employees would sometimes revolt, and leaders would sometimes prioritise their own interests above those of their employees.

This dilemma has been dubbed 'the Hitler problem': in essence, can Hitler be viewed as a transformational leader?[7] Is he in the same category as Martin Luther King, or other more moral leaders? If not, who sets the standards for what constitutes morality, using what criteria, and validated by whom? Aware of these problems, Burns proposed that 'transformational leadership has an inherently ethical component'.[8] In due course this led to the notion of 'authentic transformational leadership', from which sprang authentic leadership theory (ALT). Bernard Bass is particularly associated with the application of transformational leadership theory to business organisations. Writing with Paul Steidlmeier in 1999, he sought to differentiate between 'authentic' and 'inauthentic' transformational leadership.[9] Authentic transformational leaders take genuine care to serve the needs of their followers, whereas inauthentic ones prioritise their own self-interest. This meant that 'leaders' such as Hitler or North Korea's Kim Jong-un are in fact not leaders at all. No bad transformational leaders meant no problems for the theory. This was a handy get-out-of-jail-free card for theorists, but one that many others, including myself, have found unconvincing.[10] A builder is still a builder even if the quality of their work is atrocious. Oblivious to this, ALT has now been extended to embrace all good things, and sets an impossible level of expectation far beyond what leaders can ever actually accomplish.

The tone of the literature is captured in the following definition of authentic leadership, from Walumbwa et al.'s controversial paper in *JOM*. They describe ALT as

> *a pattern of leader behavior that draws upon and promotes both positive psychological capacities and a positive ethical climate, to foster greater self-awareness and an internalised moral perspective, balanced processing of information, and relational transparency on the part of leaders working with followers, fostering positive self-development* (italics in the original).[11]

The word 'positive' runs throughout many of the publications advocating authentic leadership, and establishes it as a part of the movement known as 'positive psychology'. Fred Luthans and Bruce Avolio contributed a chapter to a book on positive psychology in 2003 where they fully own this connection. They write: 'As a positive construct, descriptive words include *genuine, reliable, trustworthy, real,* and *veritable.* Positive psychologists conceive this authenticity as both *owning* one's personal experiences (thoughts, emotions, or beliefs, "the real me inside") and *acting* in accord with the true self (behaving and expressing what you really think and believe).' They approvingly cite the example of the polling organisation, Gallup, which has been 'focusing on positive psychology's application to the workplace by identifying and fitting employee talents and strengths into the right job ... which in turn significantly relates to desired organizational outcomes such as productivity, profit, customer service, safety, and retention'.[12] As with other mainstream leadership theories a unitarist interest is simply assumed. All we need is a sufficiently positive attitude to bring it to the fore and make good things happen. This risks producing what David Collinson has termed 'Prozac leadership', in which an unremittingly positive focus creates a dangerously inaccurate impression on the part of leaders about their own efficacy and the health of the organisations they lead.[13]

Walumbwa, this time writing with Tara Wernsing in the prestigious *Oxford Handbook of Leadership,* expands on these conceptions to argue that ALT has four dimensions, consisting of self-awareness, relational transparency, balanced processing (i.e. the ability to objectively handle data before making decisions) and an internalised moral perspective that facilitates ethical decision making.[14] It seems that authentic leaders are paragons of perfection and candidates for canonisation. In Table 7.1, I list just some of the characteristics that they have been said to possess.[15] I invite you to wonder whether any human being could possibly exhibit such a vast range of exemplary behaviour.

I could fill this chapter with similar quotations, but you get the picture. There seems to be no limit to the results that authentic leaders can produce. They satisfy followers' basic needs,[16] encourage followers to be more authentic in their own behaviours,[17] and cause them to display moral courage.[18] They are also claimed to produce superior business results.[19] Authentic leaders, it is said, exemplify high moral standards, integrity and honesty, 'and their favourable reputation fosters

Table 7.1 *The nature of authentic leadership*

'The authentic leader is confident, hopeful, optimistic, resilient, moral/
ethical, future-oriented, and gives priority to developing associates to be
leaders ... an authentic leader is true to him/herself and the exhibited
behaviour positively transforms or develops associates into leaders
themselves'.
Luthans and Avolio, 2003, p. 243

Authentic leaders are people for whom '(a) the role of the leader is a central
component of their self-concept, (b) they have achieved a high level of self-
resolution or self-concept clarity, (c) their goals are self-concordant, and (d)
their behaviour is self-expressive'.
Shamir and Eilam, 2005, p. 399

'Authentic leaders use their natural abilities, but they also recognise their
shortcomings, and work hard to overcome them. They lead with purpose,
meaning, and values. They build enduring relationships with people.
Others follow them because they know where they stand. They are
consistent and self-disciplined. When their principles are tested, they
refuse to compromise. Authentic leaders are dedicated to helping
themselves because they know that becoming a leader takes a lifetime of
personal growth'.
George, 2003, p. 12

Authentic leadership is 'a pattern of leader behavior that draws on and
promotes positive psychological capacities and a positive ethical climate,
to foster greater self awareness, an internalised moral perspective,
balanced processing of information, and relational transparency on the
part of leaders working with followers, fostering positive self-
development'.
Walumbwa et al., 2008, p. 94

Authentic leadership is based on '*authenticity*, which entails the
discovery of the authentic self through meaningful relationships within
organizational structures that support core, significant values;
intentionality, which implies visionary leadership that takes its energy
and direction from the good intentions of current organizational members
who put their intellects, hearts and souls into shaping a vision for the
future; a renewed commitment to *spirituality*, which calls for the

Table 7.1 (*cont.*)

rediscovery of the spirit within each person and celebration of the shared
meaning, with purpose of relationship; a *sensibility* to the feelings,
aspirations and needs of others, with special reference to the multicultural
settings in which many leaders operate in the light of the increasing
globalizing trends of life and work'.
Bhindi and Duignan, 1997, p. 119

An authentic leader is 'one who (1) is self-aware, humble, always seeking
improvement, aware of those being led and looks out for the welfare of
others; (2) fosters a high degree of trust by building an ethical moral
framework; and (3) is committed to organizational success within the
construct of social values'.
Whitehead, 2009, p. 850

'Authentic leaders exhibit a higher moral capacity to judge dilemmas from
different angles and are able to take into consideration different
stakeholder needs'.
May et al., 2003. p. 248.

positive expectations among employees, enhancing their levels of
trust and willingness to cooperate with the leader for the benefit of
the organization'.[20] Bruce Avolio and a number of his colleagues,
including Walumbwa, go even further. They argue that 'the influence
of authentic leaders extends well beyond bottom-line success; such
leaders have a role to play in the greater society by tackling public
policy issues and addressing organizational and societal problems'.[21]
Here, business leaders are encouraged to regard themselves in
a messianic fashion. Their job, essentially, is to save the world.
In these respects, as in others, ALT is less an advance on transformational leadership than a rebranding of it. Just as with transformational leadership, authentic leaders possess an extraordinary ability
to influence others and effect positive change. There is no real discussion of conflict or power in the literature on authentic leadership,
leading to the production of what Alessia Contu calls 'a managerialist, patriarchal and paternalist fantasy ... where management

assumes its primary, legitimate role and everyone else fulfils their position in this (presumed) consensus based way of life.'[22]

No wonder that authentic leadership has become a booming industry. Harvard Business School, fad surfer par excellence, now offers executive education courses in it. The school's marketing blurb for this asserts that the programme was developed by 'leadership visionary Bill George'. It promises that 'you'll uncover the unique characteristics that let you lead with authenticity – enabling you to become the type of leader you most admire'.[23] And if even half of the claims made by Harvard, Fred Walumbwa and others are right then the costs involved (in Harvard's case, US$15,500 for five days) is money well spent. However, it might be advisable to postpone celebrations just a little longer. The 'theory' is mostly empty rhetoric, and while I concede that the empirical studies offered in its support are a masterclass, they are unfortunately a masterclass in faulty research methods. They are designed so that they can *only* discover positive results that favour the theory. It is time to apply some critical analysis.

FAULTY THEORISING, UNSUBSTANTIATED ASSUMPTIONS AND TAUTOLOGOUS REASONING

Much of the early writing on transformational leadership had its origins in recounting the war stories of business leaders, notably Lee Iacocca of Chrysler.[24] So it also goes with ALT. Bill George is a former CEO of Medtronic, and as we have seen above is now credited by Harvard Business School as the architect of the programme it offers on authentic leadership. He published a widely cited co-authored book in 2003 entitled *True North*, followed by an equally well cited co-authored article in *Harvard Business Review* in 2007.[25] Much of the subsequent literature reads as little more than variations on the themes outlined by George. Yet it is sobering to reread his original book. It is a collection of inanities that was only taken seriously because its author was a former CEO. Typical of the text, we read:

True North is the internal compass that guides you successfully through life. It represents who you are as a human being at your deepest level. It is your orienting point – your fixed point in a spinning world – that helps you stay on track as a leader. Your True North is based on what is most important to you, your most cherished values, your passions and motivations, the sources of satisfaction in your life.[26]

It struck a chord for several reasons. The demise of Enron in 2001, mired in accountancy scandals, was still fresh in people's minds. Worse was to come with the 2008 financial crash. There was a yearning for 'genuine' and 'good' leaders who cared about more than the bottom line. In addition, 'issues of authenticity have become a pervasive part of our culture, our institutions, and our individual selves'.[27] Reality TV has fed on this obsession, promising to present people as they 'really' are, whether it is eating ants in a jungle or performing idiotic tasks to become a dodgy tycoon's apprentice. Strip away the artifice, the story goes, stay true to what you really are and people will like you for it. They will then be more willing to do your bidding.

What If Your Real Self Is a Jackass?

We have already seen, however, that a core assumption of AL is that authentic leaders have only positive moral qualities. Quite why has not been explained. I suppose that it is part of the same mind-set exhibited by transformational leadership theorists, who argue that only good leadership counts as leadership. William Gardner, Bruce Avolio and Fred Luthans tell us that authentic leaders pursue 'an integrated set of goals that reflect personal standards of conduct', they are 'intrinsically motivated' so that they 'often become so engrossed in their work that they are motivated solely by a sense of curiosity, a thirst for learning, and the satisfaction that comes from accomplishing a valued task/objective', resulting in 'the total immersion of the self at work'.[28] They also reveal aspects of themselves to others so as to 'create bonds based on intimacy and trust', and will encourage others in the organisation to do the same. It is a marvellous image.

In the 1965 Hollywood comedy *The Great Race*, Jack Lemmon played the cartoonish chief baddie, Professor Fate. He wore a black hat and cape, and invariably twirled his moustaches when hissing venomous threats. The movie's hero, The Great Leslie, was played by Tony Curtis. Leslie always dressed in a spotless white suit, his teeth sparkled when he smiled and any woman who met him swooned at his feet. ALT is the academic equivalent of The Great Leslie. It presents a black-and-white view of leadership, shorn of all complexity and any motivation other than the desire to do good. Yet, in the real world, no human being possesses traits that are wholly positive or wholly negative. The philosopher Martin Heidegger wrote in *Being and Time* that people are neither authentic or inauthentic, but rather more or less so.[29] We are constituted by our presence and interaction with other people, so that different aspects of our nature and what we think of as our inner self continually come to the fore and retreat into the background. No one is constantly authentic in the terms described by the authentic leadership literature. I rather suspect that anyone who tried would be so sanctimonious that we would find them unbearable.

Erving Goffman recognised this long ago. His seminal text *The Presentation of Self in Everyday Life*, published in 1959, described social interaction as a performance in which we are all engaged. We project ideal images of ourselves to fulfil certain roles, satisfy our needs and build our relationships with other people. But Goffman also pointed out that this impacts on how we actually see ourselves. Our performances change us, since oftentimes

> the performer comes to be own audience; he comes to be performer and observer of the same show . . . In everyday terms, there will be things he knows, or has known, that he will not be able to tell himself. This intricate manoeuvre of self-delusion constantly occurs . . . Perhaps here we have a source of what has been called

'self-distantiation', namely, that process by which a person comes to feel estranged from himself.[30]

Put differently, we have many selves rather than one. Like a shape shifter, different versions of who we think we are come to the fore depending on context. Jeffrey Pfeffer has pointed out that leaders sometimes must project more optimism and confidence than they possess.[31] For that matter, we all do. No matter how bad I feel, when I enter a classroom I have to put those feelings aside and convince my students that I am wholly focused on their education. It wouldn't do to burst into tears and tell them that my dog has just died, my house has burnt down and I have been declared bankrupt. How does this square with any suggestion of a unitary inner identity, consisting only of positive attributes?

Jackie Ford and Nancy Harding argue that the notions of authenticity found in the literature seem to imagine an 'ontologically fixed entity having an inner self securely bounded from the exterior world. The model is thus located in a binary of inside/outside. The authentic leader will be a moral person who, being moral, is good "on the inside"; through revealing their inner goodness this person will be an authentic leader.'[32] This is an image of leadership that may be consoling but which is actually impossible to practice, and which none of us has ever really encountered. It begs a key question: what if your dominant inner self is a jackass? Why does ALT fixate only on the positive attributes that are said to constitute authenticity?

Gail Fairhurst gets to the core of this issue. She discusses the example of Linda Wachner, then CEO of apparel maker Warnaco.[33] Wachner was profiled by *Fortune* magazine in 1993 as one of the seven 'toughest' bosses in the US.[34] She had a brutal attitude towards people. On one occasion, she ordered a colleague to fire people at random to show that he was serious about improving performance. The *Fortune* profile reported that she had lectured senior executives in terms like this: 'You're eunuchs. How can your wives stand you? You've got nothing between your legs.' Her rationale was that this approach

172 [IN]AUTHENTIC LEADERSHIP THEORY

ensured that the company was run 'efficiently', and that if people
didn't like it they could leave. As Fairhurst notes: 'Wachner may be
lacking many things, but personal insight does not seem to be among
them. The "real" Linda Wachner surfaces in her display of negative
traits.'[35] Interestingly, the now infamous movie producer, Harvey
Weinstein, was also among the seven bosses profiled. In 2017 numerous women made allegations against him of sexual assault and rape,
bringing his career to an ignominious end. His behaviour too was
consistent. Whatever inner soul he possessed seems to have been
untroubled by attacks of conscience. Weinstein was an authentic
bastard. Yet these displays of authenticity would be dismissed by
authentic leadership theorists as ... inauthentic. Such Pollyannaish
views of human nature suggest that if only Wachner and Weinstein
looked deeply enough inside themselves they would find a purer version of who they really are that they could bring forth and showcase to
the world. I confess to some doubts.

Ultimately, ALT rests on a primitive view of identity and self-
awareness. Identity is presented as a simple construct, consisting of
little more than positive attributes that are consistent across time and
circumstances. Gaining insight into our identity merely requires that
we look inwards, and we shall find it. As Helena Liu, Leanne Cutcher
and David Grant have argued, 'such idealized notions of authentic
leadership overlook the role of power in the co-construction of leadership narratives as well as within the socio-historical context in which
leadership takes place'.[36] But it is impossible to 'transcend the world
that we occupy. We exist in a context, variable over time and can never
be separate from this. We must always interact with people, events,
etc. and cannot be disinterested spectators of our own particular
context.'[37] ALT is little more than a series of fables, designed to
reassure us that leadership is simpler than it is and that introspection
can lead us all to salvation.

Handily enough, for consultants, it turns out that we also
need 'development' in authentic leadership: acquiring the insights
needed for it isn't so simple after all. As Jeffrey Pfeffer has

caustically observed 'The idea that one would and could be trained to become or at least appear authentic oozes with delicious irony.'[38] But it is even worse than that. Drawing on existential philosophy, Puck Algera and Marjolein Lips-Wiersma argue that tension, conflict and struggle is inherent to human existence.[39] This militates against the emergence of the integrated and harmonious sense of self that is presumed in the literature on authentic leadership. What is authentic or otherwise is something that each of us must discover for ourselves. It cannot be created or developed for us by others. Or, as Jackie Ford and Nancy Harding eloquently put it,

> Any such programmes would require that participants learn how to deny their own subjectivities in the quest of learned 'authenticity'. We anticipate that participants would engage in activities designed to develop their abilities to reflect upon themselves and to better 'know themselves', but the self they would reflect upon would be a collective organizational self, one devoid of agency or freedom of thought.[40]

Much of this is because, like transformational leadership in its heyday, the original impulses that drove the theory quickly gave way to a primary focus on organisational efficiency.[41] Authenticity is only valued if it helps the bottom line, a potential contradiction that seems to escape its advocates. But it is a useful tool when selling consultancy or training services to businesses.

Theory as Tautology

Sverre Spoelstra, Nick Butler and Helen Delaney have argued that many leadership theories are formulated as tautologies that are guaranteed confirmation when tested by conventional methods. As they say:

> what are we to make of the hypothesis that 'agreeableness is positively related to ethical leadership' when, as the authors

themselves note, ethical leaders are '*by definition* ...
altruistically motivated, caring, and concerned about their
followers and others in society' (Brown and Treviño, 2006: 603;
emphasis added]? ... It is, after all, difficult to imagine a world in
which leaders who are altruistic, caring and concerned come
across as disagreeable. It is like testing the hypothesis 'all
bachelors are unmarried' – the design of the theory ensures
empirical confirmation.[42]

In line with this, ALT presents leadership as all good things to everyone. But maintaining this line means that its theory confounds cause
with effect. Essentially, the effects that are attributed to authentic
leadership frequently turn out to be identical to what is claimed to
have caused them. In Table 7.2, I list some hypotheses, propositions
and statements that I have found in publications that are little more
than ugly tautologies.[43] They were written to conceal rather than
reveal. Where I draw on multiple hypotheses from the same paper
I discuss them together. The commentary alongside them is my
translation.

Increasingly, researchers seek to find pre-determined answers
rather than discover a series of objective truths, some of which might
clash with their theory. And if you are setting out to establish mind-
boggling tautologies along the lines that trustworthy leaders are more
trusted than untrustworthy ones (see below), it is scarcely surprising
that you will succeed. It would be hard not to. Ironically, ALT turns
out to be deeply inauthentic in the way its theorists approach empirical data. This is a profound disgrace to the academy, as I will now seek
to show.

TURNING BASE METAL INTO GOLD – AL RESEARCH AS ALCHEMY

Consider what is often described the 'romance of leadership'. This
stream of thought draws on the influential work of James Meindl,
Sanford Ehrlich and Janet Dukerich in 1985. They argued that we

Table 7.2 *Theory as tautology*

What is claimed	Translation
'Authentic leadership behaviour is positively related to follower perceptions of leader behavioural integrity.' *Leroy et al., 2012, p. 257*	Leaders who behave with integrity are seen as behaving with integrity.
'Hypothesis 1. Authentic leadership is negatively related to leaders' job stress.	H1: When leaders behave in ways that they prefer, they are less stressed.
Hypothesis 2. Authentic leadership is positively related to leaders' work engagement. . . .	H2: Happy leaders are more engaged with their work.
Hypothesis 6. The indirect effect of authentic leadership on job stress through leader mental depletion is moderated by the extent of follower interaction, in that the more authentic the leaders are, the less job stress they perceive with increasing follower interaction, and vice versa.' *Weiss et al., 2018, pp. 311–312*	H6: Happy leaders with happy followers enjoy meeting up with them.
'*Hypothesis 2*: Employee-perceived authentic leadership mediates the relationship between supervisor-perceived authentic leadership and employee trust.' *Hsieh and Wang, 2015, p. 2334*	H2: Trustworthy leaders are trusted more.
'Authentic leadership is related to both performance and trust. When followers perceive that their leaders are authentic, they also will believe they can trust those leaders.' *Clapp-Smith et al., 2009, p. 237*	Trustworthy leaders are more likely to be trusted than those who are untrustworthy, and people will work harder for them.
'*Hypothesis 1:* authentic followership is positively related to basic need satisfaction. . . .	H1: When people feel that they can be themselves, their basic needs are satisfied.

Table 7.2 (cont.)

What is claimed	Translation
'Hypothesis 3: Authentic leadership strengthens the relationship between authentic followership and basic need satisfaction.' Leroy et al., 2015, pp. 1682–1684	H3: When leaders behave nicely so do their followers, who are also happier.

have a tendency to overattribute responsibility for organisational outcomes to leaders. Humans love stories, and there is no story simpler than that Leader A has caused Outcome B. The famous evolutionary biologist Stephen Jay Gould explains it well:

> We are story-telling creatures, products of history ourselves. We are fascinated by trends, in part because they tell stories by the basic device of imparting directionality to time, in part because they so often supply a moral dimension to a sequence of events: a cause to bewail as something goes to pot, or to highlight as a rare beacon of hope.[44]

This explains the widespread confusion between correlation and causation in popular thinking, and even in many academic publications. The effect is particularly strong when there is a gap between two events in organisations. A new leader is appointed, and performance goes up or down. Either way, people have a natural tendency to explain the outcome concerned by attributing responsibility to the leader. The leader is good or bad, authentic or inauthentic, visionary or uninspired, a genius or a dolt. The problem is that our stories about the leader are rarely separated from our knowledge of the outcomes for which we are holding them responsible. So precisely the same leadership behaviours can be described in opposite ways, depending entirely on the outcome. Thus, if an organisation succeeds, the leader was authentic. If it fails, the leader was inauthentic – but the behaviour of the leaders in question might well have been identical. We are simply seeing retrospective attributions for complex organisational processes. Yet as Owain Smolovic-Jones and Keith Grint point out: 'it is quite likely that authentic leaders have failed throughout history and will continue to do so in the future. Perhaps the phenomenon of the "halo", therefore, goes some way to explaining the apparently strong link found between authenticity competencies and organizational performance ... It is a selective reading of history.'[45]

The work of Phil Rosenzweig is crucial to a deeper understanding of this process. His book *The Halo Effect: How Managers Let Themselves be Deceived* looks in detail at a number of well-known companies, such as Cisco and ABB, and a number of leaders, such as Cisco's John Chambers and ABB's Percy Barnevik.[46] In both these cases periods of spectacular success were followed by problems and setbacks. This is to be expected. No one is constantly successful, and the phenomenon of regression to the mean suggests that either superior or inferior performance is likely to be followed by something closer to the average. This helps explain why football teams who sack a manager after a poor performance usually show a temporary improvement in performance, while a manager who is praised after a run of successes usually shows a decline in performance.[47] In the cases of Cisco and ABB this played out to the letter.

The critical insight offered by Rosenzweig is that the behaviours of their leaders had not changed. But they were described differently, particularly by the business press, depending on our knowledge of organisational outcomes. Rosenzweig provides the following eulogies attracted by Barnevik when his company was on the up. *Harvard Business Review* described him as 'a corporate pioneer' building 'the new model of the competitive enterprise'; *Fortune* magazine offered the view that 'If lean and mean could be personified, Percy Barnevik would walk through the door'; *Business Week* opined that 'The hard charging executive of ABB has seen the future and it contains no boundaries ... despite a manic drive and a fast-track career, Barnevik is ... surprisingly unpretentious and accessible'; *Forbes* claimed that 'Barnevik relishes taking a scythe to corporate bloat.'[48] But when performance dipped so did the narrative around its leader. He had 'built walls around himself'; he had been 'high-handed in his treatment of the board'; he had 'monopolised the flow of information', and much more.[49]

The long and the short of it is that retrospective attributions of responsibility to leaders for success or failure are unreliable when we are already aware of organisational outcomes. We simply exaggerate a leader's responsibility for success or failure, and we craft images of positive or negative leadership behaviours (such as *authenticity* or *inauthenticity*) to be consistent with our attributions.

Can this explain some of the 'findings' that are cited in support of ALT?

Questionnaires and Confirmatory Biases within ALT

Leadership research in general is fascinated by surveys and questionnaires. Mats Alvesson and Dan Karreman mischievously suggest that: 'Sometimes one even gets the impression that leadership "as such" – practices, interactions, relations – is of less interest for researchers than questionnaire filling behavior.'[50] The assumption, of course, is that the data obtained from questionnaires accurately captures what people feel about complex issues. This is doubtful. Alvesson and Karreman go on to say:

> Responses to abstract formulations in questionnaires are usually remotely distanced from actions, events, feelings, relations, articulation of opinions, and so on, emerging in everyday life. That a person is asked to put an X in a particular response alternative from among the five or so possibilities in a questionnaire may say rather little of what or how that person feels or thinks or behave.

Experience is flattened into a number or a tick. This lends itself to the kind of faulty attributions that I have just discussed.

Let's take one paper and subject it to some examination. This was originally published in 2010 with Fred Walumbwa as the lead author, and later retracted.[51] It is important to note that it was retracted for problems with its statistical analysis and not for its overall design, which is typical of research into authentic leadership. At the time of writing it has over 500 citations on Google Scholar. It was also published in the most prestigious journal in the field of leadership studies – *Leadership Quarterly* (*LQ*). I think it is fair to wonder how this happened.

To begin with: what was the big claim of the paper that merited publication in *LQ*? Its abstract tells us that 'authentic leadership behavior was positively related to supervisor-rated organizational citizenship behavior and work engagement ... These relationships were mediated by the followers' level of identification with the supervisor and their feelings of empowerment.'[52] My translation of this is as follows: 'Supervisors with authentic leaders (that is, good ones) do more organizational citizenship and feel more engaged with their work. Moreover, followers of supervisors who feel empowered by their supervisor help contribute to this effect.' This seems like a statement of the blindingly obvious. It is difficult to imagine anyone arguing that 'bad leaders inspire followers to do more organizational citizenship, that bad leadership makes people feel more engaged with their work, and that followers who don't identify with their leader feel more empowered'. It is comparable to arguing that the ground gets wet when it rains, but it is dry when the weather is sunny and warm.

Now look at their methods in more detail. Data were obtained 'from employees in two telecom firms that were each located in a separate major city in China. One was located in northern China and the other in southern China. One company was a state-owned firm, and the other was jointly owned by the government and a foreign private company.'[53] We are given no further information about the companies' history, profitability, or general approach to managing people. Context, it seems, is viewed as unimportant in assessing leadership. The ALQ was employed, and other survey instruments were used to assess identification with supervisors, empowerment, work engagement, and organisational citizenship behaviour. The authors report that these were distributed over several waves, with two-week gaps between them, to minimise common source/method bias.

In essence, people were asked to assess the leadership style of their supervisors. But they were only asked to evaluate how authentic they were, in the terms embodied in the ALQ. Had other leadership instruments been employed, then it is likely respondents would have framed their perceptions of leadership in terms of the survey instrument concerned. Imagine that I am asking people about how satisfied they are with the food they eat. But I only ask them about meat products. Does this enable me to conclude that meat products are associated with higher levels of satisfaction, and thus that eating meat increases people's satisfaction with food? But this is the causal leap that Walumbwa et al. then take. They conclude that 'Our results support the propositions concerning a positive link between authentic leadership and follower work engagement as well as follower OCB. Thus, the supervisors' authenticity does seem to play a significant role, in terms of the relationships we reported above with both employee work engagement and supervisor rated OCB.'[54]

I also doubt that a short time lag between surveys is sufficient to establish causality, even if it is enough to escape the accusation of using cross-sectional data for causal modelling purposes. This is all the more the case when we consider alternative explanations for the causal claims being made – specifically, the halo error and romance of leadership theory. Recall that we tend to over-attribute responsibility for organisational outcomes to individual leaders. Assuming that the organisations where these data were gathered were doing reasonably well, it is likely that employees would have a favourable attitude towards at least some of their leaders, and then when asked to describe their favourable feelings in terms of authentic leadership they would do so. All we can conclude, at best, is that when people think well of their leaders, for whatever reason, this positive attitude is correlated with other good things, such as positive citizenship behaviour, and a sense of empowerment. But it doesn't follow that authentic leadership specifically has caused these things: it could be that correlational bias (which may arise from multiple factors) has caused people to perceive their leaders as authentic, or at least as more effective than ineffective.

We should also note that *all* six of the hypotheses proposed in this paper were confirmed. This level of confirmation is now widespread in management and leadership research, and is itself a cause for concern. No genuinely open-ended study can possibly produce only hypotheses that will be confirmed, unless they are so transparently obvious and tautological (that is, useless) that this is inescapable. The other possibility is that our authors had more hypotheses than those they reported in their study, but deleted them from the final paper because the results were not statistically significant. Openly reporting them would be good practice, but it would mean that the theory being promoted has less predictive value than its authors would like to suggest.

It is well known that people tend to subject conclusions that they don't like to much tougher scrutiny than conclusions that concur with their preferences. Brendan McSweeney points out that these biases, often unmotivated, may also be motivated – that is, they may be driven by a desire to defend a particular theory in which a researcher has acquired a vested interest.[55] This is facilitated by the availability of funding streams, belonging to a group that exerts conformity pressures, beliefs about how journals might respond to certain ideas and simply being influenced by what is fashionable. All this and more seems evident in the case of ALT. But the authors offer a conclusion that suggests something else is also at play: 'Interventions aimed at enhancing the authentic leadership of supervisors would seem beneficial to the extent they improve followers' positive work behaviours.'[56] This is a consultancy calling card, complete with promises of major benefits, simplistic prescriptions for success and the suggestion that 'interventions' may help. It is a motivation that does not help the disinterested pursuit of knowledge.

Experimental Work and Confirmatory Biases

Such is the bias towards questionnaires that relatively little experimental work has been done in the name of ALT. But I highlight here an exception – a paper by Nick Steffens and several of his colleagues, published once again in the *Leadership Quarterly* in 2016. Its main claim is as follows: 'Study 1 shows experimentally that compared to a leader who advances personal interests, a leader who advances the interests of a collective is (a) perceived as offering more authentic leadership and (b) more likely to inspire followership.'[57] I can't avoid noting again how flimsy this sounds. But what contortions the authors go through on their way to telling us, in effect, that leaders who promote a common good are more valued than those who pursue selfishness.

They report that they gathered data from 74 students. No details are given, including whether they were undergraduates or postgraduates. Missing data left a final sample of 73. The practice of using student samples to draw inferences about relationships at work is by itself dubious. Few of them have much experience of the world of business. Some journals now refuse to publish papers where the data comes predominantly from students. Regardless, those in this study were presented with a one-page commentary article on a senior Australian politician who had switched his support from the then prime minister to a challenger. In one version of the article, the headline was changed to read: 'Bill Shorten changes his mind to advance personal interests'. The other read: 'Bill Shorten changes his mind to advance collective interests'. AL was then assessed with a 5 point Likert scale on several items such as 'Bill Shorten shows that he understands his strengths and weaknesses'; 'Bill Shorten states what he means'; 'Bill Shorten shows consistency between his beliefs and actions'; and 'Bill Shorten carefully listens to alternative perspectives before reaching a conclusion'.

Consider that the first headline is a depiction of selfishness and will contaminate any responses that are obtained. Of course, the second headline is equally likely to skew responses. With those headlines, I suspect you could have presented any list of items from any leadership theory and the 'collective condition' would have scored higher. All this tells us is that when people are given negative information about a leader, they will rate that leader as a poor leader on whatever measurement of leadership that you present them with. And when they are given positive information about a leader the opposite will happen.

Problems of Causality in Leadership Studies

All this compounds the problem of determining causality in leadership studies. Take any of the dimensions of authentic leadership, such as self-awareness, and consider the problems of causality that it reveals. Researchers claim that authentic leaders are self-aware, and that their self-awareness produces more authentic, committed, motivated and productive followers. Yet the self-awareness of leaders is largely assessed by responses obtained from followers, who generally don't possess the gift of mind-reading. Leaders may come across as more self-aware when they share information with followers, and are more likely to engage in plausible self-disclosures when the followers in question are committed, motivated and productive. Rather than self-awareness causing the various effects that are claimed for it, the 'effects' themselves may create the attribution of self-awareness.

Look also at how the survey tools being used bias respondents towards only positive responses. Table 7.3 shows sample items that Walumbwa et al. provided from the ALQ in their 2008 *JOM* paper.[58]

In my view, *any* leader who is liked, has a reputation for basic competence and has had the good fortune to preside over positive

Table 7.3 *Authentic leadership questionnaire sample items*

Self-awareness
1. Seeks feedback to improve interactions with others.
2. Accurately describes how others view his or her capabilities.

Relational transparency
3. Says exactly what he or she means.
4. Is willing to admit mistakes when they are made.

Internalised moral perspective
5. Demonstrates beliefs that are consistent with actions.
6. Makes decisions based on his/her core beliefs.

Balanced processing
7. Solicits views that challenge his or her deeply held positions.
8. Listens carefully to different points of view before coming to conclusions.

outcomes would score highly on these and similar items. Recall the halo error. Once we make the attribution of responsibility for success to a leader *of course* we will then score them highly when presented with inherently positive statements. Researchers have moved beyond merely having a bias for positive results. In a stunning display of confirmatory bias, they now design studies *where only positive results are possible.* One might as well ask children whether they think that Santa Claus is a fat old man with a white beard who rides across the sky on a sleigh and delivers presents on Christmas Eve.

Problems of spurious measurement and implausible precision have also beset the parent field of positive psychology. In particular, a well cited paper from 2005 claimed to establish a critical positivity ratio of 2.9.[59] If you have a ratio of 2.9 positive to negative emotions you will flourish mentally and in all other ways. Sadly, the maths turned out to be flawed.[60] As with the development of the ALQ, this hasn't stopped the paper's authors from arguing that there is a critical positivity ratio, even if we don't yet know quite what it is. Undaunted by the lack of evidence, one of them, Barbara Fredrickson, has gone on to publish a best-selling book built around the original claim.[61] The positive psychology movement's founder, Martin Seligman, describes her on its cover as 'the genius of the positive psychology movement'. I think we can supplement the positivity ratio with an empty bombast ratio – that is, the ratio of empty bombast to valid claims on the part of positive psychologists and ALT researchers is about 2.9.

Meta-analyses and Root Constructs

Because of this, I have argued that some of the positive benefits claimed for authentic leadership could be found for any leadership theory, if that was measured instead. Support for this view is now emerging from a number of meta-analyses that have been published. One such review suggests that '(1) the relationship between authentic and transformational leadership is large in magnitude, suggesting construct redundancy $(\rho = .72)$; (2) neither AL nor transformational leadership add noticeable incremental validity beyond the other construct'.[62] Similar points are made in the meta-analysis by Julia Hoch and several of her colleagues. With typical academic under-statement they conclude that 'the combination of a relatively large number of dissertations or theses (44% of the samples), high heterogeneity, and the low number of samples per relationship suggests the authentic leadership results should be interpreted with caution'.[63]

Bruce Avolio, William Gardner and Fred Walumbwa may have anticipated the possibility of such findings when they wrote that 'authentic leadership is ... a root construct that transcends other theories and helps to inform them in terms of what is and is not "genuinely" good leadership'.[64] This is a useful insurance policy against construct redundancy. Any overlap is simply because authentic leadership *incorporates* transformational or ethical leadership. Of course, this begs the question of why it is needed at all.

You might imagine that all these issues are vigorously debated by authentic leadership theorists. This is not the case. One of AL's main advocates, and a co-author with Fred Walumbwa of two papers that have been retracted, is Bruce Avolio. He has said that 'although often requested ... I have never written critiques of other people's work, nor do I ever respond to them, as I have focused on the act of creation as being my most important contribution to advancing leadership theory, research and practice.'[65] This ensures that the critical literature can be conveniently ignored. It is an interesting view of science, and I wonder how we would feel today about such theories as those of evolution and relativity had Darwin, Einstein and their followers decided to focus on 'creation' rather than respond to criticisms of their work.

As *Star Trek*'s Dr McCoy never said of ALT, 'This is science, Jim, but not as we know it.'

CONCLUSION: HOW LEADERSHIP THEORY IS DEVELOPED

By now, I think we can identify how leadership 'theory' is often developed. First, find some positive-sounding adjective that you can place in front of the word 'leadership'. We already have 'transformational', 'servant', 'spiritual', 'complexity' and 'authentic' leadership. This is a crowded marketplace. So, let's say I latch on to 'athletic' and start to imagine a theory of 'athletic leadership'. I speculate that successful athletes are committed, fixed on a vision of themselves winning, incredibly driven and hardworking, and that they demand the very best from themselves and from the teams around them. When they experience a setback they immediately look for lessons, and when they succeed they imagine tiny improvements that will lead to further success. I scan the sporting literature for quotations from athletes that back up these hunches, while taking care to delete any that come from those implicated in numerous doping scandals. Then I look at interviews with CEOs to see how often they reproduce the same attitudes, I interview a few to gather further supporting data, or I invent some quotations from CEOs that I 'can't name for confidentiality reasons'. Things are looking up. Now I'm imagining an Athletic Leadership Questionnaire – the ALQ. It will have items such as:

1. My supervisor/leader/manager is highly focused on positive results.
2. My supervisor/leader/manager is resilient in the face of setbacks.
3. My supervisor/leader/manager is driven and hardworking.

One more step remains. I find an organisation willing to administer the survey. I promise that there will be a benefit in it for them – more athletic leadership, which is correlated with business success. To support my case, I show its leaders quotations from CEOs and athletes that seem to confirm the point. If their organisation is lacking in athletic leadership, I will help them to develop it. In come my results. Because of halo effects, I find – as my hypotheses predicted – that athletic leaders produce followers who are also more athletic, and that they produce better business results as well. If the results are fuzzy I can do a bit of p-hacking. But someone then points out that the mind-sets and skills I have attributed to athletic leaders are already captured by such existing theories as transformational leadership and authentic leadership. No problem. *My* theory is a 'root construct' from which the others spring. It underpins all forms of effective leadership and business success. Besides, I focus on 'creation' and never respond to criticisms anyway.

On the surface, my theory is a success. My bank balance is certainly booming. But all I have really done is compile a long list of halos, and bloated my publication record with useless research. Such is the sorry state that ALT, the most ironically named of leadership theories, has now reached. Of course, it isn't alone in this. John Antonakis and his colleagues studied 110 papers on leadership in top journals over the previous ten years that made explicit or implicit causal claims about 'leadership'. They concluded that researchers 'failed to address at least 66% and up to 90% of design and estimation conditions that make causal claims invalid'.[66] Leadership research in general may be flooded with type 1 errors.

The Nobel prize winning physicist Richard Feynman once wrote: 'The only way to have real success in science, the field I'm familiar with, is to describe the evidence very carefully without regard to the way you feel it should be. If you have a theory, you must try to explain what's good about it and what's bad about it equally.'[67] Without this, we have pseudo-science. Researchers into authentic leadership have fallen into this trap, willingly. For now, they show no desire to escape from it.

8 The Promises, Problems and Paradoxes of Evidence-Based Management

INTRODUCTION

I have already noted how poor much management research is, and how little of it is of interest to anyone, including often the people who write it.[1] Those who advocate 'evidence-based-management' (EBM) address this problem head-on. They argue that researchers should identify those research findings that will help managers to improve decision making. It is time to get rid of folklore, fiction and fantasy and to base management action on hard empirical evidence. In one sense, these issues have been around for many years – see, for example, my discussion of 'rigour' and 'relevance' in Chapter 1. However, advocates of EBM aspire to take these debates to a higher level, and their cause has been helped by the status of those who have championed it. For example, its key moment in capturing widespread attention was undoubtedly an address by the then president of the Academy of Management, Denise Rousseau, to the AOM's 2005 conference. Her talk was published in the *Academy of Management Review* the following year.[2] Many saw it as an attractive proposition, and it is not hard to see why. Clearly, the idea of EBM deserves to be taken seriously. But that does not mean it should be accepted uncritically. There is little point in escaping from one trap only to become ensnared in another. My intention in this chapter is to explore what EBM promises and look at the criticisms of it that have emerged. In my view, both the advocacy of EBM and some of the criticisms levelled at it are overblown. Is there is a third way which can preserve EBM's welcome focus on addressing real world problems without having to adhere so closely to the managerialist agenda that accompanies it at present?

The writing on EBM draws repeatedly on the precedent of 'evidence-based medicine'. We have had an explosive growth of interest in the management version of this approach. Beyond the journal literature, several books from key figures have also been produced, aimed at both management and academic audiences. Their overall intention is to have a transformative impact on management practice. The importance of impact on 'the real world' is heightened, and one supposes that theory development is in principle subordinate to the need to inform management practice. This is certainly the thrust of the definition offered by Eric Barends, Denise Rousseau and Rob Briner, as follows:

> *Evidence-based practice is about making decisions through the conscientious, explicit and judicious use*
> *of the best available evidence from multiple sources by*

1. **Asking:** translating a practical issue or problem into an answerable question
2. **Acquiring:** systematically searching for and retrieving the evidence
3. **Appraising:** critically judging the trustworthiness and relevance of the evidence
4. **Aggregating:** weighing and pulling together the evidence
5. **Applying:** incorporating the evidence into the decision-making process
6. **Assessing:** evaluating the outcome of the decision taken *to increase the likelihood of a favorable outcome* (emphasis in the original).[3]

But nothing is ever that straightforward. Critics of EBM have challenged its alleged privileging of a management voice above that of other organisational actors, and questioned its belief that we have enough good evidence from which supposedly best practices can be identified. From this perspective, the search for EBM is at best misguided, and may even be part of an attempt to strengthen managerial power at the expense of other organisational stakeholders. It has also been accused of attempting to enforce a positivist and functionalist paradigm within management studies.[4] The debate is sometimes framed like this: pluralism in research versus a stifling homogeneity (OR: rigorous research versus a chaotic cacophony of subjective opinions). It is also dichotomised as a choice between a defence of management power versus its attempted problematisation (OR: engaging with the world as it really is rather than as we would like it to be). I find these dichotomies often unhelpful, and seek to move beyond them in this chapter.

THE PROMISES AND THE PROBLEMS WITH EBM

A sense of urgency pervades the pro-EBM literature. This is driven by a recognition that many organisational interventions occur despite a significant body of evidence suggesting that they will have either no positive benefits, or prove harmful. While many practitioners are devoted to what they see as 'best practice', Edward Lawler has noted that 'In some cases, there is simply no evidence that validates what are thought to be best practices, while in other cases there is evidence to suggest that what are thought to be best practices are inferior practices.'[5] Notoriously, downsizing remains a popular management practice despite abundant empirical evidence that it reduces trust, lowers morale and damages both productivity and profitability.[6] It may be the management equivalent of bloodletting to cure and prevent diseases. Many organisations also continue to spend a great deal of time and money on conducting annual appraisal interviews despite the abundant evidence that they generally do more harm than good.[7]

The solution, as Denise Rousseau envisages it, is that scholars should 'provide, maintain, and update online, user-friendly, plain language summaries of the practice principles that the best available evidence supports, while sharing information regarding their effective use as well as their limitations'.[8] Managers often see management research as indifferent and irrelevant to their needs.[9] They can't bear to read it, and don't understand its jargon when they do. It could be that how we write is so different from the norm that it constitutes a new language – say, Desperanto? As envisaged by advocates of EBM, summaries of best practice that are derived from research can ease this problem, by providing managers with an accessible, empirically validated basis for more thoughtful, rational and effective action. Rob Briner and Neil Walsh also suggest that management students should be taught the skills and principles used to conduct systematic reviews so that they can evaluate them more thoroughly.[10]

But here advocates of EBM are compelled to acknowledge a problem: the first of many. As Denise Rousseau, Joshua Manning and David Denyer noted, the sources of evidence on many management issues are 'seldom assembled or interpreted in the systematic fashion needed to permit their confident use'.[11] There is a lack of coherent, systematic and agreed knowledge that can be transmitted to managers, either during their formal education in business schools or afterwards. Looking at the obscure topics and impenetrable jargon that fill the pages of our journals, this is not surprising. The result is that research is misused or misunderstood, and that limited and inconclusive findings are often over-generalised. Rousseau and her colleagues view the reluctance of academics to address these issues, by producing the literature reviews that are deemed necessary, as a quirk of the academy, suggesting that organisational theorists have come to value novelty over convergence. This compels them to engage in ever more abstruse theoretical squabbles, in an effort to differentiate themselves within what has become an increasingly crowded marketplace for ideas. There is obviously a great deal of truth in this (see Chapter 6). The result is a neglect of practice that should be corrected, through a collective effort of will. This radical reorientation is a key goal of the EBM movement.

However, it may be a bridge too far to assume that there is enough agreed-upon knowledge to enable the production of the integrated studies that EBM advocates. For example, Jeffrey Pfeffer has suggested that incentive pay does not motivate improved individual job performance.[12] In contrast, an overview by Sara Rynes, Barry

Gerhart and Laura Parks concluded the opposite, and proposed several mechanisms whereby it is claimed that improved job performance will result.[13] While enthusiasts for EBM seem to believe that accumulating and summarising more and more studies will produce 'convergence', despite the fact that many of them reach contradictory conclusions, the problem may be more deeply rooted than is imagined. There are conflicts between many study designs and theoretical paradigms. As a result, there are numerous important issues where there is no research convergence merely awaiting discovery, and to be then reported in practitioner-friendly summaries. Rather, discord and deeply rooted vested interests have so far resisted reconciliation.

The study of human resource management showcases this problem perfectly. Despite decades of work and the publication of hundreds of studies, 'we are still in no position to assert with any confidence that good HRM has an impact on organisation performance'.[14] This might explain why attempts to offer evidence-based guidelines for management practice are often astonishingly vague. For example, Denise Rousseau applies the rich body of literature on decision making, including the Nobel Prize winning work of Daniel Kahneman, to organisations.[15] She urges managers to draw on multiple criteria for making decisions rather than one, usually finance oriented. Far too many decisions default to this solitary criteria. Her advice is sound enough. But how should we identify these criteria? When is more criteria enough? How much weight should we attach to each? We simply don't know, and it is no good pretending that we do.

Other practice suggestions can be patronisingly simplistic. Take the contents of a new feature on the Academy of Management's website named 'AOM Insights'. This summarises articles published in AOM journals with an emphasis on their implications for practice. One such entry is headed 'A simple, no-cost way to get employees to go the extra mile'. This draws on a paper in the *Academy of Management Journal* to argue that when leaders use humour they have a positive effect on their relationships with 'subordinates', who in turn are more likely to go the extra mile.[16]

Unfortunately, the summary doesn't provide a handy compendium of appropriate jokes, purged of juvenilia, racism, sexism and homophobia. Nor have its authors apparently heard of the sitcom *The Office*, in which the hapless manager David Brent claims to his incredulous employees that he is 'a friend first and a boss second. Probably an entertainer third.'[17]

Moreover, the urge to produce convergent studies ignores the critical question of why some issues are studied and attract funding rather than others, or to offer a clear view of how research priorities should be determined. Managers, for example, might well be interested in studies into how downsizing can be 'improved' so that it enhances rather than damages shareholder value. They are unlikely to be equally fascinated by studies into how resistance to downsizing can be made more effective. Foxes and hounds come together for a hunt but have fundamentally different interests in the outcome. Thus, studies purporting to explore how downsizing can be 'improved' would be more likely to attract industry support, and access to organisations for case studies than would proposed studies of resistance.

Accordingly, the research process which produces the evidence on which EBM bases itself is not value-free and objective. Nor is it necessarily of the highest quality, as I tried to show in the previous chapter, using the example of 'authentic leadership'. As Lois Weiner has noted, researchers sometimes report data selectively, choose informants for interviews that they believe will be particularly sympathetic to a given point of view and become cheerleaders for various interventions rather than dispassionate researchers into their effects. Proponents of EBM have yet to indicate how studies which offer divergent findings, often caused by such factors, can be integrated so that they offer definitive conclusions on heavily contested issues.

Instead, the problem is evaded by rooting the case for EBM within an overtly positivist paradigm, despite occasional claims to a more pluralistic theoretical orientation. Thus, it is claimed that

Evidence is the essence of human knowledge. It deals with the regularities our senses and measuring tools can detect. Scientific evidence is knowledge derived through controlled test and observation ... evidence-based management is the complimentary (sic) use of scientific evidence and local business evidence.[18]

Knowledge is depicted here as objective, value-free and weighted in favour of methods such as experimentation that are overwhelmingly quantitative in nature. Certain forms of knowledge and research methods are favoured over others. I noted, at the outset of this chapter, that the EBM movement draws explicitly on the precedent of evidence-based medicine. But, as Kevin Morrell and Mark Learmonth point out, medical and social knowledge are different.[19] That said, even within healthcare there have been numerous controversies on such issues as the relative weight that should be attached to some forms of evidence over others; the problems that have been found in attempts to change practice in the light of evidence; and how various professional groups respond, or ought to respond, to different forms of evidence.[20] While similar issues arise in the case of EBM, the challenges are mostly sidestepped by its advocates. A narrative is adopted in which the world of management practice is simply 'out there', awaiting impartial discovery. The issue of how to adjudicate between different truth claims is purely technical – we need to do more studies, until the issue in question is resolved. I am not so sure.

In a sophisticated discussion of the problems faced by business schools in addressing real world problems, John Mingers puts his finger on a key problem with the nature of management research: 'Empiricism fails to get to grips with real-world problems because of its scientistic reduction of complex multi-dimensional and multi-causal problems to that which can be measured.'[21] In Chapter 7, I gave examples of this in relation to leadership research. Mingers also points to a fundamental problem with constructionist research, arguing that it 'fails from the opposite direction, accepting complexity and multi-dimensionality within language and discourse but eschewing the causal force of nondiscursive structures'. While positivist approaches exaggerate how much we know, constructionists often exaggerate how little we know, or can know. False claims of certainty and indiscriminate professions of ignorance both weaken the prospect of producing valid, reliable and reader-friendly summaries of evidence that can guide action.

A critical problem, from the standpoint of determining what evidence should be used and of assessing its objectivity, is that precisely what is studied, and how it is studied, itself reflects powerful sectional interests. Managers are not merely waiting for research to facilitate subtle changes in direction. Rather, they are committed to many of their practices, which reflect strongly held views of the world and are perceived as being in their own interests. Denise Rousseau and Sharon McCarthy have themselves anticipated that managers may be resistant to possible research findings – such as any that suggests they should decentralise decision making, and place less emphasis on powerful, charismatic and visionary models of leadership.[22] Evidence suggesting that these might be mistaken is also likely to clash with inbuilt pedagogic models within business schools, and the expectations of themselves that many managers have been trained to adopt.

As Sumantra Ghoshal noted, many unsound, questionable and downright damaging management theories have had a tenacious grip on practice.[23] His argument was focused with particular force on agency theory. In Ghoshal's view, this had produced a preoccupation with self-interest among managers who then engaged in behaviours inimical to their organisations' long term interests. Immediate support came from leading management thinker Jeffrey Pfeffer, who argued that the bad theories in question become self-fulfilling.[24] That is, business schools teach them as though their empirical basis were much sounder than it is, students emerge with an enriched theoretical lexicon but a diminished sense of social responsibility, and poor management practices become institutionalised to such an extent that, although they fail to deliver on their original intentions, they become naturalised and therefore are assumed to be beyond interrogation.[25] Many have become part of the neoliberal zeitgeist and are hard to shift.

This creates a twofold problem for EBM. Firstly, it places limits on the kind of research that is likely to be conducted. Funding increasingly follows lines of inquiry deemed practical, applied and 'relevant' to current rather than hypothetical future business needs. Secondly, the assumption that summaries of research findings will be welcomed by managers, and that insight alone will be sufficient to reorient their practice, may be in error. Management studies is not unique in this respect. We also know a lot about climate change, yet many of us still prefer inaction to the pain of changing our lifestyles.

THE EVIDENCE BASE FOR EBM

A key paradox within the debate is that the evidence base on which EBM rests is itself flimsy. An overview written in 2009 by Trish Reay, Whitney Berta and Melanie Kohn noted that 53.6 per cent of the papers on EBM that they identified argued for or against EBM purely on the basis of the author's opinion, rather than offering any empirical evidence in either direction. Beyond opinion, other weak forms of evidence are often adduced on the issue. For example, a book written by Jeffrey Pfeffer and Bob Sutton has become a core text of the movement, as evidenced in the fact that a special issue of the *Academy of Management Learning and Education* was devoted to it in 2007.[26] Several contributors challenged what they saw as an excessive use of the authors' own consulting experience, an over-reliance on US-based sources for information, the repeated use of various CEOs' first names (thereby over-attributing agency to them, while displaying signs of sycophancy), and the difficulty that both researchers and managers might face in adjudicating between the competing truth claims of rival data sets and theoretical interpretations. Mark Learmonth has also commented on what he described as its 'unremittingly pro-top-management tone – to the exclusion of any "evidence" that might cause us to reflect in a serious and sustained manner on the legitimacy of conventional management goals (profitability, control and so on)'.[27]

Pfeffer and Sutton's book, in particular, is a good example of what Peter Bloom and Carl Rhodes describe as the 'idolisation of the CEO'.[28] It plays down the complexity of the CEO role and sidesteps the paradoxes that are part of its DNA.

Moreover, the dearth of replication in organisation studies means that rogue findings or poorly designed studies often go unchallenged, and can become conventional wisdom.[29] Consider the problems with management research that I discussed in Chapters 4 and 5. The truth is that the evidence cited in support of many management ideas, where it exists at all, is often weak, inconclusive and flawed. All this poses a problem for literature reviews that seek to produce actionable knowledge based on robust evidence. There may not be enough of it to serve this purpose, nor much prospect of it emerging. Bill Starbuck, in an analysis which questions the value of over-reliance on 'statistical significance', points out that social scientists habitually 'overstate the generality of their observations. In particular, researchers often conceal the ambiguity in their observations by focusing on averages and using hypotheses tests about averages to convert ambiguities into apparently clear conclusions.'[30] Triangulation and replication may be unlikely to address this problem, since twenty defective studies repeating each other's mistakes, or making twenty new ones, will still fail to produce useful insights. An over-emphasis on data drawn from one country (the US), rooted in its particular model of the market economy, is particularly vulnerable to these challenges, since it invites the suggestion of an ethnocentric approach to research and a misguided presumption of universality.[31] However powerful the statistical calculations employed in such endeavours, the risk of over-generalisation remains.

Interpreting Evidence and Informing Practice

Evidence has to contend with our pre-existing attitudes and biases, and it is the latter which often wins out. Consider the different reactions of American voters to the actions of Donald Trump, and how these mirror the already existing party loyalties that people have.

Confirmatory biases ensure that we seek out evidence that confirms our views and try to ignore that which doesn't. One study presented subjects with fictionalised reports of studies on capital punishment. It found that both supporters and opponents rated as stronger the studies consistent with their prior beliefs, and pointed to what they saw as numerous problems with the others.[32] Yet advocates of EBM are inclined to assume that academic experts agree or can agree about the evidence supporting certain specific practices, and about which practices are most important for professionals.[33] It is sometimes acknowledged that people reject research findings for many reasons, perhaps particularly when they have passionate feelings on whatever issue is being addressed. But it is then assumed that better research protocols and improved communication will somehow make them more amenable.[34]

One key problem with this argument, among many others, is that there isn't much agreement on what should count as evidence. For example, while Edwin Locke and Gary Latham unambiguously extol the benefits of goal setting,[35] Lisa Ordonez and her colleagues draw on a variety of sources to argue that 'the beneficial effects of goal setting have been overstated and that systematic harm caused by goal setting has been largely ignored'.[36] Locke and Latham, meanwhile, assert that while there may be some harm caused by goal setting, the precise form and extent it takes has not been demonstrated. In the process, these writers have vigorously clashed on the critical issue of what should count as evidence in adjudicating this issue. In a further riposte, Ordonez and her colleagues suggest that 'journalistic accounts, case studies and anecdotes should all be used to raise questions, focus attention, and develop ideas that should be subject to rigorous, causal analyses'.[37] Gary Latham and Edwin Locke, by contrast, maintain with equal vigour that only data drawn from a purely positivistic approach has any role in informing an analysis of the question.[38]

Richard Adams, Palie Smart and Anne Huff identify a further problem.[39] In Chapter 2 I criticised the increased use of journal ranking as a proxy measure of the quality of papers. But it now seems that systematic reviews generally use only journal-level proxies rather than evaluating the quality of individual studies. This bias is likely to miss many high-quality studies but also to include relatively poor studies that might be best ignored. This is one reason why extra information may generate doubts about action rather than clarity on the way forward.[40] The result can be stasis – the opposite of the EBM movement's intentions.

PRIVILEGING MANAGERIAL DEFINITIONS OF REALITY AND EVIDENCE

A further critical issue in the field is that the intended audience for management research envisaged by proponents of EBM is entirely composed of managers. This, of course, raises questions about the overall role and purpose of business schools. Do they exist only to serve the needs of managers? Or should their research aim to appeal to other stakeholders, such as governments, trade unions, employees and our wider society? The EBM literature tends to conflate employee/managerial interests in a manner that is even less credible since the Great Recession of 2008 and the problems to which it has given rise. It is *assumed*, in spite of much evidence to the contrary, that the managerial voice articulates a universal interest, and that what preoccupies managers must also preoccupy other organisational actors, to the same degree and from the same perspective. It follows that it is this management interest that researchers should work to serve. Imagine if medical schools were told that their research should aim to meet the needs of the pharmaceutical industry, political scientists that their work must above all be relevant to those politicians who are in government, physicists that their work should be geared to the needs of the nuclear power industry, and computing/IT departments that their main constituency was henceforth to be Silicon Valley. It is this skewed logic that animates much of the writing on EBM.

Thus, the literature on EBM depicts 'irrational' management action – i.e. that which damages a wider organisational interest – as something that flows from a simple absence of knowledge, rather than self-interest, malign intent or wilful ignorance.[41] Yet it is clear that action which damages a hypothetical collective organisational interest is often undertaken in the full awareness that wider interests are being endangered. For example, Eileen Applebaum and Rosemary Batt document predatory rent seeking behaviours by private equity firms that are more concerned with the short-term enrichment of their funds than adding long-term value, often with destructive results.[42] Studies of Enron's collapse suggest that the organisation's key leaders may have been well aware that their business model was unsustainable, but set this inconvenient truth aside in the interests of their own short-term personal interests.[43]

Nor is it clear that when evidence is accumulated it will point unambiguously in a straightforward direction. A study of the evidence gathered on an initiative to reduce burglary rates found that the policy implications were ignored when they conflicted with the preferred options, and biases, of those making actual decisions. Even the analysis of the data presented in official reports differed markedly from that of those who conducted the research.[44] Interestingly, in view of the tendency in the EBM literature to stress the role of senior managers, an examination of town planning in Denmark showed that the greater the power held by individuals or groups, the less they felt the need to assemble evidence or consider means–end justifications when making decisions.[45] Consistent with this, a study of health prioritisation in New Zealand during the 1990s explored how different government agencies all gathered evidence on the issue, driven by the conviction that policy should be informed by better evidence, but then reached very different policy conclusions.[46] These decision dynamics are not unusual, and are well known. The garbage can model of decision making argues that a great deal of decision making is accidental and reflects an often random association of problems and solutions.[47] It posits that relatively independent processes within organisations converge to an eventual decision, in place of linear progress from the recognition of problems to the identification of viable solutions.

Plentiful evidence also exists to show that organisational leaders often persist with high levels of commitment to obviously failing courses of action.[48]

Reflecting this awareness, Kevin Morrell and Mark Learmonth argued that 'there are often no unambiguous or unanimous solutions to dilemmas in the workplace. There are often irreconcilable tensions between fairness and care on the one hand, and profit or efficiency on the other.'[49] You would never guess as much from reading the EBM literature.

Rather, its privileging of a managerial voice is often explicit and crude. Rob Briner, David Denyer and Denise Rousseau suggest that decision making informed by EBM should also consider 'the perspectives of those people who might be affected by the decision'. But they also affirm that 'the start of the process is the practitioner's or manager's problem, question or issue'.[50] The assumption here is that managers are the 'experts' on the multiple issues that confront most workplaces, and are rightly the ultimate arbiters of what matters. Presumably, the rest of us are expected to gape admiringly at their daring deeds while being kept at a safe distance from decision making. It is equally plausible to suggest that expertise may be more widely distributed than such hierarchical models acknowledge.

It would be naïve, I suggest, to assume that what can be characterised as a 'consulting' model of business engagement will value all research questions equally, producing a pot of knowledge from which managers will select only those options that have a particular logical force. Jeffrey Pfeffer noted, in 2007, that a greater reliance on funding from companies and well-off alumni has led to a decline in research on topics that attempt to measure social impact as well as economic efficiency.[51] Despite this, some have argued that the future of business schools would be more secure if academics were to adopt a greater focus on the practical problems faced by managers.[52] Accepting this logic means that researchers should become more oriented to business sources for funding rather than less. If managers and employees invariably shared identical interests this might not matter. But if this isn't the case, and if the interests of particular stakeholders are privileged above those of others, it will directly affect the kind of questions that get asked, what research gets done, what sort of knowledge is accumulated and hence summarised in practitioner-friendly summaries, and what its eventual impact on practice is likely to be. Integrative literature reviews will therefore draw on data that is inherently biased towards the priorities of powerful interest groups, and on findings which reflect sectional rather than unitarist interests.

A study into smiling behaviours by employees in service settings, written by Patricia Berger and Alicia Grandey, is often cited by writers on EBM. It epitomises the problem I am discussing. Its authors conclude that their research 'provides evidence for the continued interest in encouraging service with a smile on the part of employees on the front lines. Even in brief encounters, maximal smiling by employees made customers respond similarly, and they perceived the employees as providing quality service and felt satisfied with their encounters overall.'[53] From an EBM perspective, a practical conclusion would be that managers should 'encourage' employees to maintain a certain frequency of smiling behaviours towards customers, and utilise performance management systems to that end. If this improves customer satisfaction and sales, who could object? One could imagine using mystery shoppers to conduct 'smile audits', with staff receiving feedback and eventually training in how to smile more often – perhaps at key moments of the sales process. Personal problems such as divorce, family illness or bereavement would be irrelevant: after all, the needs of the organisation, as determined by its managers, come first. Those deemed to have an insufficiently sunny disposition would eventually – with regret – be terminated.

This idea could be taken further. Student satisfaction surveys are increasingly common in universities. Barger and Grandey's research might suggest that academics should maintain a certain level of smiling behaviour before, during and after lectures, and that these behaviours should be carefully monitored (perhaps through CCTV?), linked to appraisal systems and considered during tenure and promotion decisions. Somehow, I don't imagine that either of the authors would be keen on this occurring within their own work environments.

THE SOCIAL CONSTRUCTIONIST CRITIQUE CRITIQUED

From this perspective, the narrative driving EBM is viewed largely as an attempt to impose uniformity on the currently pluralistic field of organisation theory. As Mark Learmonth notes: 'Not only does it limit (what counts as) legitimate research methodologies to those that natural science finds acceptable; more directly politically, the emphasis on what works tends to assume elite definitions of effectiveness. That is, constructions of "what works" are often interest serving.'[54] However, given that businesses now often have more power than nation states, there is an even more pressing need for managers to consider the ethical and moral implications of their decisions. But a heavy emphasis on 'what works' sidesteps this crucial issue, and slips instead into a performative discourse in which the bottom line is all that seems to matter. Imagine that I conduct some research which shows that productivity and profits could be improved if a small random sample of employees were to be publicly flogged each morning. From the standpoint of EBM, I should present my findings to managers and urge that they be put into practice. It would be entirely consistent with the troubling lack of concern for any ethical framework within the literature on EBM. Denise Rousseau has a chapter in the *Oxford Handbook of Evidence-Based Management* that she edited entitled 'Envisioning evidence-based management'.[55] This contains two pages that discuss ethics – the only place in the *Handbook*'s 419 pages where it is considered. The discussion relies heavily on a discussion of an air strike in Afghanistan, which has little obvious connection to EBM.[56]

Social constructionist perspectives also question the positivistic stress of EBM on causality. As even mainstream researchers, such as Gerald Davis, have sometimes acknowledged: 'while there is a lot of sound and fury, it is difficult to point to many areas of settled science when it comes to organization'.[57] Karl Weick stresses how much uncertainty is bound up with organisational scholarship, and queried whether the idea of 'settled science' – which he describes as an oxymoron – was even a meaningful goal.[58] In terms of EBM, these critiques challenge the absence of discussion on power, question the assumption that a managerial interest has a universal applicability, and query the absoluteness of the evidence base on which many EBM claims (for example, on the relationship between goal setting and the work-based performance of individuals) are erected.

The problem, however, is that it is all too easy to avoid the question: 'what is the alternative?' Some of us write about organisational problems in the spirit of ghouls who gather at the scene of a disaster to film it, but never offer any help. It is not an approach that has much to recommend it. A case in point is Stewart Clegg's analysis of how power is manifest in organisations.[59] This describes management as the practice of power and domination, intended to affect the behaviour of others and also of oneself. Power over others is exercised in multiple ways, through coercion, the framing of meaning, the imposition of culture, the use of moral panics, and latterly through the management of social capital and knowledge. But, despite an impressive overview of these issues, Clegg at no point feels compelled to suggest how coercive power can be resisted, or to discuss how power relations can be re-imagined within the modern workplace in order to attenuate at least some of its most baleful effects. I am by no means decrying the value of problematising power in this manner. But I am pointing out that when critique remains the *only* purpose of analysis the phenomenon in question invariably emerges unscathed, and hence remains securely in place.

To draw an analogy with medical practice that is for once appropriate, this may be like a doctor who is content to diagnose a patient's problems but who always refuses to prescribe any treatment. The EBM movement, on the other hand, promises a degree of certainty that is more apparent than real, and which institutionalises the managerial voice into a determining standpoint within the research process. Can we find a way through this tangle of contradictions that can provide a more fruitful perspective on the quest for evidence-based management?

A CRITICAL REALIST ALTERNATIVE

John Mingers has postulated four aspects of what it means to be critical in management studies.[60] Each of these is consistent with a critical realist epistemology, and are central to my argument that we need to advance theoretically from the critique that EBM has so far attracted. They are:

1. *Critical thinking – the critique of rhetoric.* This means evaluating the extent to which conclusions flow from premises, whether premises are justifiable, and whether/how language is being used in emotive and misleading ways. In this context, it means that we might challenge the fundamental premise of most writing on EBM: that the practitioner audience to whom research findings should be addressed is composed entirely of managers. Society as a whole has a vested interest in business issues. When our economy faces problems none of us are immune. It is therefore useful to acknowledge that issues such as organisational effectiveness are of vital interest to stakeholders beyond a managerial elite, and are pressing questions for academic inquiry.

2. *Being sceptical of conventional wisdom – the critique of tradition.* Advocates of EBM tend to view management practice as a taken-for-granted activity beyond interrogation. There is little critique of such management priorities as the need to increase shareholder value. A critical approach would query this, and highlight other priorities, such as social cohesion, fairness and long-term effectiveness.

3. *Being sceptical of one dominant view – the critique of authority.* Again, as discussed above, EBM advocates take management power for granted, and proposes that those priorities advocated by managers should dominate the research agenda of management academics, who would feel even more compelled to develop research programmes deemed 'relevant' by a management audience. This does not mean endless deconstructions of power dynamics for their own sake, but could extend to the exploration of more emancipatory forms of organisation in which some of the more oppressive manifestations of power are removed. In Chapter 10 I discuss the notion of 'critical performativity' and how it can help with this task.

4. *Being sceptical of information and knowledge – the critique of objectivity.*
   This means that we must question the validity of that knowledge which is
   currently available, recognising that it is never value-free and objective.
   Thus, it is important to recognise that much apparently objective knowledge
   is socially constructed and reflects sectional rather than universal interests.

I argue that these points must be integrated into the discourse around
EBM, in order to avert an uncritical adaptation to whatever it is that
a managerial elite deems to be important at any particular point in
time. The objective of inquiry remains to reduce uncertainty – that is,
to increase what is known and reduce what is not known. This also
compels a recognition that the positivistic split between facts and
values is fallacious, since all social theories are evaluative as well as
descriptive. Management straddles the domain between the objective
and the subjective, and while aspiring to achieve greater certainty
about the world must recognise that elements of uncertainty and
subjectivity will always remain. To suggest that improvements in
research techniques will somehow yield 'better' end products and
thus overcome this problem is to miss the point. Rather, there is
space for both knowledge production *and* a contest about values,
ethics, meaning, interpretation, significance and importance.

Knowledge is therefore always provisional. But not all representa-
tions of the world are equally good or valid. Rather, 'some represen-
tations constitute better knowledge of the world than others'.[61]
Despite the fervour of some enthusiasts who have held conferences
to promote their worldview, the world is not flat, and the moon land-
ings did take place.[62] Of course, each account of reality that we
develop is constrained, pinched and tenuous. But with sufficient
respect for the evidence, such accounts can move us ever closer to
a more reliable depiction of the world as it is. This implies that
research can seek to develop a progressive reduction of uncertainty
and the creation of spaces where ethical and other issues can find
a greater purchase in the research process than the traditional positivist approaches favoured by advocates of EBM normally allow.

I suggest that critical realism can have a transformative impact on the discussion of EBM in six key and positive respects.

1. Advocates of EBM have suggested that integrative literature reviews should provide managers with definitive insights into 'what works'. It follows that managers will be able to take particular courses of action with a high degree of confidence that they will have predictable effects. On the other hand, critics have argued that the evidence base behind management 'science' is so affected by the interpretive tropes used by humans to process information that any degree of certainty is impossible. A critical realist epistemology, on the other hand, would suggest that literature reviews should aspire to the more modest goal of *the progressive reduction of uncertainty*. Evidence is emergent and open, rather than definitive and closed. As Roy Bhaskar expressed it: 'reality is a potentially infinite totality, of which we know something but not how much'.[63] But while total certainty about anything is impossible to achieve, in either the physical or social sciences, critical realism denies that all truth claims are equally valid or equally invalid. Some causal explanations approximate more closely to reality than others. Literature reviews should therefore aim to acknowledge both what is known and what is unknown, and identify what is generally agreed by the social scientific community as well as what remains in dispute. For example, such reviews should clearly discuss what light the evidence base sheds on those causal theories that have been debated within the research community, and where we can be more or less sure that they are incorrect.

2. Literature reviews should make critical use of a wide range of evidence types – including qualitative and quantitative research, case studies, journalistic accounts and anecdotes. Such forms of evidence can inform the development of theories that will lead to continuously improved forms of empirical research in due course. Research should therefore avoid privileging particular methods of data collection and analysis above others. Choices of method ought to be appropriate to the object of study. Thus, in opposition to purely positivistic and functionalist theoretical paradigms, the goal of social science is viewed as being to generate *plausible* rather than definitive hypotheses about causal relationships, from which fresh streams of research can be developed. Both quantitative and qualitative

methods have strengths and limitations, including the difficulty of generalising from inherently limited data sets. But if they are properly appraised in integrative literature reviews they may still serve the aim of reducing uncertainty and increasing insight.

3. A critical realist perspective recognises that our perceptions of the social world are constructed by disparate interest groups, and that the interpretations of the world held by these interest groups often reflect competing rather than unitarist material interests. It follows that the discussion of the role of evidence in management practice should not privilege either the interests or the insights of one organisational grouping above others in its attempt to produce actionable knowledge. Too often, in discussions of either EBM or the 'relevance' of management research, it is assumed that what is socially useful and academically rigorous needs to be deemed useful above all by managers. But, as Chris Grey has pointedly asked, 'by what fiat are the users of management research held to be the corporations and the managers?'[64] It follows that integrative literature reviews would seek to reach beyond a management audience. Rather, the evidence should be synthesised and addressed to the wide variety of audiences who have a vested interest in business practices – including employees, customers, trade unions and government. Accordingly, and in a project of greater inclusivity, it may be more fruitful to re-envisage the field as one concerned with 'evidence-based organising' rather than with 'evidence-based management'.

4. Issues of ethics and values should have a central place in management research. These cannot be reduced to 'what works' or to what managers decree as having immediate, practical significance. It means that ethical principles should guide the selection of research topics as well as the practice of empirical research, and be informed by greater concerns than immediate business success. The bald invocation of 'what works' often masks deeper issues of social power, and is rarely designed to liberate the voices of actors perceived as being marginal in various social forums. In terms of EBM, the question 'what works' can therefore be reframed as 'what works for who? Why? For how long? In whose interests?' Integrative literature reviews should explicitly address such questions, thereby openly acknowledging the limitations of any knowledge that is generated.

5. Critical realism recognises ambiguity and indeterminacy, but also embraces the challenge of identifying what actions, policies and solutions

are more or less likely to have a positive impact on organisational practices and wider social well-being. It therefore seeks to move beyond critique and towards a positive engagement with the multiple stresses facing the world we inhabit. I return to this issue, in the context of assessing the contribution of critical management studies, in Chapter 10. This means recognising and seeking to explain the power-saturated organisational contexts in which organisational theory seeks to find traction. But it also acknowledges those aspects of organisational reality other than power and domination which must be addressed.

6. We need to recognise that human action is impelled by many factors, in addition to and sometimes in place of rational reflection. It follows that merely making evidence available may not be sufficient to change the behaviour of managers or other organisational actors. While rational action should remain a key goal, it should also be recognised that social action flows from socially constructed perceptions of reality that are in part created by the working out of conflicts between vested interests located within organisational structures. As with the notion of progressively reducing uncertainty, this suggests that we embrace the goal of progressively reducing irrationality and increasing the space for rational thought and action, without imagining that this process can ever be completed.

CONCLUSION

It is easy to see why has EBM appealed to many. There is growing disquiet at the disconnect between our research and the outside world, where most of it has little influence. I can't fault the suggestion that we need better research which speaks to real problems, and that uses evidence to guide decision making. But I can fault the very narrow definition of evidence that is offered by advocates of EBM. While I am not a fan of theorising for its own sake, it is also striking how little EBM has contributed to theory development in management studies. As Kevin Morrell, Mark Learmonth and Loizos Heracleous point out, the literature has focused on a simplistic narrative that equates management and medicine, ignores the enormous differences between these two fields and underestimates the problems of gathering evidence within medicine. As a result, 'advocates are repeating something that is becoming less interesting'.[65] This is certainly my impression. EBM may already have gone from a fad to obsolescence without ever touching the consciousness of most managers.

I am also critical of the idea that management research is really only of interest to practising managers. We should aim to serve a much broader constituency than that. At the same time, it is unsatisfactory to engage solely in the deconstructionist and textual games that many postmodernists seem to find so fascinating. This turns research into a parlour game for those few initiated into the charms of academic life but of little interest to anyone else. We can do better. Given the problems that we face, the need to do so is urgent. In Chapter 9, I flag at least some issues where management research can make a much more powerful contribution to public debate than it does at present.

9 Reclaiming Meaningful Research in Management Studies

As I have argued frequently in this book, management research tends to neglect really important issues. It turns us into experts on trivial issues who explore unimportant relationships between insignificant variables. Researchers focus on either the blindingly obvious or the deservedly obscure. In Chapter 7, I discussed the extent of this problem in leadership studies. 'Gaps' that no one has ever noticed and no one cares about are 'filled'. Much of this research, as I argued in Chapter 6, is written in impenetrable jargon and overloaded with references to the work of philosophers, preferably obscure ones, all to disguise the insignificance of what is going on. The authors of such work seem to revel in their inability to express themselves in the English language. Clarity, simplicity and meaning are mortal foes, to be put to the sword in every sentence.

Yet if we are to rediscover some purpose beyond progressing our careers we need to address issues that matter, particularly where our disciplinary insights can add value. We should even aim to be much less pompous in our writing. Here, I take only one example of the kinds of issues that need much more attention in our research – the influence of technological change on work, organisations and management.

TECHNOLOGY AND THE FUTURE OF WORK

Whether to be afraid of mechanisation or to welcome it as 'progress' is, of course, an age-old issue. Most famously, English textile weavers in the nineteenth century destroyed weaving machinery that they felt was taking away their jobs. They were known as the Luddites. This name is still used to mock anyone resisting such modern conveniences as online dating, self-checkout facilities at the supermarket, and online banking. Yet the Luddites were not the first. Back in 1589 William Lee invented a stocking frame knitting machine and visited Queen Elizabeth I to seek patent protection. His hope was that it would dispense with wearisome, expensive and labour-intensive hand knitting – and, of course, make him rich. Elizabeth refused his request, asking him to 'Consider what the invention could do to my poor subjects.'[1]

Opposing such pessimism, we have the optimistic refrain that technological innovation will open up endless opportunities to eliminate drudgery, increase our leisure time and enable more of us to make greater use of our creative talents. Matt Ridley is among a group of writers that includes the Harvard psychologist Stephen Pinker and the Oxford economist Max Roser, and who are sometimes known as 'the new optimists'. They note that more people are better fed, live healthier lives for longer, and are at less risk of being murdered or killed in wars than any time in human history. Much of the credit for this can be attributed to technology, innovation and what the libertarian economist Deirdre McCloskey describes as 'trade tested betterment'.[2] The phrase conjures up images of ships sailing into Venice's Grand Canal, stuffed with silks, spices and other delights from the East, to be unloaded and haggled over at Rialto Bridge. She writes:

> Since 1800 the ability of humans to feed and clothe and educate themselves, even as the number of humans increased by an astonishing factor of seven, has risen, per human, by an even more astonishing factor of ten. We humans now produce and consume *seventy* – 7 × 10 – times more goods and services worldwide than in 1800 ... In the best run countries, such as France or Japan or Finland ... real income per person, conventionally measured, has by now increased to roughly $100 a day. Income has risen ... by a *factor* of thirty (italics in the original).

McCloskey terms this 'the great enrichment'. Ridley, in his 2015 book *The Evolution of Everything*, hails the technological progress we have made since the Industrial Revolution in tones of quasi-religious fervour.[3] Like McCloskey, he argues that its continued progress will lead to virtually limitless prosperity in the near future. Maybe. But maybe not. The problem with all such analysis is its reluctance to acknowledge the possibility of problems likely to arise between now and the advent of Utopia. The Great Recession of 2008 reflected the difference between the 'efficient markets' hypothesis, which assumes that prices tend to reflect all available information and are therefore rational and change only in response to more information, and the distortions imposed by human greed, over-confidence, speculation and asset inflation.[4] The over-financialising of our economy, in which more and more people seek to make money out of money rather than through trading in goods and real services, is also a far cry from the world of thrifty and daring bourgeois traders so celebrated by McCloskey.

This led to the Great Recession. We still suffer from its effects. The International Labor Organization (ILO) Global Wage Report for 2017 shows that real wage growth globally started to recover from the Great Recession in 2010.[5] But it fell by 1.7 per cent in 2015 to its lowest level in four years. It is not only incomes that have been affected. The ILO noted in its 2015 World Employment and Social Outlook report that three-quarters of the world's workforce were on temporary or short-term contracts.[6] Are these blips in the grand narrative of historical progress, or will the upward trajectory chronicled by McCloskey resume once more? Or was that upward trajectory itself a blip, now giving way to a new normal that resembles the distant rather than the more recent past?

THE PROBLEMS OF MECHANISATION

We could do worse than turn to George Orwell, who was fond of testing ideas to destruction. In 1937, he published *The Road to Wigan Pier*, republished in 2001 by Penguin as a Modern Classic.[7] It is famous for its first part, in which Orwell brilliantly explores the poverty-stricken lives of people in the working-class towns of

Northern England. In the book's second part he advocates socialism as a solution, but also explores that ideology's contradictions and the limitations of the movement that had grown up around it. In particular, he discusses how the idea of socialism had become bound up with Utopian notions of indefinite technological progress. Writers such as H.G. Wells, and others whose reputations have faded into oblivion, were prolific advocates of such a linkage. Orwell was not convinced. The relevance of his thoughts on this is not confined to socialist ideologies, but could equally well be applied to the challenges being wrought by technological progress today.

Orwell pointed out that technological innovation makes life softer and easier. Machines mechanise more and more human activities, and do them better than we can. Orwell argued that the need for physical strength and courage is steadily diminished. Aeroplanes were still a relative novelty in 1937. But, in the future, 'The aeroplane, like the motor-car, will be made foolproof; a million engineers are working, almost unconsciously, in that direction. Finally ... you will get an aeroplane whose pilot needs no more skill or courage than a baby needs in its perambulator.' There were, he asserted, few human activities that could not be affected by such processes. What, then, is left for human beings? Work, after all, is not just about earning money. What is work to one person might well be play to someone else.

One of the best, and funniest, fictional illustrations of this can be found in Mark Twain's classic novel Tom Sawyer, published in 1876.[8] Tom is set the task of painting a fence. But when the time comes to do the job 'all gladness left him and a deep melancholy settled down upon his spirit ... Life to him seemed hollow, and existence but a burden.' Eventually, a friend called Ben Rogers comes along and draws Tom into conversation. But Tom pretends to be so absorbed in his work that he doesn't hear him. Eventually he relents and gradually begins to convince Ben that he *likes* the job he is doing. As he says: 'Well, I don't see why I oughtn't to like it. Does a boy get a chance to whitewash a fence every day?' In no time at all Ben begins agitating to help with the painting. The more Tom refuses the keener Ben becomes. Eventually

Tom permits him to paint some of the fence in return for an apple. More boys wander along and are eventually allowed to paint the fence in return for such delights as a kite and a dead rat on a string. As Twain wrote:

> Tom said to himself that it was not such a hollow world, after all. He had discovered a great law of human action, without knowing it – namely, that in order to make a man or a boy covet a thing, it is only necessary to make the thing difficult to attain. If he had been a great and wise philosopher ... he would now have comprehended that Work consists of whatever a body is *obliged* to do, and that Play consists of whatever a body is not obliged to do.

The first part of Orwell's book is also an excellent study of community feeling and solidarity in Northern mining towns. These people were miners. But this meant much more to them than simply earning a living. The physical effort and dangers of the job built a sense of camaraderie and kinship that was crucial to the identity of whole communities. What would people do if this was all taken from them? Even changes in work organisation can threaten traditional ties that bind. In 1951, Eric Trist and Ken Bamforth explored the introduction of 'longwall' mining techniques in the British mining industry after its nationalisation in 1945. It replaced a 'hand-got' system which relied on small-group organisation at the coalface. With the former system:

> Stable relationships tended to result, which frequently endured over many years. In circumstances where a man was injured or killed, it was not uncommon for his mate to care for his family. These work relationships were often reinforced by kinship ties, the contract system and the small group autonomy allowing a close but spontaneous connection to be maintained between family and occupation.[9]

The new system enabled the more efficient use of technology and improved productivity. Yet as Trist and Bamforth could not help noting:

Anyone who has listened to the talk of older miners who have experienced in their own work-lives the change-over to the longwall cannot fail to be impressed by the confused mourning for the past that still goes on in them together with a dismay over the present coloured by despair and indignation ... Those with rehabilitation experience will recognise it as similar to the quality of feeling expressed by rehabilitees when ventilating the aftermath in themselves of an impairment accepted as irreversible.

As an aside, I discussed in Chapter 6 our current predilection for over-theorising and the tendency to stuff our papers with scores of references. Trist and Bamforth's work, by contrast, is a model of elegant writing. It offers no mega-theoretical framework for the issues it explores and has only four references. Yes, four – this is not a misprint. Such a paper would today be desk rejected by every academic management journal.

Returning to the main issue, work is never just work. It brings a meaning to our existence that goes far beyond the immediate tasks that we perform. When it changes and technology moves to the fore, we often mourn for the past and fall into despair. Orwell concluded that 'the logical end of mechanical progress is to reduce the human being to something resembling a brain in a bottle'.[10] He was not of course suggesting that this end would be achieved or was imminent. But he was proposing it as a direction of travel into which humanity seemed to be inescapably locked, and which posed fundamental questions about what it means to be human.

These issues struck with special force after the 1984–1985 miners' strike in Britain. This took place when 20,000 miners were made redundant and twenty collieries were slated for closure. The yearlong strike that followed was the most bitter and savage industrial dispute in British history. Those communities affected entered a spiral of decline from which many have not yet recovered. Of course, this was only partly as a result of mechanisation. It also owed much to the government's determination to destroy the powerful National Union of Mineworkers. The then prime minister, Margaret Thatcher, famously referred to the miners' leader, Arthur Scargill, as 'the enemy within'. But the basic question remains of how to find meaning and identity in a world in which traditional work suddenly disappears.

Today we can see that we have made even more progress towards the dystopian goal Orwell identified. We rely on labour-saving gadgets such as washing machines and vacuum cleaners to save time and energy. So, we instal rowing machines and treadmills to burn up the energy that we have just saved. We could defy these trends by washing all our clothes by hand, after we have dumped our washing machines and vacuum cleaners in the local recycling centre. I have yet to meet anyone who has done so. If we reject the treadmill solution we can choose instead to grow fat on our sofas while surfing channels. With the aid of remotes, we don't even have to get on our feet and walk a few yards to our TVs. The energy expenditure is effectively zero. It is not surprising that a world-wide obesity epidemic is perfectly in sync with our technological progress. A study published in *The Lancet* in 2014 suggested that nearly one-third of the world's population is now overweight or obese.[11]

Such processes have profound influences on the world of work. Billy Wilder's 1960 movie *The Apartment* is a classic. Jack Lemmon stars as CC ('Bud') Baxter, a lowly employee in a national insurance corporation who is keen to climb the corporate ladder. In pursuit of this cause, he allows his senior managers to use his apartment for their extra-marital liaisons, himself often wandering the streets alone while they do so. When Baxter is pictured at work he is one of countless drones hunched over their desks as he manually enters numbers into an old-fashioned computer. Baxter's face is wreathed in boredom and his head nods in sync to the clattering noise the machine makes as it crunches his data. It is safe to assume that such jobs have long been mechanised. The CC Baxters of today would be doing something else, while it is unlikely that senior executives still require the services he offers them in this movie. Moreover, who would want to bring such dreary work back once again? As with insurance workers, so it has always been with repetitive and non-creative job tasks. We no longer have people manufacturing hansom cabs, lamplighters who light gas lights in our city streets one by one, small children working as bowling alley pinsetters whose job is to set up the pins after each bowler knocks them down, telephone operators who connect international calls, or ice cutters dangerously carving blocks of ice from ponds in the winter to enable food to be preserved in the summer. Nor do we have bus conductors to sell and inspect tickets, while driverless trains and even driverless buses may be soon be upon us.

The Internet, meanwhile, has been a hugely disruptive technology. It personifies what the economist Joseph Schumpeter, as far back as 1942, called the 'creative destruction' of capitalism.[12] Since we increasingly download whatever we want to watch on TV, DVD shops have become an historical curiosity. Teenagers today may not even know what they were. For that matter, there is less and less need to visit a cinema if we wish to see the latest movies. We surf and shop from home, thereby decimating the high street. Many of us visit bookstores only to note what is available, and then buy books more cheaply online. This is known as 'showrooming'. A 2012 study found 35 per cent of US consumers reporting that they did this regularly, and not just for books.[13] It doesn't stop us complaining that our favourite shops have closed and that our town centres are boring and lifeless. Estate agents and travel agents may be next in line, since the Internet puts all middle-person jobs in jeopardy. At each step, we lose yet more opportunities for human interaction. Is there theoretically a point short of 'the brain in a bottle' scenario, where human vocal chords will deteriorate from lack of use and assume the same superfluous status as our appendix?*

We may be on the verge of a transformation of the world of work, organisation and management that surpasses anything seen in the

---

* For those who have read too many of the humourless articles that fill our journals, I should probably explain that this is a joke.

past. Klaus Schwab has described what is in prospect as 'the fourth industrial revolution'.[14] What does it mean for the world of work and organisations? Back in 1933, John Maynard Keynes voiced the fear that that a future of greater unemployment would be inevitable, since 'our discovery of means of economising the use of labour (is) outrunning the pace at which we can find new uses for labour'.[15] So far, this fear has been groundless. But what of the future? In 2013 Carl Frey and Michael Osborne conducted a detailed analysis of 702 occupations, ranging across such industries as healthcare, transportation, management and education. They concluded that 47 per cent of total US employment was at risk.[16] A Spanish food-processing firm, El Dulze, now uses robots to pick heads of lettuce from a conveyor belt and reject those that don't fit with company standards. Another low-skilled job is being lost. It has been suggested that low-wage jobs have five times the potential to be mechanised as their higher-paid counterparts.[17]

Look at the Amazon Go store, opened in Seattle in January 2018. As they enter, customers scan an Amazon Go smartphone app and are monitored by cameras and sensor equipment while they put items in their basket or back on the shelf. They are then billed automatically on their credit cards when they leave. There are no checkouts, and therefore no exit queues or cashiers. Unless you enjoy twiddling your thumbs in long lines, what's not to like – apart, maybe, from being under surveillance, possibly losing your job, and certainly minimising the chance of some social interaction when shopping? But depersonalised customer experiences are now routine. Writing in *McKinsey Quarterly* in 2017, W. Brian Arthur recorded the following:

> A year ago in Oslo Airport I checked in to an SAS flight. One airline kiosk issued a boarding pass, another punched out a luggage tag, then a computer screen showed me how to attach it and another where I should set the luggage on a conveyor. I encountered no single human being. The incident wasn't important but it left me

feeling oddly that I was out of human care, that something in our world had shifted.[18]

Nor are cashiers and other low-paid positions the only ones that are at risk. Frey and Osborne calculate a 99 per cent probability that tele-marketers and insurance underwriters will be passé by 2033, that the same fate will befall sports referees and that there is a 91 per cent chance of tour guides becoming redundant. A report written by Richard Berriman and John Hawksworth on behalf of PricewaterhouseCoopers in 2017 estimated that 'up to 30% of UK jobs could potentially be at risk of automation by the early 2030s'.[19] It went on to point out that the risks were even higher in some sectors than others – 56 per cent in transportation and storage, 46 per cent in manufacturing and 44 per cent in wholesale and retail. Previous technological revolutions always saw jobs replace those that were lost. But history offers no promissory notes for the future.

Richard Susskind and Daniel Susskind explore the significance of all these developments for the professions, including health, education, the law and architecture.[20] In each, there is the real prospect of people being displaced by machines. A breast clinic in New York has found that using algorithms reduced false positives for breast cancer by 39 per cent. In essence, it has proven much more reliable than humans. An AI system known as Watson is being used to support cancer diag-nosis and to help physicians develop treatment plans. Another system, the Knowledge Interpretation Toolkit, scans new literature and helps to develop hypotheses for further research. What is the future for doctors? We can at least speculate that we may need far fewer of them, and that their role will fundamentally change. As Susskind and Susskind observe: 'We are not convinced that the concept of a "job" will of itself be coherent in decades to come. Certainly, in an era of radical and ongoing change, the notion of a "single job for life" will be regarded as quaint, if not misconceived.'

Nor have we begun to grapple with the implications of block-chain technologies in finance. It is, in many ways, a financial extension of the Internet. Blockchain uses what are known as 'distributed ledgers' to store information and record transactions that occur, including all our income and payments. The technology may be in its infancy but more than $1 billion of venture capital found its way into developing its commercial applications in 2014 and 2015.[21] Spending on it is now doubling annually. Regulators, governments and banks are anxiously studying its implications. Some enthusiasts that I have spoken to argue that it will make all our transactions so transparent that tax evasion and tax avoidance will become well-nigh impossible. Governments will be able to raise more money and spend less of it on backroom services and staff. Diminishing costs of trade will also increase prosperity. Both developments, they suggest, might enable a new global attack on poverty. They may also threaten the very existence of the banking and finance sectors on which so many of us depend for our jobs. To the chagrin of traditionalists, banks have already closed many high-street branches as more and more of us bank online.* They may have seen nothing yet.

Of course, this process may only be partial, with aspects of jobs automated and husks remaining. Matthew Lawrence and his colleagues suggest that 'an estimated 60 per cent of occupations have at least 30 per cent of activities which could be automated with already-proven technologies'. [22] An OECD report published in 2018 follows a similar trajectory.[23] It looked carefully at 32 of the 35 countries within the OECD. One key finding was that only about 14 per cent of jobs were 'highly automatable' – that is, there was a 70 per cent or more probability of automatisation. Moreover, there was wide variation between countries. Generally speaking, the more educated and skilled areas of the world, such as Europe, were less likely to see this. What seems more likely than the outright disappearance of work is that its nature will change, with many tasks now performed by

---

*   On 1 December 2017, the Royal Bank of Scotland announced that it was closing 62 of its branches in Scotland. This was more than one in three of its total in the country, and cost 158 people their jobs (www.bbc.co.uk/news/uk-scotland-scotland-business-4217 9432). Such news items that have become so typical that they now barely produce any reaction – apart from those who lose their jobs.

humans undertaken by machines. Consider the possibility of driver-less freight lorries. At this point, no one has figured out how they could be loaded and unloaded entirely without human involvement. The OECD report is also careful to point out that automation will create many new jobs, as it has always done. But the key questions will be: what will these new jobs, and the work that remains in old jobs, consist of and how will it feel to employees? Peter Fleming is among those argue that that we will see a proliferation of poorly paid jobs, where the skill set required is so low that it is cheaper to employ people rather than replace them with machines.[24] It is scarcely an inspiring thought.

Even if jobs are not lost completely, there is already growing evidence that a significant proportion of the workforce is now under-employed. Roland Paulsen cites a number of studies that suggest the average employee engages in what he terms 'empty labour' for between 1.5 and 3 hours per day.[25] That is, they surf the Internet, watch porno-graphy, and pretend to work while actually soldiering and gossiping with friends. As opposed to 'burnout' this can result in what Phillipe Rothlin and Peter Werder describe as 'boreout', where people feel under-stretched, unmotivated and, above all, bored.[26] If technology further reduces the demands on our cognitive abilities maybe this will be the fate of us all – until we are made completely redundant.

Is this far-fetched? In his book *Domo Deus: A Brief History of Tomorrow*, Yuval Noah Harari explores how technology and data are increasingly colonising our lives.[27] He notes that '99% of human qualities and abilities are simply redundant for the performance of most modern jobs'. Uber, he points out, manages millions of drivers with only a small number of managers. There are few obvious limits. A musicology professor has invented a computer program that com-poses symphonies, concertos and operas. Recordings of some of these have been released, and sold well. Concertgoers presented with a performance of Bach's music and one composed by a computer program that imitated his style were unable to distinguish between them. Perhaps novels, screenplays, painting, plays and poetry will be next. Given the recycled nature of many Hollywood movies (explosion; shooting; car chase; sex scene; another explosion: plot twist – The End) I would not be surprised to learn that computer algorithms already generated many of them.

Traditionally, we have valued the intuitive abilities that humans alone seem to possess, and which have played such a critical role in organisational decision making. Lately, the sheen has worn off this advantage, as the full range of misconceptions and biases that lead us to irrational thoughts has become ever more apparent.[28] Machines are better than us at processing data, error prevention and system coordination. Would a machine that lacks emotions, prejudices and intuition, but which is able to analyse all available data, have decided on Brexit? Would such a machine in charge of the Royal Bank of Scotland have been so driven by hubris that it embarked on the most expensive and ultimately disastrous bank acquisition in history, that of ABN Amro? Would it don a combover wig plus orange makeup, and promise to build a wall between Mexico and the United States?

LETHAL AUTONOMOUS WEAPONS

But the lack of emotion and intuition in decision making can also be fatal. Drone technologies still require human operatives to guide them. An intense ethical debate now rages about lethal autonomous weapons (LAWs). In an eerie echo of *The Terminator* movies, they select installations or people without human guidance. Some of those involved in developing the artificial intelligence on which these weapons rely, including Tesla's Elon Musk and Alphabet's Mustafa Suleyman, have argued that such technologies represent a third revolution in warfare. They are, they suggest, the sequel to gunpowder and nuclear weapons and should be banned.[29] We now have what are known as automated 'hardkill' active protection systems. These include radar-guided guns on ships that identify and attack oncoming missiles, rockets, artillery fire, aircraft and surface vessels. Autonomous drones seem imminent. Many missile defence systems have autonomous targeting capabilities. They still operate within limits and guidelines set by humans. But for how much longer? In the future, will wars be ordered by machines, fought by machines and won and lost by machines? Will they take account of civilians, or treat all human beings as disposable but biodegradable units of collateral damage? Yet history suggests that attempts to ban weapons of mass destruction will fail so long as one side imagines that it can use them to its own advantage. Nor can they be un-invented. In this view (*realpolitik*), treaties are signed until it is convenient to break them. As Steven Pinker put it: 'If a nation decides not to learn war anymore, but its neighbor continues to do so, its pruning hooks will be no match for the neighbor's spears, and it may find itself at the wrong end of an invading army.'[30] We may already be on a road that forbids U-turns.

The new optimists scoff at any suggestion that the future might get worse when in the last two centuries it has become steadily better. They neglect to consider that the cognitive capacity of humans has not kept pace with the technological innovations we have instigated. Isaac Asimov remarked in 1988 that 'The saddest aspect of life right now is that science gathers knowledge faster than society gathers wisdom.'[31] Nothing much has changed. Why is this? Rush Dozier describes hate as 'the nuclear weapon of the mind.'[32] He traces its prevalence to our evolutionary past, when a fight-or-flight response in the face of a perceived threat gave us a positive survival advantage but also made us suspicious of others and inclined to exaggerate our differences with them. While we have also acquired other positive instincts, we remain in essence hairless apes who have replaced bows and arrows with nuclear, chemical, biological and lethal autonomous weapons. Steven Pinker, new optimist par excellence, convincingly shows in his 2011 book *The Better Angels of Our Nature* that violence, including fatalities from wars, has steady declined.[33] True. Wars a thousand years ago were bloody, brutal and barbaric, as they are today. But they didn't threaten the survival of our species. This has changed. One crazy decision by a leader driven to madness – say, a Hitler, a Kim Jong-un or a Trump – can have globally catastrophic consequences.

Pinker's latest book, *Enlightenment Now: the Case for Reason, Science, Humanism and Progress,* considers such possibilities, before concluding that they are implausible.[34] Drawing directly on the words of Kevin Kelly, founding editor of *Wired* magazine, he emphasises that 'The more powerful technologies become, the more socially embedded they become.' Pinker adds: 'Cutting-edge technology requires a network of co-operators who are connected to still wider social networks, many of them committed to keeping people safe from technology and from each other.'[35] This is true – up to a point. But the more autonomy we grant weapons systems, inch by inch, the less true it is. A social network may only be as strong as its weakest link. Think of the pivotal and mostly forgotten role of Stanislav Petrov, who died in 2017. He worked at a Russian nuclear early warning centre. On 26 September 1983 he received computer readouts indicating that US missiles had been launched. Protocol indicated that he should immediately alert his superiors. Instead, he reported a computer mal-function, and spent an anxious twenty-three minutes waiting to see if he and the Soviet Union would be incinerated.[36] Perhaps his superiors would have read the report of a nuclear attack as Petrov did, and reacted accordingly. Perhaps.

Context is everything. If income growth, secure employment and meaningful jobs are in jeopardy the stable social conditions and networks that are required for rational decision making by leaders and by the Stanislov Pavlovs of this world might also be under threat. Steven Pinker may be crediting both individuals and social systems with far more wisdom and greater powers of restraint than they pos-sess. Time will tell.

IMPLICATIONS FOR MANAGEMENT

I suggested earlier that, in many cases, automation may be only par-tial, and it is worthwhile returning to this theme here. Volvo sold over 50,000 of its XC90 range between 2002 and 2018 in the UK. No driver or passenger in an XC90 was killed within that timeframe. This can only be a cause for celebration. One reason is that the XC90 helped pioneer the use of camera and radar systems which alert drivers to hazards ahead. But the system goes further. It stops the car automatically if its algorithms judge that the driver is getting too close to another vehicle. No wonder the XC90 is often viewed as perhaps the safest car on the road.[37] But consider again the route of travel we are on. The skill required to drive cars has gone down another notch, and the driver's role in making critical decisions is further diminished. And if this improves safety, who could possibly object?

Now take one step beyond this. We may soon reach the position where driverless cars are safer than those driven by humans. If governments decide that people should be banned from driving themselves, in the interests of public safety, another human function will disappear. Resistance might be viewed as akin to those who opposed making the wearing of seatbelts compulsory, in the name of individual freedom. Isolated 'individuals' (how appropriate that word feels) may sit in their cars and engage in deep thoughts about the meaning of the universe. Or they may travel silently and alone from Destination A to Destination B, watching last night's soap opera on their iPhone or iPad while ingesting pharmaceutical substances to blunt their overwhelming sense of boredom and pointlessness.

There are glimmers of discussion of what this means for management and organisations, but so far only glimmers. Xavier Ferràs-Hernández poses some intriguing questions in an article entitled 'The future of management in a world of electronic brains.[38] He reports that researchers in artificial intelligence predict that what they call 'the singularity' will be reached by around 2040 – that is, artificial intelligence will equal human intelligence. Some theorists predict that this will be the prelude to the development of artificial super intelligence (ASI). Debates are rampant as to whether this will mean the destruction of humanity or, alternatively, enable the abolition of disease, poverty and even death as we know it.[39] Forget Orwell's scenario of 'a brain in a bottle'. The possibility of downloading the contents of our minds onto a computer means that we may face the prospect of 'a brain on a microchip'. I should say that in my own view much of this is little more than fanciful speculation, and that while *aspects* of human intelligence (e.g. data input, storage, retrieval and analysis) can be mapped onto computational models of the mind, consciousness is an altogether more complex business.[40] In terms of timescales, Robin Hanson concludes that, if we project future possibilities from past rates of progress, we will have to wait between two and four centuries to develop 'a broadly capable human level AI'.[41] But even if the projections of singularity enthusiasts are too optimistic/pessimistic (choose which applies, depending on your preference), and whether the time required is shorter or longer, it is in that direction that we are unmistakably travelling.

Think of the consequences for management. Even if they fall short of a multifaceted human intelligence and consciousness, machines will be increasingly able to anticipate market trends, evaluate strategic choices, and outline appropriate responses. Moreover, much of the work within organisations will be done by machines. Robot-operated factories are already commonplace. Data processing is done online. Computer programs make complex statistical calculations rather than people. There will be fewer human beings to be influenced, persuaded and motivated by managers, fewer annual appraisals to conduct, fewer salary negotiations to be scheduled and fewer strikes to be resolved when these break down. Will management therefore become obsolete too? And if that were to be the case, there may be no need for business school professors to teach classes and write books complaining about the poor quality of management research.

THE DEMISE OF CORPORATIONS?

The nature of organisations is also changing around us. Gerald Davis pointed out in 2016 that the number of public corporations in the United States had dropped by half since 1997. He attributes much of this to the growth of information technology, which is producing what he calls a 'regime change' in the costs of organising. Specifically:

> Information and communication technologies have made it much
> cheaper to organise commercial activity on a small and provisional
> basis rather than investing in long-term institutions such as
> corporations ... Moreover, computer controlled production
> technology is getting more powerful, cheaper and smaller. As such
> the economies of scale that made corporations so dominant in the
> 20th century are flipping into diseconomies of scale.[42]

3D printing, or additive manufacturing, uses computers to create
layers of materials that form objects. It is in its infancy, but could
conceivably make manufacturing even cheaper, smaller in scale, and
less labour dependent. Alysia Garmulewicz and a number of her colleagues view it as a 'disruptive' technology, an overused term that for
once might just be right.[43] This also means that different forms of
organisation are more viable, such as cooperatives, mutuals and what
Davis calls 'commons-based peer production', where people around
the world co-operate with varying degrees of formality to produce
goods and services. Wikipedia is an example. It is produced without
legal contracts between it and contributors and without departments
to bill users who consume its content. Looking up Wikipedia on
Wikipedia (for free), I find that as of mid-2017 it had only 280 paid
employees. In such environments, what use are management theories
that originated in corporations, and which assume the immutability
of hierarchy, functional specialisation, divisional organisation and the
pyramid model of decision making? They may serve no more purpose
in the twenty-first century than does the medieval practice of using
leeches for bloodletting, to flush out the bad humours of black bile,
yellow bile, blood and phlegm.

This means that we may also have to rethink what it means to
be human in a world dominated by machines. If they are as good as us
at most things and better than us at many, by what right do we claim
dominion over the world around us and the species that inhabit it?
Xavier Ferràs-Hernández wonders, for example, whether in the future
a machine could be the legal owner of a company. I would say: if not,

why not, especially if all or most of the company's 'employees' are themselves machines? The ethical issues are obviously enormous. What constraints need to be placed on machine-guided decision making, particularly when the decisions could have far reaching implications on humans, such as rendering them superfluous, redundant, unemployable, impoverished and maybe even vaporised? We have barely begun to consider any of these issues. The editors of *Academy of Management Perspectives* reported on a search they had made of many major journals using such key terms as 'artificial intelligence', 'robot(ics)' and 'automation'. The journals included *Journal of Management Studies, Organization Science* and *Journal of Applied Psychology*. Their search mostly drew a blank, while *Academy of Management Journal* and *Strategic Management Journal* had 'published a grand total of six papers, since inception, remotely connected to these concepts'.[44] Note the word 'remotely'. What a disgrace this really is. If our field's coverage of the banking crisis is any guide it is unlikely that this will change any time soon.

Yuval Noah Harari also poses what is surely an obvious problem: 'In the twenty first century we might witness the creation of a massive new unworking class: people devoid of any economic, political or even artistic value, who contribute nothing to the prosperity, power and glory of society. This "useless class" will not merely be unemployed – it will be unemployable.'[45] He is not alone in this view. A review of the impact of technology on the UK labour market by Matthew Lawrence and his colleagues argued that 'In the absence of policy interventions, the most likely outcome of automation is an increase in inequalities of wealth, income and power.'[46] If this were to happen, then it seems to me that there is an obvious lesson from history. Where and when have the dispossessed been content to meekly accept their lot, and why should they? We are more likely to see resentment, resistance and revolution. There is already a dangerous disconnect between the political 'elites' and many voters. In the United States, concern at job losses and a craving for simple solutions helped get Donald Trump into the White House. In the UK, it helped drive the electorate towards Brexit. If deindustrialisation, deskilling, insecurity and inequality continue to rise then even more extreme measures may begin to seem appealing.

I am not suggesting that management scholars should now engage in futurology, a pastime rife with charlatanism and littered with failed predictions, both gloomy and positive. Nor am I myself pessimistic about the future. But I am arguing that we can identify major trends and challenges now that will have a profound impact on the nature of work, organisations and management in the near future. We cannot predict how they will play out. However, we can explore their implications, the better to clarify the choices we face as a species. Progress is not inevitable. It depends on the decisions that we make individually and collectively. The bleak possibilities considered by Harari assume that society remains constituted more or less as it is, with wealth, power and decision making concentrated in the hands of a privileged elite whose guiding purpose is the promotion of share-holder value. Our field has witnessed animated debates about such views of corporations, and spilled much ink in discussing alternatives. These debates acquire renewed force in the context of the changing world of work. The inescapable questions that are posed include: for whose benefit are these changes being introduced? Who will reap the gains and who will endure the pains? What action can be taken by governments and an active and increasingly enraged citizenry to ensure that material advances are used for the benefit of the many rather than just a few? What are the implications for how companies are organised, and even for their very existence?

Rutger Bregman is among a growing number of voices who suggest that at least part of the solution lies in providing everyone with a universal basic income. Finland and Canada have already embarked on experiments with the idea.[47] Other countries are follow-ing suit, or considering doing so.[48] Blogging on the website of the Institute for Public Policy Research, Matthew Lawrence has argued that we need new models of ownership to ensure that the benefits of the boost in production that will undoubtedly occur through automation are shared more widely. How would this work? Consistent with Bregman's ideas, he suggests the creation of a citizens' wealth fund that would have a portfolio of assets and which would 'act to spread wealth by paying out a universal citizen's dividend to all or particular groups of the population, and by investing in the provision of universal basic services'.[49] Luc Soete, who made major contributions during the 1990s when similar concerns were expressed about the job-destroying possibilities of 'the information society', has flagged similar solutions.[50] Steven Pinker also endorses the idea of some kind of universal income, and points out that 'it could turn the slow-motion disaster of robots replacing workers into a horn of plenty. Many of the jobs that robots will take over are jobs that people don't particularly enjoy, and the dividend in productivity, safety and leisure could be a boon to humanity *as long as it is widely shared*' (my emphasis).[51] The phrase in italics here is a rather important caveat.

Who knows where such ideas may lead? But of one thing we can be certain. Any industrial revolution that benefits a tiny few and impoverishes the rest will produce social explosions on a scale that may surpass anything we have seen before in history. At this stage, we are better at identifying questions than we are at providing the answers. Doing so requires responses from scholars across many disciplines. These must include those of us who study management and organisations. I have argued that our scholarship has been disgracefully slow to deal with major events in our recent past, such as the banking crisis. It is all the more negligent in its failure to consider the challenges we face today, never mind tomorrow. We have become complicit in the manufacturing of our own irrelevance.

There are numerous other issues that would benefit from insights derived from our field. Terrorism is, among other things, an organisational phenomenon. So is totalitarianism. What can our discipline say about how terrorism and totalitarianism are organised and managed? What does management studies have to add? At present, the answer is nothing. On climate change, poverty, and hunger we are a ghostly apparition hovering on the fringes of debates conducted by others. In the end, if we have nothing to say on the biggest challenges that confront our world perhaps there is a case to be made that we should go out of business. We need a commitment to meaningful research that addresses problems which are far more important than building our careers.

Or, as the Terminator might say, 'Hasta la vista, baby'.

10 Putting Zest and Purpose Back into Academic Life

Throughout this book, I have documented growing problems with the quality of academic life, how academics do their jobs, and a habit of over-theorisation within management studies that is handcuffed to the fetish of prioritising where something is published rather than what is written. Some suggestions have been made about how we should address these problems. But we need more than formal measures by powerful agencies. I think we also need a shift in our own mind-sets. A certain fatalism has gripped academics about our working lives and publishing practices. We are, it is said, evaluated, harassed, exhausted and even bullied as never before. Universities and regulatory bodies are more concerned with monitoring where we publish than whether we have something meaningful to say. Careers thrive if we 'play the game' and languish if we don't. (By the way, how high is your h-index today, and what is your total number of citations on Google Scholar?) There is, we often say, nothing that we can do about it. As I have noted before in this book, it is even increasingly common to hear people speak of 'the publishing game'.

I recall attending a presentation at a conference in which an early-career-stage academic introduced some fascinating data, and pondered what to do with it. A senior scholar who was present put his hand up and immediately identified four 'stories that you could tell' around the data, each of them radically different from the other. Note the problem. There was no commitment to finding the best and most accurate interpretation of the data. Rather, the objective was to fashion a compelling 'story' that would end up in a 'leading journal'. Publishing has become an end in itself rather than a means to an end – the dissemination of good ideas. If it only has the mercenary purpose of furthering our own careers why not surrender to the zeitgeist and play the game as well as we can? Why not bend the rules, and cheat 'just a little bit', if the game has little intrinsic meaning and it brings a prized trophy that bit closer to home? Each time we talk about 'the publishing game' we legitimise this mind-set and undermine the idea of dispassionate inquiry that is so central to a worthwhile academic life. Surely we should aim to make our research matter more than a 'game', by making a real difference to the world in which we live.

To do otherwise also corrupts whatever impulse brought us into academia in the first place. People might become investment bankers to become rich, but no one becomes an academic with that primary purpose in mind. We become academics because we are interested in the life of the mind, we love writing, and we want to develop new and innovative ideas. If we lose sight of this there seems little point in choosing an academic career when there are plentiful more lucrative alternatives. Rather than academics playing the game, the game can drive us in directions we never dreamed of travelling and monopolise our thoughts to the exclusion of all else.

Eliza Byington and Will Felps characterise some of these dynamics as 'an iterated public-goods social dilemma, where the actions that benefit individual scholars are bad for the field as a whole'.[1] Specifically, when we submit papers we can contribute to the collective good by engaging in ethical and credible research prac-tices. Alternatively, we can 'defect' to the dark side by using QRPs and even fraud to enhance our prospects of publication. As they point out, the more of us who defect the more damaging it is to the whole field. Ultimately, defectors may be among those who are adversely affected. Who wants to work in an area that invites public ridicule and con-tempt? Yet 'if we accept that scholars are just as likely to be self-interested and opportunistic as other humans, then noncredible research will be common as long as it is rewarded. To expect otherwise is to reward A while hoping for B.'

On one level, this requires changes to our systems of incentives. Perhaps academics need to be rewarded for the quality of their ideas rather than the quantity and place of publication. Perhaps, also, we need less emphasis on journal, business school and university league tables. We may also need to put less importance on getting research grants. As Scott Lilienfeld points out, these have become a major requirement to advance careers.[2] In truth, much of the research that we do doesn't need grant income. The need to compete for it says more about the corporatised environment in which we work than it does about how to do good research. But, to get grants, 'a strong track record of positive results can be a virtual necessity'. All of this creates perverse incentives and distorts academic life.

Beyond the macro level, we as individuals have choices to make. Noam Chomsky famously addressed the question of the 'responsibility of intellectuals' in 1967, in the context of the USA's war in Vietnam. He railed against the reluctance of many intellectuals to speak out against it and the willingness of others to endorse it. As Chomsky put it: 'It is the responsibility of intellectuals to speak the truth and to expose lies.'[3] But to speak the truth and expose lies also implies that we deal with important issues. By these criteria, our field – mired in trivia and obscurantism – has yet to reach first base.

Getting there means that each of us must decide how much emphasis we want to put on building our careers, and what having a career means. Mats Alvesson, Yiannis Gabriel and Roland Paulsen argue the point like this: 'Our first priority must be a reorientation of social research away from the omnipresent requirement to continuously publish in "high-quality" journals, to the overriding goal and ultimate purpose of creating original knowledge that matters to society.'[4] This is a noble goal. It expresses what brought most of us into academic life in the first place. We did not aspire to the status of hamster on a treadmill, doomed to spend eternity moving in small circles. Nor did we aspire to bore people by writing what is very often little more than tedious rubbish. Yet compliance has been more common than resistance, as academics have conformed in the desperate hope of carving out some limited space where they can still feel free.[5] In the main, this has merely enabled the managerialist agenda to advance in ever more intrusive directions. Others have internalised the view that publication in top journals and working in top universities is fundamental to their identity and self-esteem, a bulwark against the crushing sense of failure that is now omnipresent in academic life.

Yet there must be a life and a sense of purpose beyond that of working in a highly ranked university. I argued in Chapter 2 that such ambitions dominate some people's lives, to the exclusion of virtually all else. If there is anything worse than having these desires thwarted, it can only be achieving them. Many of those who work in 'top' universities have acquired the thousand-yard stare often found among war veterans, as they lurch from one publishing and grant-getting offensive to the next. They have internalised the masochistic expectations of managers and peers and administer sadistic punishments for perceived failure to each other – a classic example of 'concertive control'.[6] I wonder how many younger academics at such institutions arrive in a blaze of glory after publishing a few papers in 'world-leading journals', only to find with horror that they are now expected to maintain barking-mad work norms for decades to come. The human costs are off balance sheet, and are incalculable in any event.

The eminent sociologist Gary Marx has reflected with candour and humour on his own intensely successful early career at Harvard, followed by disappointment and then further forms of success. As he argues, there is a price to be paid when we cease to love the *process* of academic creation and become fixated only on particular sorts of *outcomes*. Marx also points to the law of diminishing returns. Early trophies feel marvellous but later ones can seem like Groundhog Day. He pointedly urges academics 'not to make your career your life'.[7] For when the music stops, the applause fades and speaking invitations dry up it is easy to see one's whole-life achievements as little more than an empire built out of sand.

I also greatly admire Ann Cunliffe's words on the pressures and perils of career building. Reflecting on the difficulties she encountered as a non-mainstream researcher in getting published and achieving tenure in the US, she writes as follows:

I would be damned if I would conform. I believed in my philosophical orientation, that research is about the meanings people give to their lived experience, and I wanted to do what *I* thought was interesting. I did not want to be bored for the rest of my career. So I *would* find way of getting my work published in quality journals and I *would* make a contribution to knowledge but in my own way if I could only figure out what that way would be.[8]

Of course, there is always another route. Steve Kerr was once an academic, and acquired early fame for publishing an article entitled 'On the folly of rewarding A, while hoping for B'.[9] He then became a senior executive at General Electric and Goldman Sachs. Interviewed in 2018 for a piece in the *Journal of Management Inquiry* celebrating his 'folly' paper he commented on his GE career as follows:

When I was at GE, we used to tell people GE's the kind of place you could have a bad marriage and never know you're having it because you won't get to be home long enough to find out. Nine out of 10 people say: 'Get away from me I am not interested in this type of lifestyle.' The 10th person says, 'That sounds good to me.' Now, you can't populate a society like that, but we didn't need a society at GE. We needed a relatively small number of people at GE who would respond positively to the notion that if you do well, you will get wealthy. Alternatively, if you do poorly, you'll likely be fired, possibly in a humiliating manner. If you don't like this type of arrangement, don't come.[10]

Leaving aside the promise of great wealth, how is this appalling prospectus any different from the norms of some prominent universities and business schools? Is it acceptable, or worthwhile? There is, in my view, more to life than publishing in 'top' journals. Nor can we create a more humane world by building inhumane universities. I have nothing against publishing in well-regarded journals, and have done so myself. But it has become such a compelling addiction for many academics that they define themselves completely by how many papers they have published, and where. If some were offered the chance to publish in a top journal on condition that they murder their entire family they would probably respond: 'What's the catch?' It is time to rediscover passionate scholarship, to dare to care, and to remember what brought us into this profession in the first place. As C. Wright Mills put it: 'Scholarship is a choice of how to live as well as a choice of career.'[11] Or, I would add, it is meaningless.

MOVING ON FROM EXHAUSTED TOPICS

On which point, there can be few pursuits more meaningless than continuing to mine a seam of knowledge that has been exhausted. In Chapter 6 I noted the observation from Mats Alvesson and Yiannis Gabriel that some scholars seem to rewrite the same paper over and over again, on change, leadership, diversity or whatever label they have chosen to identify themselves with.[12] There often seems a reluctance to say that enough is enough, and admit that a particular area of inquiry has been researched to such an extent that there may be no truly important insights remaining to be unearthed.

We might be close to that point with theorising around how communication constitutes organisations, an approach sometimes referred to as 'CCO'. This has been fruitful, and has influenced much of my own work. I am not alone. Entering 'communication constitutes organizations' into Google Scholar I find 916,000 hits, nearly 18,000 of them since 2017. But it is some time now since I found anything truly fresh and inspiring in work that adopts a CCO framework. Scholarship in this area is becoming repetitious, and more obtuse than it is illuminating.

For example, Karen Ashcraft and Timothy Kuhn published a chapter in a book entitled *The Agency of Organizing: Perspectives and Case Studies* in 2018. From a broadly CCO standpoint, the chapter studies the implications of a law passed in North Carolina that required people to use the bathroom which matched the sex identified on their birth certificate. This is an important issue, and not just for those directly affected. It tells us much about the times that we now live in, and opens up another front in which the reactionary scapegoating of individuals and groups should be resisted. But, opening the chapter almost at random, I read the following:

> Against the usual view of agency, the question is not *which participants* prove to 'have' or 'exert' more or less capacity for influence (e.g., human actors wielding money or religion), but rather how *relational configurations among* participants authorize them as certain kinds of players in the first place, yielding impasse by enacting a familiar divide of nature from culture and clustering bathroom practice around the binary poles. To clarify, it is a hybrid matrix of social and material 'stuff' (note that meaning is also 'stuff', as it too materializes in practice) that acts, but only as a bundle of mutually adapting practices, *not* as some sort of programmed machine or wizard behind the curtain. If neither robot nor wizard, it may be tempting to regard this matrix as just the supporting infrastructure necessary to authorize any apparent agent (which it is), but the matrix *is* (also) action, not an inert backdrop already in place ... Agency is not somehow pre-authorized, a latent structural capacity 'one' then elects to exercise. Agency is not the property if any 'one' at all; it radiates from the *simultaneous* practice of relations that make it possible.[13]

I would translate this as follows: 'How much power I have and my ability to influence others depends on the attitudes and behaviours they and I display, and how willing people are to let me. I can't just use whatever bathroom that I think best matches my gender. Nor can anyone else.' What does '*relational configurations among* participants', with or without italics, really mean, other than how we talk to each other? The text is replete with redundant quotation marks around certain words, presumably intended to convey that although the authors are using them they wish to put an ironic distance between themselves and their own vocabulary. They use insertions within brackets after the italicised expression 'stuff', to explain what they mean by it, thereby revealing that the chosen noun doesn't really convey anything at all. After 'To clarify', things get even more tortuous, as, in their struggle to avoid admitting that they are stating the obvious, the writers tie themselves in ever tighter linguistic knots.

Back in 1971, Murray Davis argued that interesting theories are 'those which *deny* certain assumptions of their audience, while non-interesting theories are those which *affirm* certain assumptions of their audience'.[14] From this perspective, work within the CCO tradition is becoming progressively less interesting the more it simply reiterates what are now well-worn axioms within its own self-referential framework.

When I encounter such writing I begin to suspect that we are witnessing an approach that doesn't have much left to say, but is determined to make a lot of noise saying it anyway. This may be especially the case for individuals and groups that have become so tightly identified with a particular theory, method or viewpoint that it has become emotionally and intellectually impossible for them to do anything else. In this case, the CCO approach is strongly associated with scholars at Montreal University who are often known as the Montreal School. It even has its own entry in Wikipedia, which traces its development back to the work of James Taylor and the launch of a new doctoral programme in 1987. I wonder how healthy it is to become branded in this way, and then feel compelled to work only on issues associated with the brand. It can imprison rather than liberate our thinking.

Yet theorising is enhanced when it is opened up, when people shift topics, read widely outside narrow sub-disciplinary domains, respond to important events happening around them – and are willing to move on, unless and until they find a way of adding something genuinely new to previous work. A flexible approach is healthy. Bill Starbuck published a paper in *JMS* in 2010 entitled 'What makes a paper influential and frequently cited'.[15] It is a reflection on his earlier paper 'Learning by knowledge-intensive firms', which I discussed in Chapter 6. Starbuck writes as follows:

Innovative papers are much more likely to originate reactively than proactively. A researcher who focuses on and adheres to a long-range plan may make important contributions, but these contributions are not going to respond to newly arising issues in the researcher's environment. By contrast, a researcher who has a flexible research agenda can pick up new topics spontaneously.

It is also more likely that the researcher will find something interesting to say. Starbuck acknowledged that this approach creates 'the risk of flitting capriciously from one trivial and ephemeral topic to another'. True. But it is a risk well worth taking, if it helps us to avoid the even worse problem of pedalling in ever smaller cycles of pointless repetition. It might even be more fun.

RETHINKING THE PROCESS OF JOURNAL PUBLICATION

Improving our research also requires us to re-evaluate our publishing norms. Many journal editors and reviewers seem to assume that the more often papers are revised and the more that are rejected the higher our standards become. I don't think this is true. Look where it has led us. Jay Barney has written scathingly of what he calls the 'norm of completeness' in strategic management research. This 'suggests that a single paper can develop a new theory, derive testable hypotheses from this theory, develop appropriate data and methods to test these hypotheses, report results, and discuss the theoretical implications of these results – all within thirty-two manuscript pages'. Similar expectations have grown up in other areas of management research. As Barney concludes: 'This is insane.'[16] It means that the easiest response from any reviewer is to point out what is missing in a paper. Researchers struggle to accommodate multiple demands to include more issues while being berated by editors for writing too much. Increasingly, they resemble over-stretched contortionists who are worried about how they can possibly assume the positions demanded of them.

I have also already noted that our journals are painfully slow to address really important topics in the outside world, if they do at all. The financial crash of 2008 is a prime example. Part of this is due to the process we put papers through, leaving aside how long it takes to write them. Art Bedeian refers to an *AMJ* forum which

> seems to take pride in the fact that the paper elected as the journal's Best Article for 2004 required a full 24 months between initial submission and final acceptance. A third of this time was required for various reviews and 16 months were need to satisfy three referee requests for revision. Allowing, perhaps, for a 12-month lag before publication, one has to wonder about the timeliness of our discipline's research, let alone its prospects for reporting dramatic scientific breakthroughs that will change the world.[17]

This is simply ridiculous.

Rejection rates of 90 per cent plus are also common. We are surrounded by carnage. An overstatement? Not to those whose livelihood depends on publication in top-tier journals. Literature reviews are too long (or too short); the methods section provides too much detail about data collection and coding (or not enough); critical sources (probably written by the reviewer) have been 'overlooked'; the theoretical contribution isn't distinctive enough (or contradicts conventional wisdom too sharply). Regardless, we are generally encouraged to believe that reviewer comments are fair and that we should respond positively. In the journal *Industrial Marketing Management*, Peter LaPlaca and his colleagues write as follows:

> Some comments may sound harsh at times, but authors always should try to understand where the comments come from. It could be, for example, that the manuscript was not written very clearly and that reviewers therefore had a hard time understanding what the authors tried to say. Thus, adopting the proper mindset is really key for revising a manuscript successfully.[18]

Amen to that. But what to do when the reviewer or editor comments are manifestly absurd, as they often are? An example: one of my colleagues submitted a paper to 'a leading journal'. The editor desk rejected it, and then listed a dozen sources that the paper had failed to cite – *all of them the editor's own work*. The process of submitting one's work to many journals forces us to traverse a formidable obstacle course. We are required to dodge the bullet of desk rejection, overcome the hurdle of reviewer comments, and crawl through a long process of multiple revisions – all the while profusely thanking the editor and reviewers for 'their invaluable feedback'. Papers have become bloated by lengthy, pointless and boring literature reviews as authors try to anticipate every possible demand from every conceivable reviewer; reviewers are asked to suggest improvements, whatever the quality of the paper in front of them, so they do; and editors rarely call time when a paper is simply good enough to publish.

The papers that emerge from this – bloodied, misshapen, over-long, and engorged with references – have not always been improved by it. We need to regain some sense of proportionate effort. Maybe it is time to heed Matthew Spiegal's advice and, as authors, editors and reviewers, just *do less*.[19] There are many steps that could be taken in this direction. I agree with the suggestion that two rounds of revision on a paper should be enough before a firm decision to publish or not can be made. As Mats Alvesson and his colleagues point out, 'This would forestall "the escalation of commitment" dynamic which locks reviewers and authors into a process usually ending up in tepid or overlong articles or bitter and costly rejections.'[20] It might even help everyone to actually enjoy the process, to at least some extent.

In contrast, I recall having dinner with a number of academic colleagues that included a senior editor of one of our best-known journals. I described some research I was doing – on research malpractice, actually – and we had an animated and useful discussion of its possible implications. The editor then said meaningfully: 'But if you send it to us, we would push you really hard to develop a contribution to theory.' He didn't say why. Notice also that he had not yet read the paper. But he had already made up his mind that it was destined for multiple rounds of revisions. Quite why the imperative of a theoretical contribution has conquered the world I don't know: I can't offer a 'theoretical contribution' that explains it. But I do know that it has seriously damaged our field (see Chapter 6), and it is high time that we grew out of it. I have no objection to papers that develop theory. They are important. But it is preposterous to insist that *every* paper must do so, or for that matter that they should all follow the same template – introduction, methods, findings, discussion, implications, limitations and yawn. We need more innovative and varied forms of writing. We also need papers that contain fascinating data but which may lack, as yet, a solid theoretical framework. They might stimulate others to think of one. We need at least some papers that have stronger implications for practice than they do for theory. It might even be a good idea to write more books.

FOR CRITIQUE WITH PURPOSE – THE PROBLEMS OF CRITICAL MANAGEMENT STUDIES

Lastly, I want to comment on the importance of critique *with a purpose*. In particular, critical management studies (CMS) has, since the late 1980s, captured a lot of attention for its criticisms of positivist and functionalist research. It has challenged the tendency by mainstream scholars to see the goals and actions of senior managers as an unproblematic given that expresses an explicit unitarist interest: *We are all in this together*. For example, improving shareholder value may be attractive to some (i.e. those who own shares), but may be much less attractive to those who don't, and who do the work on which shareholder value depends – employees. Thus, 'resistance to change', an old warhorse on many organisational behaviour courses, is not always an irrational aberration that must be overcome. It is often a quite sensible response to sordid working conditions, capricious management, low pay, insecure employment and many other brutal manifestations of the so-called 'gig economy'.

Millions are affected by this. To be precise, it is estimated that 2.8 million people in the UK held gig enconomy jobs in 2017. Of these, 56 per cent were aged between 18 and 34. In days gone past these were prime years for beginning a family and building a home. Yet one in four of such workers earned less than £7.50 an hour.[21] For many, what were once commonplace aspirations have become unattainable fantasies, not far removed from that of winning the lottery. Resistance is growing, and a relatively new and small trade union, the Independent Workers Union of Great Britain, is attracting attention for its work among the low-paid, including those who work for courier firms and as university cleaners. One imagines that researchers in management and organisation studies, particularly those within the tradition of CMS, should have much to say about all these issues.

Rather than doing any such thing, much of CMS has retreated into the comforts of faux theorising that I have repeatedly criticised in this book. I have inflicted enough examples to strain the patience of even the most tolerant of readers, and don't intend to add more. But what is mostly absent is any compelling account of the world in which we live, and *some serious suggestions of what we can do about it.* We have criticism without any purpose other than publication, often expressed in prose that lacerates the reader, and which is over-freighted with references to a canon of sources whose work is treated as Holy Writ. The inspiration behind such writing is often in inverse proportion to the perspiration required to read it. Andre Spicer, Mats Alvesson and Dan Karreman, all well-known critical scholars, have written that '(CMS) is in crisis, less so in terms of employment and careers for its proponents, than in terms of moral and social relevance.'[22] In a similar vein, Anthony Hopwood observed:

> less and less effort is being put into really probing fieldwork. More superficial understandings at a distance seem to be getting ever more common. At the same time there is a growth in seemingly endless minor theorizing. I say minor because so much of the theorizing seems to be a repetition of existing theoretical work,

summarizing time and time again what is already known and usually doing more to add to the publication listings of the authors than to advance wider understandings of the managerial craft and its organizational and societal contexts.[23]

There is considerable irony in that what began as something critical of the mainstream has become, for many, little more than an astute career move to boost their prestige and their salaries. The Academy of Management now has a CMS sub-division with over 700 members. CMS has become part of the mainstream, and shares at least some of its vices – introspection, verbal effluvia and an over-fondness for theory in place of discussing practical implications. It is perhaps not entirely coincidental that CMS has failed to impact on the wider public consciousness. Its publications do a great job – of inciting apathy. Nor has it offered any serious *practical* challenge to the ortho-doxies of power and neoliberalism. Rather, CMS sometimes resem-bles a firefighter who spots an inferno but decides to write a report on it rather than help to extinguish the flames. I argue that this is partly because many scholars in this tradition have retreated into forms of meta-theoretical discourse that increasingly distance them from the world outside the CMS conference circuit. Meanwhile, those with most power remain unfazed by the pinpricks they are dealt by critical scholarly journals.

By contrast, look at James Bloodworth's book *Hired: Six Months Undercover in Low Wage Britain*.[24] Bloodworth reports on stints working in an Amazon warehouse, as a homecare worker, labouring on a building site, as a 'renewals consultant' for the Admiral Insurance group and as a taxi driver working for Uber. Academics would call this ethnography. But Bloodworth is a journalist and not an academic, so he simply says that he is writing a book about the changing nature of Britain. Living in squalid, temporary accommodation he meets a cross-section of impoverished, sick and desperate people rendered perpetually insecure by the growing casualisation of work in our economy. Solidarity is not always their dominant instinct. Many of them express hostile attitudes towards immigrants and each other. These are not saints, but nor are they only sinners. They share many of my aspirations and yours – for enough money to live on, a house they can call home, and some certainty that their jobs will be there the day after tomorrow. Bloodworth mercilessly exposes the reality of life in the gig economy, and if he doesn't offer an action plan to fix it he at least stimulates readers into thinking for themselves about what must and should be done.

Why aren't more CMS scholars producing work of this interest and significance? Of course, Bloodworth was able to take six months to research his book, and any academic today would struggle to do the same. Nevertheless, I sense that even if it were possible few of us would be interested. Playing metatheoretical games with Big Words and Big Names has become more alluring than trying to make a difference. Anyway, it is often cold outside.

The problem is that intense theorising and problematisation alone don't answer the question: what are we to do? Reflecting on this, Paul Thompson suggested that 'CMS is predisposed to problematize everything and resolve nothing.'[25] Critique as an end in itself seems to me an extraordinarily pointless agenda that produces only radical posturing, and endless citations of Foucault, Bourdieu, Lacan, Butler ('Judith the Obscure'*) and, on a brave day, Karl Marx.

It is encouraging to note that dissatisfaction with this is growing within the camp of CMS itself. In particular, it has been suggested that CMS should embrace an agenda of *critical performativity*. Early CMS scholars criticised what they described as 'performativity', defined as a preoccupation with improving organisational outcomes without regard to either the value of their ends, or the ethics of the means chosen to accomplish them.[26] Unfortunately, this led some to repudiate any attempt to improve the world of work, and to treat every attempt at liberation or progress as a new form of oppression that must be 'problematized'. In contrast, Andre Spicer and his colleagues suggest that:

---

* I cheerfully admit to pilfering this pun from an online review of one of Butler's books on Amazon.

'critical performativity' means 'engaging with theories of management to create social change through productive engagement with specific theories of management'. Critical performativity also moves beyond the cynicism that pervades CMS. It does so by recognising that critique must involve an affirmative movement along-side the negative movement that seems to predominate in CMS today.[27]

In short: they advocate criticism with the aim of promoting change, and suggest that critics declare what they are for as well as what they are against. This means 'attempting to create a sense of what could be',[28] rather than the barren feeling that one sometimes gets from CMS work that it is 'against everything'.

To be sure, this isn't free of problems, and has attracted criticism. It has been argued that the idea of critical performativity exaggerates the ability of individual scholars to significantly change management discourse and practice,[29] and that academics may end up compromising their values by engaging with practitioners.[30] It is not my purpose here to review this back-and-forth, other than to note that making some effort to influence the world beyond the seminar room is better than making none at all, and that maintaining scholarly values is as much of a problem these days when we remain within the corporatised academy as it is when we venture outside it. The great strength of ideas on critical performativity is that they open the possibility of dealing with issues that really matter, while using language that people can understand, instead of over-relying on the often curious formulations of such people as Jacques Lacan and other assorted luminaries. This doesn't mean forfeiting a critical edge. It simply gives that edge a sharper sense of purpose. And about time too.

CONCLUSION

Management research is in a parlous state. But its condition is not yet terminal. Nevertheless, we have to face the fact that the world does not owe us a living. Great institutions have come into being and passed away throughout human history. By contrast, how puny is the standing of business schools and what a limited mark they have made on society. They are a relatively recent confection and are vulnerable to changing tastes. Expensive buildings help to create the illusion of permanence. But institutions are, first and foremost, human constructions. They only endure if enough people give them legitimacy, provide them with resources, and believe that they add value. Martin Parker, the *enfant terrible* of critical management studies, has responded to these issues by arguing that business schools should be abolished, and replaced instead by 'schools of organising' that would take a much broader view of the purposes of management education and research. Business schools, he suggests, are irremediably tainted by their curriculum's (relatively) uncritical treatment of capitalism, power, shareholder value and pretty much everything else. Their research reflects 'the wider dominance of neoliberal accounts of people and markets'.[31] They have become citadels of shame. It is time to bring in the wrecking balls.

I am not (yet) ready to go that far. However, I do argue that, at this stage, our research is more of a weakness than a strength. Once the paying public tumbles to this, the game will be up. Our fate will be determined by many forces, including our own willingness to take action. It is my hope that this book provokes discussion about what forms that action should take and how we should view the work that we do. We need to reclaim more traditional academic values.

The Academic Vocation?

Max Weber delivered a speech in 1918 at Munich University entitled 'Science as a vocation'. In it he reflected as follows:

> Ideas occur to us when they please, not when it pleases us. The best ideas do indeed occur to one's mind ... when smoking a cigar on the sofa; or ... when taking a walk on a slowly ascending street; or in a similar way. In any case, ideas come when we do not expect them, and not when we are brooding and searching at our desks. Yet ideas

certainly would not come to mind had we not brooded at our desks and searched for answers with passionate devotion.[32]

Weber's words speak to two sides of academic creation – hard work, and the space and time to think, often aimlessly. Modern academic life increasingly stresses the disciplinary side of this complex process. It sets targets, monitors how we spend our time, and measures and audits our outputs. This technocratic approach shrinks the space where our imaginations might otherwise be free to roam and play at will. It replaces autonomy with a leash, and intrinsic motivation with the extrinsic drive to succeed in performative games where means have become ends, thereby corrupting both. In doing so, it threatens the spirit of 'passionate devotion' that Weber rightly saw as essential to all true academic endeavour.

Throughout this book I have argued that universities, governments and societies must do much more to rebuild an environment in which the disinterested pursuit of truth and knowledge is once more enshrined as the core purpose of academic life. In addition, academics are neither helpless nor free of the obligation to act. We need to see publishing in top journals as a means to an end rather than an end in itself. We need to ask bigger and more critical questions about the world of organisations than we do at the moment. We need to do work that matters.

In doing so, perhaps we need to realise that we have nothing to lose but our h-indexes.

Notes

INTRODUCTION

1. Mingers, J. (2015) Helping business schools engage with real problems: the contribution of critical realism and systems thinking, *European Journal of Operational Research*, 242, 316–331. The quotation is on p. 316.
2. Brooks, C., Fenton, E., Schopohl, L., and Walker, J. (2018) Why does research in finance have so little impact? *Critical Perspectives on Accounting*, DOI: doi.org/10.1016/j.cpa.2018.04.005.
3. Starbuck, W. (2003) Shouldn't organization theory emerge from adolescence? *Organization*, 10, 439–452. This quotation is on p. 442, and the one that follows is on p. 449.
4. Harley, B. (in press) Confronting the crisis of confidence in management studies: why senior scholars need to stop setting a bad example, *Academy of Management Learning and Education*.
5. Shymko, Y., and Roulet, T. (2017) When does Medici hurt da Vinci? Mitigating the signalling effect of extraneous stakeholder relationships in the field of cultural production, *Academy of Management Journal*, 60, 1307–1338. The following quotation is on p. 1307.
6. Carney, D., Cuddy, A., and Yap, A. (2010) Power posing: brief nonverbal displays affect neuroendocrine levels and risk tolerance, *Psychological Science*, 21, 1363–1368.
7. All these quotations are from the paper's abstract on p. 1363.
8. See www.ted.com/talks/amy_cuddy_your_body_language_shapes_who_you_are, accessed 12 September 2017.
9. See www.nytimes.com/2014/09/21/fashion/amy-cuddy-takes-a-stand-TED-talk.html, accessed 12 September 2017.
10. Cuddy, A. (2015) *Presence: Bringing Your Boldest Self to Your Biggest Challenges*, New York: Little Brown.
11. Ranehill, E., Dreber, A., Johannesson, M., Leiberg, S., Sul, S., and Weber, R. (2015) Assessing the robustness of power posing: no effect on hormones and

risk tolerance in a large sample of men and women, *Psychological Science*, 26, 653–656.

12. Gelman, A., and Fung, K. (2016) The power of the 'power pose', *Slate Magazine*, 19 January, www.slate.com/articles/health_and_science/sci ence/2016/01/amy_cuddy_s_power_pose_research_is_the_latest_exam ple_of_scientific_overreach.html, accessed 12 September 2017.

CHAPTER I

1. This is a long-standing issue in the academic management community. For a relatively recent and valuable discussion, see Hodgkinson, G., and Starkey, K. (2011) Not simply returning to the same answer over and over again: reframing relevance, *British Journal of Management*, 22, 355–369.

2. See Gordon, R., and Howell, J. (1959) *Higher Education for Business*, New York: Columbia University Press; and Pierson, F. (1959) *The Education of American Businessmen*, New York: McGraw-Hill.

3. Taylor, F. (1911) *The Principles of Scientific Management*, New York: Harper.

4. Conti, R. (2013) Frederick Winslow Taylor, in M. Witzel and M. Warner (eds.) *The Oxford Handbook of Management Theorists*, Oxford: Oxford University Press, pp. 11–31. The quotation is on p. 11.

5. See Taylor, 1911, p. 14.

6. You can see a clip of this at www.youtube.com/watch?v=8NPzLBSBzPI, accessed 7 December 2018.

7. See Taylor, 1911, pp. 44–46.

8. See Taylor, 1911, p. 46.

9. Cooke, B. (2003) The denial of slavery in management studies, *Journal of Management Studies*, 40, 1895–1918.

10. See Taylor, 1911, p. 40.

11. See Taylor, 1911, p. 59.

12. Braverman, H. (1974) *Labor and Monopoly Capital*, New York: Monthly Review Press.

13. Harry Braverman reproduces much of this testimony (Braverman, 1974, pp. 64–67).

14. See Taylor, 1911, p. 83. The italics are in the original.

15. See Taylor, 1911, p. 47.

16. It also reflected his recent background in the Trotskyist movement, which he had noisily departed in 1940 after a prolonged ideological dispute with

Leon Trotsky himself. See Burnham, J. (1941) *The Managerial Revolution*, New York: Pelican Books.

17. Wrege, C., and Perroni, A. (1974) Taylor's pig-tale: a historical analysis of Frederick W. Taylor's pig-iron experiments, *Academy of Management Journal*, 17, 6–27. The quotation is on p. 6.

18. Stewart, M. (2009) *The Management Myth: Why the Experts Keep Getting it Wrong*, New York: Norton. The quotation is on p. 48.

19. Mayo, E. (1922) Industrial peace and psychological research. II. Industrial unrest and 'nervous breakdown', *Industrial Australian and Mining Standard*, 67, 63.

20. Bruce, K., and Nyland, C. (2011) Elton Mayo and the deification of human relations, *Organization Studies*, 32, 383–405.

21. Bynum, B. (2000) Discarded diagnoses, *The Lancet*, 356, 4 November 1615.

22. See the full text of this astonishing document at www.pbs.org/wgbh/aia/part4/4h3106t.html, accessed 7 February 2018.

23. Van Maanen, J. (2013) Hold the Mayo: some comments on the origins of organizational ethnography, *Journal of Organizational Ethnography*, 105–107. The quotation is on p. 107.

24. Roethlisberger, F., and Dickson, W. (1939) *Management and the Worker: an Account of a Research Program Conducted by the Western Electric Company, Hawthorne Works, Chicago*, Cambridge, MA: Harvard University Press. The quotation that follows is on p. 575.

25. Mayo, E. (1933) *The Human Problems of an Industrial Civilization*, New York: Macmillan. The quotation is on p. 103.

26. Mannevuo, M. (2018) The riddle of adaptation: revisiting the Hawthorne studies, *Sociological Review*, 66, 1242–1257.

27. See Mayo, 1933, p. 57.

28. See Harvey, A., Denfield, K., and Montague, P. (2010) Monetary favors and their influence on neural responses and revealed preference, *Journal of Neuroscience*, 28, 9597–9602; and Klein, O., Doyen, S., Leys, C., Gama, P., Miller, S., Questienne, L., and Cleermans, A. (2012) Low hopes, high expectations: expectancy effects and the replicability of behavioural experiments, *Perspectives on Psychological Science*, 7, 572–584.

29. See www.ncbi.nlm.nih.gov/pmc/articles/PMC3921203/ and skepdic.com/cleverhans.html, both accessed 5 March 2018.

30. Gillespie, R. (1991) *Manufacturing Knowledge: a History of the Hawthorne Experiments*, Cambridge: Cambridge University Press. The quotation is on p. 58.
31. See Mayo, 1933, p. 103.
32. Hanlon, G. (2017) *The Dark Side of Management: a Secret History of Management Theory*, London: Routledge. The quotation is on p. 180.
33. Carey, A. (1967) The Hawthorne studies: a radical critique, *American Sociological Review*, 32, 403–416. See also a highly effective criticism in Viteles, M. (1953) *Motivation and Morale in Industry*, New York: Norton.
34. See Carey, 1967, p. 408.
35. Jones, S. (1992) Was there a Hawthorne effect? *American Journal of Sociology*, 98, 451–468. The quotation is on p. 460.
36. Levitt, S., and List, J. (2011) Was there really a Hawthorne effect at the Hawthorne plant? An analysis of the original illumination experiments, *American Economic Journal: Applied Economics*, 3, 224–238. The quotation is on p. 226.
37. See Van Maanen, 2013, p. 107.
38. See Gordon and Howell, 1959, p. 357. The following quotation is on p. 359.
39. Schmidt, R. (1958) Executive decision making, *Academy of Management Journal*, 1, 36–44. The quotations are on p. 36.
40. Thompson, J. (1956) On building an administrative science, *Administrative Science Quarterly*, 1, 102–111. The quotation is on p. 105.
41. Peters, T., and Waterman, R. (1982) *In Search of Excellence*, New York: Harper and Row.
42. Starkey, K., and Tiratsoo, N. (2007) *The Business School and the Bottom Line*, Cambridge: Cambridge University Press, pp. 132–133.
43. Pfeffer, J., and Fong, C. (2002) The end of business schools? Less success than meets the eye, *Academy of Management Learning and Education*, 1, 78–95. The quotation is on p. 88.
44. Tsui, A. (2017) Ivory tower, value-free ideal, and responsible science, in Honig, B., Lampel, J., Baum, J., Glynn, M., Jing, R., Lounsbury, M., Schüßler, E., Sirmon, D., Tsui, A., Walsh, J., and Witteloostuijn, A. (2017) Reflections on scientific misconduct in management: unfortunate incidents or a normative crisis? *Academy of Management Perspectives*, 32, 412–442, DOI: 10.5465/amp.2015.0167. The quotation is on p. 418.
45. Hambrick, D. (1994) What if the academy actually mattered? *Academy of Management Review*, 19, 11–16. The quotation is on p. 13.

46. Starkey, K., and Madan, P. (2001) Bridging the relevance gap: aligning stakeholders in the future of management research, *British Journal of Management*, 12, S3–S26.

47. Hammer, M., and Champy, J. (1993) *Reengineering the Corporation: a Manifesto for Business Revolution*, New York: Harper Business Books.

48. https://money.cnn.com/magazines/fortune/fortune_archive/1993/08/23 /78237/index.htm, accessed 30 August 2018.

49. Shapiro, E. (1995) *Fad Surfing in the Boardroom*, Cambridge, MA: Perseus Books.

50. Kilduff, M., and Kelemen, M. (2001) The consolations of organization theory, *British Journal of Management*, 12 (SI), S55–S59.

51. Grey, C. (2001) Re-imagining relevance: a response to Starkey and Madan, *British Journal of Management*, 12 (SI), S27–S32. The quotation is on p. S29.

52. Learmonth, M., Lockett, A., and Dowd, K. (2012) Promoting scholarship that matters: the uselessness of useful research and the usefulness of useless research, *British Journal of Management*, 23, 35–44.

53. Li, D.X. (2000) On default correlation: a copula function approach, *Journal of Fixed Income*, 9, 43–54.

54. See criticism from Nicolas Taleb, author of *The Black Swan*, quoted at www.wired.com/2009/02/wp-quant/, accessed 17 August 2018.

55. McSweeney, B. (2009) The roles of financial asset market failure denial and the economic crisis: reflections on accounting and financial theories and practices, *Accounting, Organizations and Society*, 34, 835–848.

56. Tushman, M., and O'Reilly, C. (2007) Research and relevance: implications of Pasteur's quadrant for doctoral programs and faculty development, *Academy of Management Journal*, 50, 769–774. The quotation is on p. 769.

57. See Starkey and Tiratsoo, 2007, p. 84.

58. Antebey, M. (2013) *Manufacturing Morals: the Values of Silence in Business School Education*, Chicago: University of Chicago Press.

59. Irwin, A. (2019) Re-making 'quality' within the social sciences: the debate over rigour and relevance in the modern business school, *Sociological Review*, 67, 194–209. The quotation is on p. 197.

60. Kocieniewski, D. (2013) Academics who defend Wall St. reap reward, *New York Times*, 27 December, www.nytimes.com/2013/12/28/business/ academics-who-defend-wall-st-reap-reward.html, accessed 7 March 2018.

61. See Mingers, J. (2015) Helping business schools engage with real problems: the contribution of critical realism and systems thinking, *European Journal of Operational Research*, 242, 316–331. The quotation is on p. 321.

62. Weick, K. (2001) Gapping the relevance bridge: fashions meet fundamentals in management research, *British Journal of Management*, 12 (SI), S71–S75. The quotation is on p. S74.

63. Gardner, J. (1968) *No Easy Victories*, New York: Harper, p. 90.

CHAPTER 2

1. Courpasson, D. (2013) On the erosion of 'passionate scholarship', *Organization Studies*, 34, 1243–1249. The quotation is on p. 1244.

2. Alvesson, M., Gabriel, Y., and Paulsen, R. (2017) *Return to Meaning: a Social Science with Something to Say*, Oxford: Oxford University Press. The quotation is on p. 5.

3. Wilsdon, J., Allen, L., Belfiore, E., Campbell, P., Curry, S., Hill, S., Jones, R., Kain, R., Kerridge, S., Thelwall, M., Tinkler, J., Viney, I., Wouters, P., Hill, J., and Johnson, B. (2015) *The Metric Tide*, London: Higher Education Funding Council.

4. Power, M. (1997) *The Audit Society: Rituals of Verification*, Oxford: Oxford University Press. The following quotation is on p. 97.

5. Power, M. (2003) Evaluating the audit explosion, *Law and Policy*, 25, 185–202. The quotation is on p. 190.

6. Kalfa, S., Wilkinson, A., and Gollan, P. (2018) The academic game: compliance and resistance in universities, *Work, Employment and Society*, 32, 274–291. The quotation is on p. 275.

7. Foucault, M. (1977) *Discipline and Punish*, London: Allen and Unwin; see pp. 201–202.

8. Head, S. (2011) The grim threat to British universities, *New York Review of Books*, 13 January, www.nybooks.com/articles/2011/01/13/grim-threat-british-universities/, accessed 17 March 2018.

9. Kaplan, R., and Norton, D. (1992) The balanced scoreboard: measures that drive performance, *Harvard Business Review*, January–February, 71–79.

10. Nørreklit, H. (2003) The balanced scoreboard: what is the score? A rhetorical analysis of the balanced scoreboard, *Accounting, Organizations and Society*, 28, 591–619. See p. 591.

11. Woodman, C. (2016) Warwick University plc: neo-liberalism, authoritarianism and resistance, *Prometheus*, 34, 39–48.

12. Busch, L. (2017) *Knowledge for Sale: the Neoliberal Takeover of Higher Education*, Cambridge, MA: MIT Press. See p. 17.

13. Muller, J. (2018) *The Tyranny of Metrics*, Princeton, NJ: Princeton University Press. See p. 16.

14. See Norton and Kaplan, 1992, p. 71.

15. Alvesson, M., and Spicer, A. (2017) (Un)conditional surrender? Why do professionals willingly comply with managerialism? in T. Huzzard, M. Benner, and D. Karreman (eds.) *The Corporatization of the Business School: Minerva Meets the Market*, London: Routledge, pp. 92–110. See p. 94.

16. For a detailed case study, see Pelletier, K., Kottke, J., and Sirotnik, B. (2018) The toxic triangle in academia: a case analysis of the emergence and manifestation of toxicity in a public university, *Leadership*, DOI: 10.1177/1742715018773828.

17. The *FT* requires registration to access this list. However, it can be found at http://library.mcmaster.ca/find/ft-research-rank-journals, accessed 17 August 2018.

18. The Association of Business Schools achieved chartered status in 2014 and is now known as the Chartered Association of Business Schools. I refer to it here as the ABS to avoid confusing switches in terminology when discussing various iterations of its Guide.

19. See https://charteredabs.org/academic-journal-guide-2018-available-now/, accessed 17 August 2018.

20. See www.abdc.edu.au/pages/abdc-journal-quality-list-2013.html, accessed 17 August 2018.

21. See Nkomo, S. (2009) The seductive power of academic journal rankings: challenges of searching for the otherwise, *Academy of Management Learning and Education*, 8, 106–112.

22. www.gate.cnrs.fr/spip.php?article1002&lang=fr, accessed 17 August 2019.

23. See the following for detailed critiques: Tourish, D. (2011) Journal rankings, academic freedom and performativity: what is, or should be, the future of *Leadership*? *Leadership*, 7, 367–381; and Tourish, D., and Willmott, H. (2015) In defiance of folly: journal rankings, mindless measures and the ABS Guide, *Critical Perspectives on Accounting*, 26, 37–46.

24. Singh, G., Haddad, K., and Chow, C. (2007) Are articles in 'top' management journals necessarily of higher quality? *Journal of Management Inquiry*, 16, 319–331.

25. Smith, K., and Hitt, M. (eds.) (2005) Great Minds in Management: the Process of Theory Development, Oxford: Oxford University Press.
26. Walker, J., Fenton, E., Salter, A., and Salandra, R. (2018) What influences business academics' use of the Association of Business Schools (ABS) list? Evidence from a survey of UK academics, British Journal of Management, DOI: 10.1111/1467-8551.12294.
27. Pidd, M., and Broadbent, J. (2015) Business and management studies in the 2014 Research Excellence Framework, British Journal of Management, 26, 569–581.
28. Full disclosure: I went on to become editor of the journal in question.
29. Sparkes, A. (2018) Autoethnography comes of age, in D. Beach, C. Bagley, and S. Marques da Silva (eds.) The Wiley Handbook of Education, London: Wiley-Blackwell, pp. 479–499. The quotation is on p. 492.
30. Cunliffe, A. (2018) Alterity: the passion, politics and ethics of self and scholarship, Management Learning, 49, 8–22. The quotation is on p. 15.
31. Prasad, A. (2013) Playing the game and trying not to lose myself: a doctoral student's perspective on the institutional pressures for research output, Organization, 20, 936–948.
32. Bell, E., Kothiyal, N., and Willmott, H. (2017) Methodology-as-technique and the meaning of rigour in globalized management research, British Journal of Management, 28 (3), 534–550, DOI: 10.1111/1467-8551.12205.
33. Schüßler, E. (2017) The role of socialization for the transmission of norms, in Honig, B., Lampel, J., Baum, J., Glynn, M., Jing, R., Lounsbury, M., Schüßler, E., Sirmon, D., Tsui, A., Walsh, J., and Witteloostuijn, A. Reflections on scientific misconduct in management: unfortunate incidents or a normative crisis? Academy of Management Perspectives, 32, 412–442.
34. Segalla, M. (2008) Editorial: publishing in the right place or publishing the right thing, European Journal of International Management, 2, 122–127.
35. Macdonald, S., and Kam, J. (2007) Ring a Ring o' Roses: quality journals and gamesmanship in management studies, Journal of Management Studies, 44, 640–655.
36. Barney, J. (1991) Firm resources and sustained competitive advantage, Journal of Management, 17, 99–120.
37. Merton, R. (1968) The Matthew Effect in science, Science, 159, 56–63.
38. A partial exception was the Academy of Management Annals, excluded from the previous issue since it was unclear whether it was a journal or

a book series. From this point regarded as an annual journal, it was included in the ABS list as a four-star journal.

39. Hardy, C. (2013) Treading fine lines, *Journal of Management Inquiry*, 22, 452–456. The quotation is on p. 454.

40. Grey, C. (2010) Organizing studies: publications, politics and polemic, *Organization Studies*, 31, 677–694. The quotation is on p. 685.

41. Seeber, M., Cattaneo, M., Meoli, M., and Malighetti, P. (2019) Self-citations as strategic response to the use of metrics for career decisions, *Research Policy*, 48, 478–491.

42. Fowler, J., and Aksnes, D. (2007) Does self-citation pay? *Scientometrics*, 7, 427–437.

43. See Alvesson, Gabriel and Paulsen, 2017, p. 7.

44. Larivière, V., and Sugimoto, C. (2018) The Journal Impact Factor: a brief history, critique, and discussion of adverse effects, in W. Glänzel, H. Moed, U. Schmoch, and M. Thelwall (eds.) *Springer Handbook of Science and Technology Indicators*, Cham (Switzerland): Springer International Publishing. See p. 12.

45. Brembs, B. (2018) Prestigious science journals struggle to reach even average reliability, *Frontiers in Human Neuroscience*, DOI: 10.3389/fnhum.2018.00037.

46. Fong, E., and Wilhite, A. (2017) Authorship and citation manipulation in academic research, *PLoS One*, 12 (12), e0187394, DOI: 10.1371/journal.pone.0187394.

47. See Goodhart, C. (1975) Problems of monetary management: the UK experience, in *Papers in Monetary Economics, Volume I*, Reserve Bank of Australia.

48. See Khan, S. (2018) Doctors 'being pressurised into manipulating patient records to meet A&E targets', The Independent, 28 January, www.independent.co.uk/news/health/doctors-accident-emergency-targets-patients-records-figure-manipulate-a-e-hospitals-a8172996.html, accessed 21 February 2018.

49. See BBC Scotland (2018) A Force in Crisis, 30 April.

50. If you are curious enough, or bored enough, you can see the most recent rankings at www.usnews.com/best-colleges.

51. Gladwell, M. (2011) The order of things, *New Yorker*, 14–21 February, 68–75.

52. See www.washingtonpost.com/local/education/five-colleges-misreported-data-to-us-news-raising-concerns-about-rankings-reputation/2013/02/06/

cb437876-6b17-11e2-af53-7b2b2a7510a8_story.html?utm_term=
.127a7b33e48e, accessed 21 February 2018.

53. See www.nytimes.com/aponline/2018/07/10/us/ap-us-temple-business-
school-falsified-rankings.html, accessed 23 July 2018.

54. Guttenplan, D. (2010) Questionable science behind academic rankings,
New York Times, 14 November, www.nytimes.com/2010/11/15/educa
tion/15iht-educLede15.html, accessed 12 December 2018.

55. See Gabriel, Y. (2010) Organization studies: a space for ideas, identities
and agonies, *Organization Studies*, 31, 757–775.

56. King, E., Avery, D., Hebl, M., and Cortina, J. (2018) Systematic
subjectivity: how subtle biases infect the scholarship review process,
Journal of Management, 44, 843–853. The quotation is on p. 834.

57. Amabile, T. (1983) Brilliant but cruel: perceptions of negative evaluators,
Journal of Experimental Social Psychology, 19, 146–156.

58. Gibson, B., and Oberlander, E. (2008) Wanting to appear smart:
hypercriticism as an indirect impression management strategy, *Self and
Identity*, 7, 380–392.

59. Baumeister, R., Bratslavasky, E., Finkenauer, C., and Vohs, K. (2001) Bad is
stronger than good, *Review of General Psychology*, 5, 323–370.

60. See Gabriel, 2010, p. 764.

61. Seibert, S. (2006) Anatomy of an R&R (or, reviewers are an author's best
friends . . .), *Academy of Management Journal*, 49, 203–207. The quotation
is on p. 203.

62. Cederström, C., and Spicer, A. (2017) Going public, *Organization*, 24,
708–711. The quotation is on p. 708.

63. Jump, P. (2015) Grant income targets set at one in six universities,
THE poll suggests, *Times Higher Education*, 11 June, www
.timeshighereducation.co.uk/news/grant-income-targets-set-one-six-uni
versities-poll-suggests, accessed 20 August 2015.

64. Mills, C. (1959) *The Sociological Imagination*, Oxford: Oxford University
Press, p. 205.

65. See https://charteredabs.org/wp-content/uploads/2018/04/Chartered_ABS_
Research_Income_Report_2018-WEB.pdf, accessed 11 April 2018.

66. Karran, T., and Mallinson, L. (2017) *Academic Freedom in the U.K.: Legal
and Normative Protection in a Comparative Context*, Report for the
University and College Union, London: University and College Union.
The quotation is on p. 64.

67. Harvey, C., Kelly, A., Morris, H., and Rowlinson, M. (2010) *The Association of Business Schools Academic Journal Quality Guide (Version 4)*, London: Association of Business Schools, p. 2.

68. The ongoing negative effects of this mantra, including a proliferation of nonsense research that can't be replicated, are discussed in illuminating detail by Moosa, A. (2018) *Publish or Perish: Perceived Benefits versus Unintended Consequences*, Cheltenham: Edward Elgar.

69. Sorokowski, P., Kulczycki, E., Sorokowska, A., and Pisanski, K. (2017) Predatory journals recruit fake editor, *Nature*, 543 (23 March), 481–483.

70. Bagues, M., Sylos-Labini, M., and Zinovyeva, N. (2019) A walk on the wild side: 'predatory' journals and information asymmetries, *Research Policy*, 48, 462–477.

71. Cederström, C., and Hoedemaekers, C. (2012) On dead dogs and unwritten jokes: life in the university today, *Scandinavian Journal of Management*, 28, 229–233. The quotation is on p. 231.

72. See Grey, 2010, p. 691.

CHAPTER 3

1. The full text of this email and others can be viewed at www.dcscience.net/2014/12/01/publish-and-perish-at-imperial-college-london-the-death-of-stefan-grimm/. Coverage of Professor Grimm's death in *Times Higher Education* can be viewed at www.timeshighereducation.co.uk/news/imperial-college-professor-stefan-grimm-was-given-grant-income-target/2017369.article?storyCode=2017369 and www.timeshighereducation.co.uk/news/stefan-grimm-inquest-new-policies-may-not-have-prevented-suicide/2019563.article. See also the following in the *Daily Mail*: www.dailymail.co.uk/news/article-2861588/Professor-dead-cash-row-Cancer-scientist-said-told-fellow-academics-chiefs-treated-like-s.html. The quotation from 'a fellow academic' is taken from this report.

2. See http://felixonline.co.uk/news/5475/review-in-response-to-grimms-death-completed/.

3. See www.timeshighereducation.com/news/cardiff-plans-review-after-suicide-overworked-lecturer, accessed 9 June 2018.

4. Willetts, D. (2017) *A University Education*, Oxford: Oxford University Press.

5. See Willetts, 2017, p. 104.

6. Martin-Sardesai, A., and Guthrie, J. (2018) Human capital loss in an academic performance measurement system, *Journal of Intellectual Capital*, 19, 53–70.

7. Schüßler (2017) The role of socialization for the transmission of norms, in Honig, B., Lampel, J., Baum, J., Glynn, M., Jing, R., Lounsbury, M., Schüßler, E., Sirmon, D., Tsui, A., Walsh, J., and Witteloostuijn, A. (2017) Reflections on scientific misconduct in management: unfortunate incidents or a normative crisis? *Academy of Management Perspectives*, 32, 412–442.

8. Fochler, M., and de Rijcke, S. (2017) Implicated in the indicator game? An experimental debate, *Engaging Science, Technology, and Society*, 3, 21–40. The quotation is on p. 25.

9. See Task and Finish Group Report (2012) *Listening to Our Voices: Towards a Sustainable Future*, University of Exeter. This was an internal university report, and the quotation is on p. 4.

10. Kinman, G., and Wray, S. (2013) *Higher Stress: a Survey of Stress and Well-Being Among Staff in Higher Education*, London: University and College Union.

11. Guthrie, S., Lichten, C., van Belle, J., Ball, S., Knack, A., and Hofman, J. (2017) *Understanding Mental Health in the Research Environment: a Rapid Evidence Assessment*, Cambridge: RAND Europe.

12. Padilla, M., and Thompson, J. (2016) Burning out faculty at doctoral research universities, *Stress Health*, 32, 551–558.

13. See https://docs.google.com/spreadsheets/d/1OODoiZKeAtiGiI3IAONC spryCHWo5Yw9xkQzkRntuMU/edit#gid=0, accessed 22 February 2018.

14. See www.timeshighereducation.com/features/work-life-balance-survey-2018-long-hours-take-their-toll-academics, accessed 22 February 2018.

15. De Vita, G., and Case, P. (2016) 'The smell of the place': Managerialist culture in contemporary UK business schools, *Culture and Organization*, 22, 348–364. The quotation is on p. 354.

16. Saunders, M. (2006) The madness and malady of managerialism, *Quadrant*, March, 9–17. The quotation is on p. 17.

17. Alvesson, M., and Spicer, A. (2017) (Un)conditional surrender? Why do professionals willingly comply with managerialism? in T. Huzzard, M. Benner, and D. Karreman (eds.) *The Corporatization of the Business School: Minerva Meets the Market*, London: Routledge, pp. 92–110. The quotation is on p. 95.

18. Martin, B. (2016) What's happening to our universities? *Prometheus*, 34, 7–24. The quotation is on p. 7.

19. The original UCU forum is no longer available online. However, I downloaded its contents at the time they appeared and draw from that archive here. The full text is available from me on request.

20. Alakavuklar, O., Dickson, A., and Stablein, R. (2017) The alienation of scholarship in modern business schools: from Marxist material relations to the Lacanian subject, *Academy of Management Learning and Education*, 16, 454–468. The quotation is on p. 457.

21. See www.the-eye.wales/death-duties/, accessed 19 March 2018.

22. See www.walesonline.co.uk/news/wales-news/swansea-university-man agement-school-describes-8644690, accessed 19 March 2018.

23. Gabriel, Y. (2012) Organizations in a state of darkness: towards a theory of organizational miasma, *Organization Studies*, 33, 1137–1152. The quotation is on p. 1141.

24. Day, N. (2007) The silent majority: manuscript rejection and its impact on scholars, *Academy of Management Learning and Education*, 10, 704–718. The quotation is on p. 706.

25. Knights, D., and Clarke, C. (2014) It's a bittersweet symphony, this life: fragile academic selves and insecure identities at work, *British Journal of Management*, 35, 335–357.

26. Peters, D., and Ceci, S. (1982) Peer-review practices of psychological journals: the fate of published articles, submitted again, *Behavioral and Brain Sciences*, 5, 187–266.

27. Alvesson, M. (2012) Do we have something to say? From re-search to ros-search and back again, *Organization*, 20, 79–90. The quotation is on p. 79.

28. www.timeshighereducation.com/features/universities-need-to-plan-for-dark-future-if-academics-prefer-their-own-plan-b, accessed 27 February 2018.

29. Oswald, A. (2018) The perils of middle age, *Times Higher Education*, 28 June, 26.

30. Byron, K., Khazanchi, S., and Nazarian, D. (2010) The relationship between stressors and creativity: a meta-analysis examining competing theoretical models, *Journal of Applied Psychology*, 95, 201–212. The quotation is on p. 201.

31. See the following for fascinating and sometimes moving discussions of these issues: O'Neill, M. (2014) The slow university: work, time and well-

being, *Qualitative Social Research*, DOI: http://dx.doi.org/10.17169/fqs-15.3.2226; and Sparkes, A. (2007) Embodiment, academics and the audit culture: a story seeking consideration, *Qualitative Research*, 7, 521–550.

32. Bristow, A. (2012) On life, death and radical critique: a non-survival guide to the Brave New Higher Education for the intellectually pregnant, *Scandinavian Journal of Management*, 28, 234–241. The quotation is on p. 238.

33. For a particularly in-depth argument along these lines, see Adler, N., and Harzing, A. (2009) When knowledge wins: transcending the sense and nonsense of academic rankings, *Academy of Management Learning and Education*, 8, 72–95.

34. Alvesson, M., and Sandberg, J. (2014) Habitat and habitus: boxed-in versus box-breaking research, *Organization Studies*, 35, 967–987.

35. Jones, D. (2018) Could slow be beautiful? Academic counter-spacing within and beyond 'The Slow Swimming Club', *Journal of Management Inquiry*, 27, 420–435. The quotation is on p. 426.

36. Berg, M., and Seeber, B. (2016) *The Slow Professor: Challenging the Culture of Speed in the Academy*, Toronto: University of Toronto Press.

37. Dzeng, E. (2014) How academia and publishing are destroying scientific innovation: a conversation with Sydney Brenner, *King's Review*, 24 February, http://kingsreview.co.uk/articles/how-academia-and-pub lishing-are-destroying-scientific-innovation-a-conversation-with-sydney-brenner/, accessed 19 March 2018.

38. Harford, T. (2011) *Adapt: Why Success Always Starts with Failure*, London: Little Brown. The quotation is on p. 103.

39. See *Times Higher Education* (2018), 1 March, www.timeshighereduca tion.com/news/radical-ideas-required-cut-research-grant-waste-funders -told.

40. Vaesen, K., and Katzav, J. (2017) How much would each researcher receive if competitive government research funding were distributed equally among researchers? *PLoS/ONE*, 12, e0183967, https://doi.org/10 .1371/journal.pone.0183967.

41. Stern, N. (2016) *Building on Successes and Learning from Experience: an Independent Review of the Research Excellence Framework*, https:// assets.publishing.service.gov.uk/government/uploads/system/uploads/ attachment_data/file/541338/ind-16-9-ref-stern-review.pdf, accessed 12 September 2018.

42. Such are the direct and indirect costs of securing accreditation from many of these bodies, and the reputational impact of not being accredited, that Lowrie and Willmott suggest they have much in common with protection rackets. See Lowrie, A., and Willmott, H. (2009) Accreditation sickness in the consumption of business education: the vacuum in AACSB standard setting, *Management Learning*, 40, 411–420.

43. The report can be viewed at https://workspace.imperial.ac.uk/college/Public/Provost%27s%20Board%20paper%20Performance%20Management%20Review%20-%20FULL.pdf, accessed 20 August 2015.

44. Cited in the chairman's foreword to the Dearing Report into the future of UK higher education (1997), www.educationengland.org.uk/documents/dearing1997/dearing1997.html#for, accessed 21 August 2015.

CHAPTER 4

1. Some of the material in this chapter and in Chapter 5 has been previously published as follows: Tourish, D., and Craig, R. (2018) Research misconduct in business and management studies: theorising its causes, exploring its consequences and possible remedies, *Journal of Management Inquiry*, DOI: 10.1177/1056492618792621.

2. Martin, B. (2013) Editorial: Whither research integrity? Plagiarism, self-plagiarism and coercive citation in an age of research assessment, *Research Policy*, 42, 1005–1014. The quotation is on p. 1010.

3. Wright, D., and Breithaupt, H. (2012) To protect and serve research integrity, *Science & Society*, 13 (6), 484–486, http://europepmc.org/backend/ptpmcrender.fcgi?accid=PMC3367251&blobtype=pdf, accessed 20 November 2015.

4. Matthews, D. (2015) Secret dossier warns of scale of research fraud, *Times Higher Education*, 3 December, 6–7.

5. Abritis, A. (2015) *An Assessment of Retractions as a Measure of Scientific Misconduct and Impact on Public Health Risks* (doctoral dissertation, University of South Florida), http://scholarcommons.usf.edu/etd/5630, accessed 20 November 2015.

6. See www.singaporestatement.org/downloads/singpore%20statement_A4size.pdf, accessed 12 January 2016.

7. See www.ascb.org/files/SFDeclarationFINAL.pdf, accessed 12 January 2016.

8. See http://publicationethics.org/about, accessed 12 January 2016.

9. See http://retractionwatch.com/, accessed 12 January 2016.

10. Hiney, M. (2015) *Briefing Paper: Research Integrity: What It Means, Why It Is Important and How We Might Protect It*, Brussels: Science Europe.

11. Ferguson, C., Marcus, A., and Oransky, I. (2014) The peer-review scam, *Nature*, 515, 480–482.

12. Horbach, S., and Halffman, W. (2019) The extent and causes of academic text recycling or 'self-plagiarism', *Research Policy*, 48, 492–502.

13. Colquhoun, D. (2017) An investigation of the false discovery rate and the misinterpretation of *p*-values, *Royal Society Open Science*, 1 (3), 140216, DOI: 10.1098/rsos.140216.

14. Bishop, D. (2018) Using simulations to understand *p*-values (blog post), *BishopBlog*, http://deevybee.blogspot.co.uk, accessed 1 February 2018.

15. Ziliak, S., and McCloskey, D. (2008) *The Cult of Statistical Significance*, Ann Arbor: University of Michigan Press, p. 2.

16. See Colquhoun, 2017.

17. Wasserstein, R., and Lazar, N. (2016) The ASA's statement on *p*-values: context, process, and purpose, *American Statistician*, 70, 129–133. The quotation is on pp. 131–132.

18. Nelson, L., Simmons, J., and Simonsohn, U. (2018) Psychology's renaissance, *Annual Review of Psychology*, 69, 511–534. The quotation is on p. 514.

19. Chambers, C. (2017) *The 7 Deadly Sins of Psychology: a Manifesto for Reforming the Culture of Scientific Practice*, Princeton and Oxford: Princeton University Press and Oxford University Press. See Chapter 2, where this issue is discussed in depth.

20. Aguinis, H., Ramani, R., and Alabduljader, N. (2018) What you see is what you get? Enhancing methodological transparency in management research, *Academy of Management Annals*, 12, 83–110. The quotation is on pp. 84–85.

21. Hendry, D. (1980) Econometrics – alchemy or science? *Economica*, 47, 387–406.

22. Simmons, J., Nelson, L., and Simonsohn, U. (2011) False positive psychology: undisclosed flexibility in data collection and analysis allows presenting anything as significant, *Psychological Science*, 22, 1359–1366.

23. See www.tylervigen.com/spurious-correlations.

24. Moosa, I. (2017) Blaming suicide on NASA and divorce on margarine: the hazard of using cointegration to derive inference on spurious correlation, *Applied Economics*, 49, 1483–1490.

25. Ferguson, C., and Heene, M. (2012) A vast graveyard of undead theories: publication bias and psychological science's aversion to the null, *Perspectives on Psychological Science*, 7: 555–561.

26. Bergh, D., Sharp, B., Aguinis, H., and Li, M. (2015) The looming replication crisis in strategic management (conference paper), Annual International Conference of the Strategic Management Society, Denver, CO, 3–6 October.

27. Leung, K. (2011) Presenting post hoc hypotheses as a priori: ethical and theoretical issues, *Management and Organization Review*, 7, 471–479.

28. Bakker, M., and Wicherts, J. (2011) The (mis) reporting of statistical results in psychology journals, *Behavior Research Methods*, 43, 666–678.

29. Hubbard, R. (2016) *Corrupt Research: the Case for Reconceptualising Empirical Management and Social Science*, London: Sage. The quotation is on p. 5.

30. See Aguinis et al., 2018, p. 83.

31. DeSimone, J., Kohler, T., and Schoen, J. (2018) If it were only that easy: the use of meta-analytic research by organizational scholars, *Organizational Research Methods*, DOI: 10.1177/1094428118756743.

32. Aczel, B., Palfi, B., and Szaszi, B. (2017) Estimating the evidential value of significant results in psychological science, *PLoS ONE*, 12(8), e0182651, https://doi.org/10.1371/journal.pone.0182651.

33. Kerr, N. (1998) HARKing: hypothesizing after the results are known, *Personality and Social Psychology Review*, 2, 196–217. The quotation is on p. 209.

34. See, for example, p. 11 of *The Concordat to Support Research Integrity* (2012), produced by Universities UK. See www.universitiesuk.ac.uk/pol icy-and-analysis/reports/Documents/2012/the-concordat-to-support-research-integrity.pdf, accessed 2 August 2018.

35. Levelt Committee, Noort Committee and Drenth Committee (2012) *Flawed Science: the Fraudulent Research Practices of Social Psychologist Diederik Stapel*, http://pubman.mpdl.mpg.de/pubman/item/esci doc:1569964:7/component/escidoc:1569966/Stapel_Investigation_Final_report.pdf, accessed 20 November 2015. The quotation is on p. 53.

36. Randall, D., and Welser, C. (2018) *The Irreproducibility Crisis of Modern Science*, New York: National Association of Scholars.

37. Bergh, D., Sharp, B., Aguinis, H., and Li, M. (2017) Is there a reproducibility crisis in strategic management research? Evidence on the reproducibility

of study findings, *Strategic Organization*, 15, 423–436. This quotation is on p. 423, while the one that follows is on pp. 430–432.

38. Makel, M., Plucker, J., and Hegarty, B. (2012) Replications in psychology research: how often do they really occur? *Perspectives on Psychological Science*, 7, 537–542.

39. For a detailed account, see Reich, E. (2009) *Plastic Fantastic: How the Biggest Fraud in Physics Shook the Scientific World*, Houndmills: Palgrave Macmillan.

40. See Ioannidis, J. (2005) Why most published research findings are false, *PLoS Medicine*, 2, e124, DOI: 10.1371/journal.pmed.0020124; and Ioannidis, J. (2012) Why science is not necessarily self-correcting, *Perspectives on Psychological Science*, 7, 645–654.

41. Hubbard, R., and Vetter, D. (1991) Replications in the finance literature: an empirical study, *Quarterly Journal of Business and Economics*, 30, 70–81.

42. Open Science Collaboration (2015) Estimating the reproducibility of psychological science, *Science*, 349 (6251), DOI: 10.1126/science.aac4716.

43. For an overview, see Molden, D. (2014) Understanding priming effects in social psychology: what is 'social priming' and how does it occur? *Social Cognition*, 32 (SI), 1–11.

44. Mazar, N., Amir, O., and Ariely, D. (2008) The dishonesty of honest people: a theory of self-concept maintenance, *Journal of Marketing Research*, 45, 633–644.

45. Verschuere, B., Meijer, E., Jim, A. et al. (2018) Registered replication report on Mazar, Amir, and Ariely (2008), *Advances in Methods and Practices in Psychological Science*, 1 (3), 299–317, DOI:10.117/7/2515245918781032.032.

46. See letter from Kahneman (2012), www.nature.com/polopoly_fs/7.6716.1349271308!/suppinfoFile/Kahneman%20Letter.pdf, accessed 31 August 2018.

47. For example, the psychologist Lisa Barrett published an opinion piece in the *New York Times* in 2015 headlined 'Psychology is Not in Crisis' (1 September). See www.nytimes.com/2015/09/01/opinion/psychology-is-not-in-crisis.html, accessed 15 September 2018. See also Bartlett, T. (2018) I want to burn things to the ground, *Chronicle of Higher Education*, 11 September, www.chronicle.com/article/I-Want-to-Burn-Things-to/244488?key=ONA-J8qTe05O7njbTd0tJ5MGlT3EF5H5UcVzn-A0SjvQuzk

OG60mekK3-jrAePM-N1hXSXktZXhZb2x6RVdBSDZBTVJHZHFYRVV
POVV4Z0tjRW9RbWlmcVlqMA, accessed 15 September 2018.

48. See https://improvingpsych.org, accessed 15 September 2018.

49. Prinz, F., Schlange, T., and Asadullagh, K. (2011) Believe it or not: how much can we rely on published data on potential drug targets? *Nature*, 10, 712, DOI:10.1038/nrd3439-c1.

50. Jump, P. (2015) Reproducing results: how big is the problem? *Times Higher Education*, 3 September, www.timeshighereducation.co.uk/fea tures/reproducing-results-how-big-is-the-problem?nopaging=1, accessed 11 November 2015.

51. Ioannidis, J., Allison, D., Ball, C., Coulibaly, I., Cui, X., Culhane, A., Falchi, M., Furlanello, C., Game, L., Jurmen, G., Mangion, J., Mehta, T., Nitzberg, M., Page, G., Petretto, E., and van Noort, V. (2009) Repeatability of published microarray gene expression analyses, *Nature Genetics*, 41, 149–155.

52. Stroebe, W., and Hewstone, M. (2015) What have we learned from the Reproducibility Project? *Times Higher Education*, 17 September, www .timeshighereducation.com/opinion/reproducibility-project-what-have-we-learned, accessed 23 September 2015.

53. Pashler, H., and Harris, C. (2012) Is the replicability crisis overblown? Three arguments examined, *Perspectives on Psychological Science*, 7, 531–536.

54. See Nelson et al., 2018.

55. The studies cited in Table 4.1 are as follows:Bailey, C., Hasselback, J., and Karcher, J. (2001) Research misconduct in accounting literature: a survey of the most prolific researchers' actions and beliefs, *Abacus*, 37, 26–54. Banks, G., O'Boyle, E., Pollack, J., White, C., Batchelor, J., Whelpy, C., Abston, K., Bennett, A., and Adkins, C. (2016) Questions about questionable research practices in the field of management: a guest commentary, *Journal of Management*, 42, 5–20. Bedeian, A., Taylor, S., and Miller, A. (2010) Management science on the credibility bubble: cardinal sins and curious misdemeanours, *Academy of Management Learning and Education*, 9, 715–725. Honig, B., and Bedi, A. (2012) The fox in the hen house: a critical examination of plagiarism among members of the Academy of Management, *Academy of Management Learning and Education*, 11, 101–123. Hoover, G., and Hopp, C. (2017) What crisis? Taking stock of management researchers' experiences with and views of

scholarly misconduct, *CESifo Working Papers*, https://ideas.repec.org/p/ces/ceswps/_6611.html, accessed 1 September 2017.

56. Hvistendahl, M. (2015) China pursues fraudsters in science publishing, *Science*, 350 (6264), 1015.

57. The studies cited in Table 4.2 are as follows: Agnoli, F., Wicherts, J., Veldkamp, C., Albiero, P., and Cubelli, R. (2017) Questionable research practices among Italian research psychologists, *PLOS/One*, 12(3), e0172792, DOI: 10.1371/journal.pone.0172792. Boulbes, D., Costello, T., Baggerly, K., Fan, F., Wang, R., Bhattacharya, R., Ye, X., and Ellis, L. (2018) A survey on data reproducibility and the effect of publication process on the ethical reporting of laboratory research, *Clinical Cancer Research*, DOI: 10.1158/1078-0432.CCR-18-0227. Cossette, P. (2004) Research integrity: an exploratory survey of administrative science faculties, *Journal of Business Ethics*, 49, 213–234. Eastwood, D., Derish, P., Leash, E., and Ordway, S. (1996) Ethical issues in biomedical research: perception and practices of postdoctoral research fellows in responding to a survey, *Science and Engineering Ethics*, 2, 89–114. Fanelli, D. (2009) How many scientists fabricate and falsify research? A systematic review and meta-analysis of survey data, *PLoS ONE*, 4, e5738, DOI: 10.1371/journal.pone.0005738. Fraser, H., Parker, T., Nakagawa, S., Barnett, A., and Fidler, F. (2018) Questionable research practices in ecology and evolution, *Open Science Framework*, DOI: osf.io/ajyqg. John, L., Loewenstein, G., and Prelec, D. (2012) Measuring the prevalence of questionable research practices with incentives for truth telling, *Psychological Science*, 23, 524–532. Kalichman, M., and Friedman, P. (1992) A pilot study of biomedical trainees' perceptions concerning research ethics, *Academic Medicine*, 67, 769–775. Kerr, N. (1998) HARKing: hypothesizing after the results are known, *Personality and Social Psychology Review*, 2, 196–217. Martinson, B., Anderson, M., and De Vries, R. (2005) Scientists behaving badly, *Nature*, 435, 737–738. Necker, S. (2014) Scientific misbehavior in economics, *Research Policy*, 43, 1747–1759. Pupovac, V., and Fanelli, D. (2015) Scientists admitting to plagiarism: a meta-analysis of surveys, *Science and Engineering Ethics*, 21, 1331–1352. Ranstam, J., Buyse, M., George, S.L., and Lachenbruch, P. (2000) Fraud in medical research: an international survey of biostatisticians, *Controlled Clinical Trials*, 21, 415–427. Swazey, J., Anderson, M., and Louis, K. (1993) Ethical problems in academic research, *American Scientist*, 81, 542–553. Tijdink, J.,

Bouter, L., Veldkamp, C., van de Ven, P., Wicherts, J., and Smulders, Y. (2016) Personality traits are associated with research misbehaviour in Dutch scientists: a cross-sectional study, *PLoS One*, DOI: 10.1371/journal. pone.0163251. Titus, S. (2014) Evaluating U.S. medical schools' efforts to educate faculty researchers on research integrity and research misconduct policies and procedures, *Accountability in Research*, 21, 9–25. Titus, S., Wells, J., and Rhodes, L. (2008) Repairing research integrity, *Nature*, 19 (453), 980–982. Williams, J., and Roberts, D. (2016) Academic integrity: exploring tensions between perception and practice in the contemporary university (report), Canterbury: University of Kent Society for Research into Higher Education, www.srhe.ac.uk/downloads/WILLIAMSJoannaRO BERTSDavid.pdf.

58. www.ourcatholicprayers.com/St-Augustine-on-prayer.html, accessed 20 August 2018.

59. Krimsky, S., Rothenberg, L., Stott, P., and Kyle, G. (1996) Financial interests of authors in scientific journals: a pilot study of 14 publications, *Science and Engineering Ethics*, 2: 395–410.

60. Ngai, S., Gold, J., Gill, S., and Rochon, P. (2005) Haunted manuscripts: ghost authorship in the medical literature, *Accountability in Research: Policies and Quality Assurance*, 12, 103–114.

61. Bosch, X., and Ross, J. (2012) Ghostwriting: research misconduct, plagiarism, or fool's gold? *American Journal of Medicine*, 125, 324–326. The quotation is on p. 325.

62. Wager, E. (2009) Recognition, reward and responsibility: why the authorship of scientific papers matters, *Maturitas*, 62, 109–112.

63. Abritis, A., and McCook, A. (2017) Cash bonuses for peer-reviewed papers go global, *Science*, www.sciencemag.org/news/2017/08/cash-bonuses-pe er-reviewed-papers-go-global, accessed 30 August 2017.

64. Powell, S. (2018) Financial bonus for published research, *The Australian*, 18 July, p. 27.

65. Three prominent medical researchers at the university in question publicly criticised such incentives on precisely these grounds, arguing that they harmed the institution's reputation for research integrity (*The Australian*, 1 August 2018, p. 31).

66. Pinto, J., Leana, C., and Pil, F. (2008) Corrupt organizations or organizations of corrupt individuals? Two types of organization-level corruption, *Academy of Management Review*, 33, 685–709.

67. See Lance Armstrong's interview with Oprah Winfrey, www .youtube.com/watch?v=e_-yfFIiDao, accessed 18 January 2016.
68. Kelman, H. (1973) Violence without moral restraint: reflections on the dehumanization of victims and victimizers, *Journal of Social Issues*, 29, 25–61.
69. Kim, T., Monge, R., and Strudler, A. (2015) Bounded ethicality and the principle that 'ought' implies 'can', *Business Ethics Quarterly*, 25, 341–361.
70. Edwards, M., and Roy, S. (2017) Academic research in the 21st century: maintaining scientific integrity in a climate of perverse incentives and hypercompetition, *Environmental Engineering Science*, 34, 51–61. The quotation is on p. 53.
71. Smith, R. (2006) Research misconduct: the poisoning of the well, *Journal of the Royal Society of Medicine*, 99, 232–237. The quotation is on p. 234.

CHAPTER 5

1. Karabag and Berggren also report that confidentiality was a major concern for editors in deciding whether to complete their survey. The extreme sensitivity of the issues involved in research misconduct clearly creates particular problems in researching this area. See Karabeg, S., and Berggren, C. (2016) Misconduct, marginality and editorial practices in management, business and economics journals, *PLoS ONE*, 11: e0159492, doi.org/10.1371/journal.pone.0159492.
2. See the official report into his activities: Levelt Committee, Noort Committee and Drenth Committee (2012) *Flawed Science: the Fraudulent Research Practices of Social Psychologist Diederik Stapel*, http://pubman.mpdl.mpg.de/pubman/item/escidoc:1569964:7/compo nent/escidoc:1569966/Stapel_Investigation_Final_report.pdf.
3. Stapel, D. (2014) *Faking Science: a True Story of Academic Fraud*, trans. N. Brown, http://nick.brown.free.fr/stapel/FakingScience-20141214.pdf, accessed 16 January 2016.
4. Guffey, D., and Harp, N. (2013) Ranking faculties, PhD programs, individual scholars, and influential articles in accounting information systems based on citations to publications in the *Journal of Information Systems*, *Journal of Information Systems*, 28, 111–144.

5. Stone, D. (2015) Post-Hunton: reclaiming our integrity and literature, *Journal of Information Systems*, 29, 211–227. The quotation is on p. 214.

6. Malone, J. (2014) *Report of Judith A. Malone, Bentley University Ethics Officer, concerning Dr. James E. Hunton*, Waltham, MA: Bentley University, www.bentley.edu/files/Hunton%20report%20July21.pdf, accessed 1 December 2015.

7. See http://blog.openinnovation.net/2012/12/end-to-embarrassing-year-for-oi-research.html, accessed 11 September 2017.

8. See https://retractionwatch.com/2018/08/14/management-researcher-with-16-retractions-has-new-professorship/#more-69981, accessed 17 August 2018.

9. Woolf, P. (1991) Accountability and responsibility in research, *Journal of Business Ethics*, 10, 595–600. The quotation is on p. 598.

10. See (2015) Retraction, *Journal of Information Systems*, 29, 229.

11. See (2015) Retraction Notice, *Organizational Behavior and Human Decision Processes*, 131, 190.

12. See (2015) Retraction, *Journal of Management Studies*, 52, 849.

13. Karabeg, S., and Berggren, C. (2016) Misconduct, marginality and editorial practices in management, business and economics journals, *PLoS ONE*, 11: e0159492, doi.org/10.1371/journal.pone.0159492.

14. See (2014) Retraction, 'Technological turbulence and the impact of exploration and exploitation within and across organizations on product development performance' by Ulrich Lichtenthaler, *Entrepreneurship Theory and Practice*, DOI: 10.11111/etap.520.

15. See (2012) Retraction, 'Integrated knowledge exploitation: the complementarity of product development and technology licensing', *Strategic Management Journal*, 33, 1341.

16. See (2012) Retraction, *Journal of Management Studies*, 49, 1350.

17. Bohannon, J. (2013) Who's afraid of peer review? *Science*, 342, 6065.

18. Atwater, L., Mumford, M., Schriesheim, C., and Yammarino, F. (2014) Retraction of leadership articles: causes and prevention, *Leadership Quarterly*, 25, 1174–1180.

19. Kochan, C., and Budd, J. (1992) The persistence of fraud in the literature: the Darsee case, *Journal of the American Society for Information Science*, 43, 488–493.

20. Bar-Ilan, J., and Halevi, G. (2018) Temporal characteristics of retracted articles, *Scientometrics*, 116 (3), 1771–1783, doi.org/10.1007/s11192-018-2802-y.

21. The full report can be accessed via http://retractionwatch.com/2014/11/14/univ-no-misconduct-but-poor-research-practice-in-mgt-profs-work-now-subject-to-7-retractions/

22. Lockett, A., McWilliams, A., and Van Fleet, D. (2014) Reordering our priorities by putting phenomena before design: escaping the straitjacket of null hypothesis significance testing, *British Journal of Management*, 25, 863–873.

23. Schwab, A., Abrahamson, E., Starbuck, W., and Fidler, F. (2011) Perspective – researchers should make thoughtful assessments instead of null-hypothesis significance tests, *Organization Science*, 22, 1105–1120.

24. Stroebe, W., Postmes, T., and Spears, R. (2012) Scientific misconduct and the myth of self-correction in science, *Perspectives on Psychological Science*, 7, 670–688. The quotation is on p. 671.

25. Thielen, J. (2018) When scholarly publishing goes awry: educating ourselves and our patrons about retracted articles, *Libraries and the Academy*, 18, 183–198. Both quotations are on p. 187.

26. Berggren, C., and Karabag, S. (2019) Scientific misconduct at an elite medical institute: the role of competing institutional logics and fragmented control, *Research Policy*, 48, 428–443.

27. Macchiarini's private life was equally deceitful. An article in *Vanity Fair* in January 2016 recounted how he began an affair with an NBC TV producer who was making a documentary about him. They became engaged, and Macchiarini claimed that the Pope would officiate at the wedding, while Bill Clinton and President Obama would be in attendance. Alas, it turned out that none of these dignitaries had ever heard of him, and that he had already been married for thirty years. See www.vanityfair.com/news/2016/01/celebrity-surgeon-nbc-news-producer-scam, accessed 16 August 2018.

28. Hussinger, K., and Pellens, M. (2019) Guilt by association: how scientific misconduct harms prior collaborators, *Research Policy*, 48, 516–530.

29. See www.icmje.org/recommendations/browse/publishing-and-editorial-issues/scientific-misconduct-expressions-of-concern-and-retraction.html, accessed 7 August 2018.

30. See Stroebe et al., 2012, p. 676.

31. Nuzzo, R. (2015) Fooling ourselves, *Nature*, 526, 182–185. The quotation is on p. 183.

32. Antonakis, J. (2017) On doing better science: from thrill of discovery to policy implications, *Leadership Quarterly*, 28, 5–21. The quotation is on p. 7.

33. Hall, J., and Martin, B. (2019) Towards a taxonomy of research misconduct: the case of business school research, *Research Policy*, 48, 414–427.

34. See www.icmje.org/recommendations/browse/publishing-and-editorial-issues/scientific-misconduct-expressions-of-concern-and-retraction.html, accessed 24 August 2018.

35. Hoover, G., and Hopp, C. (2017) What crisis? Taking stock of management researchers' experiences with and views of scholarly misconduct, CESifo Working Papers, https://ideas.repec.org/p/ces/ceswps/_6611.html, accessed 1 September 2017.

36. Wicherts, J., Borsboom, D., Kats, J., and Molenaar, D. (2006) The poor availability of psychological research data for reanalysis, *American Psychologist*, 61, 726–728.

37. For an example, see Gabriel, A., and Wessel, J. (2013) A step too far? Why publishing raw datasets may hinder data collection, *Industrial and Organizational Psychology*, 287–290.

38. Ben-Yehuda, N., and Oliver-Lumerman, A. (2017) *Fraud and Misconduct in Research*, Ann Arbor: University of Michigan Press, p. 94.

39. Ziliak, S., and McCloskey, D. (2008) *The Cult of Statistical Significance*, Ann Arbor: University of Michigan Press, p. 2.

40. Francis, G. (2012) The psychology of replication and replication in psychology, *Perspectives on Psychological Science*, 7, 585–594.

41. Schwab, A., and Starbuck, W. (2017) A call for openness in research reporting: how to turn covert practices into helpful tools, *Academy of Management Learning and Education*, 16, 125–141. The quotation is on p. 131.

42. Resnik, D., Rasmussen, L., and Kissling, G. (2015) An international study of research misconduct policies, *Accountability in Research*, 22, 249–266.

43. House of Commons Science and Technology Committee (2018) *Research Integrity: Sixth Report of Session 2017–19*, 11 July, London: House of Commons.

44. Rastrollo, M., Schulze, M., Ruiz-Canela, M., and Martinez-Gonzalez, M. (2013) Financial conflicts of interest and reporting bias regarding the association between sugar-sweetened beverages and weight gain: a systematic review of systematic reviews, *PLOS Medicine*, 10, e1001578, DOI: 10.1371/journal.pmed.1001578.

45. Carrick-Hagenbarth, J., and Epstein, G. (2012) Dangerous interconnectedness: economists' conflicts of interest, ideology and financial crisis, *Cambridge Journal of Economics*, 36, 43–63.

46. See the full statement at www.aeaweb.org/aea_journals/AEA_Disclosure_Policy.pdf., accessed 29 January 2016.

47. Broad, W., and Wade, N. (1982) *Betrayers of the Truth: Fraud and Deceit in the Halls of Science*, New York: Simon and Schuster.

48. Adler, N., and Hansen, H. (2012) Daring to care: scholarship that supports the courage of our convictions, *Journal of Management Inquiry*, 21, 128–139.

CHAPTER 6

1. See http://aom.org/Publications/AMJ/Information-for-Contributors.aspx, accessed 5 August 2018.

2. Sutherland, J. (1975) *Systems Analysis, Administration and Architecture*, New York: Van Nostrand, p. 9.

3. Bacharach, S. (1989) Organizational theories: some criteria for evaluation, *Academy of Management Review*, 14, 496–515. The quotation is on p. 496.

4. Sutton, R., and Staw, B. (1995) What theory is not, *Administrative Science Quarterly*, 40, 371–384. The quotation is on p. 378.

5. Campbell, J. (1990) The role of theory in industrial and organizational psychology, in M. Dunnette and L. Hough (eds.) *Handbook of Industrial and Organizational Psychology* (volume 1), Palo Alto, CA: Consulting Psychologists Press, pp. 39–74. The quotation is on p. 65.

6. Corley, K., and Gioia, D. (2011) Building theory about theory building: what constitutes a theoretical contribution? *Academy of Management Review*, 36, 12–32. The quotation is on p. 12.

7. King, A., and Lepak, D. (2011) Editors' comments – myth busting – what we hear and what we've learned about *AMR*, *Academy of Management Review*, 36, 207–214. The quotation is on p. 209.

8. Tilcsik, A. (2014) Imprint–environment fit and performance: how organizational munificence at the time of hire affects subsequent job performance, *Administrative Science Quarterly*, 59, 639–668. The quotation is on p. 639.
9. Billig, M. (2013) *Learn to Write Badly: How to Succeed in the Social Sciences*, Cambridge: Cambridge University Press, p. 51.
10. Van Maanen, J. (1995) Style as theory, *Organization Science*, 6, 133–143. The quotation is on p. 139.
11. Weick, K. (1989) Theory construction as disciplined imagination, *Academy of Management Review*, 14, 516–531. The quotation is on p. 516. The following quotation refers, of course, directly to his paper's title.
12. Hambrick, D. (2007) The field of management's devotion to theory: too much of a good thing? *Academy of Management Journal*, 50, 1346–1352. The following quotation is on p. 1346.
13. Davis, G. (2010) Do theories of organizations progress? *Organizational Research Methods*, 13, 690–709. The following quotation is on p. 707.
14. See Hambrick, 2007, p. 1348.
15. Leavitt, K., Mitchell, T., and Peterson, J. (2010) Theory pruning: strategies to reduce our dense theoretical landscape, *Organizational Research Methods*, 10, 644–667. The quotation is on p. 647.
16. Colquitt, J., and Zapata-Phelan, C. (2007) Trends in theory building and theory testing: a five-decade study of the *Academy of Management Journal*, *Academy of Management Journal*, 50, 1281–1303.
17. Kacmar, K., and Whitfield, J. (2000) An additional rating method for journal articles in the field of management, *Organizational Research Methods*, 3, 392–406.
18. For an insightful analysis of this, see Cornelissen, J. (2017) Preserving theoretical divergence in management research: why the explanatory power of qualitative research should be harnessed rather than suppressed, *Journal of Management Studies*, 54, 368–383.
19. Edwards, J., and Berry, J. (2010) The presence of something or the absence of nothing: increasing theoretical precision in management research, *Organizational Research Methods*, 13, 668–689. The quotation is on p. 670.
20. See Hofstede, G. (1980) *Culture's Consequences: International Differences in Work-Related Values*, London: Sage; and Hofstede G., Hofstede, G.J., and Minkov, M. (2010) *Cultures and Organizations:*

Software of the Mind – Intercultural Cooperation and Its Importance for Survival, New York: McGraw-Hill.

21. McSweeney, B. (2002) Hofstede's model of national culture differences and their consequences: a triumph of faith – a failure of analysis, *Human Relations*, 55, 89–118. The quotation is on p. 92.

22. For example, see Hofstede, G. (1998) Attitudes, values and organizational culture: disentangling the concepts, *Organization Studies*, 19, 477–492. The quotation is on p. 480.

23. Google Scholar tabulates published research and the number of citations that individual academic papers, books, research theses and other publications receive. The h-index was invented by a physicist, Jorge Hirsch. It tracks all of an academic's output, and offers a means whereby a calculation can be made of how many outputs have been cited how many times. The score obtained shows how many publications have been cited h times, which becomes an academic's h-index. Many academics now track their h-index in an obsessive fashion, since it is read as a measure of their overall professional worth.

24. Hofstede, G. (2001) *Culture's Consequences: Comparing Values, Behaviours, Institutions and Organizations across Nations* (2nd edn), London: Sage, p. 385.

25. McSweeney, B. (2002) The essentials of scholarship: a reply to Geert Hofstede, *Human Relations*, 55, 1363–1372.

26. See Bothello, J., and Roulet, T. (2018) The imposter syndrome, or the misrepresentation of self in academic life, *Journal of Management Studies*, DOI: 10.111/joms.12344.

27. Clark, T., and Wright, M. (2009) So farewell then . . . Reflections on editing the *Journal of Management Studies*, *Journal of Management Studies*, 46, 1–9. The quotation is on p. 6.

28. Ferris, G., Hochwarter, W., and Bucklet, M. (2012) Theory in the organizational sciences: how will we know it when we see it? *Organizational Psychology Review*, 2, 94–106.

29. Lindebaum, D. (2016) Critical essay: Building new management theories on sound data? The case of neuroscience, *Human Relations*, 69, 537–550. The quotation is on p. 537, and the emphasis is in the original.

30. Bloom, H. (1973) *The Anxiety of Influence: a Theory of Poetry*, Oxford: Oxford University Press.

31. Alvesson, M., and Sandberg, J. (2011) Generating research questions through problematization, *Academy of Management Review*, 36, 247–271.

32. De Rond, M., and Miller, A. (2005) Publish or perish: bane or boon of academic life? *Journal of Management Inquiry*, 14, 321–329.

33. Barney, J. (2005) Where does inequality come from? The personal and intellectual roots of resource-based theory, in K. Smith and M. Hitt (eds.) *Great Minds in Management*, Oxford: Oxford University Press, pp. 280–303. The quotation is on pp. 296–297.

34. Alvesson, M., and Gabriel, Y. (2013) Beyond formulaic research: in praise of greater diversity in organizational research and publications, *Academy of Management Learning and Education*, 12, 245–263.

35. See Alvesson and Gabriel, 2013, p. 248.

36. Mills, C. (1959) *The Sociological Imagination*, Oxford: Oxford University Press. The quotations are on pp. 26 and 33 respectively.

37. Grey, C., and Sinclair, A. (2006) Writing differently, *Organization*, 13, 443–453. The quotation is on p. 445.

38. Chia, R., and Holt, R. (2006) Strategy as practical coping: a Heideggerian perspective, *Organization Studies*, 27, 635–655. The quotations are on pp. 635 and 645 respectively.

39. See Billig, 2013, p. 4.

40. See www.openculture.com/2013/06/noam_chomsky_slams_zizek_and_lacan_empty_posturing.html, accessed 23 July 2018.

41. Contu, A., Driver, M., and Jones, C. (2010) Jacques Lacan with organization studies, *Organization*, 307–315. The quotation is on pp. 307–308.

42. Gross, P., and Levitt, N. (1994) *Higher Superstition: the Academic Left and its Quarrels with Science*, Baltimore: Johns Hopkins University Press, p. 73.

43. Vidaillet, B., and Gamot, G. (2015) Working and resisting when one's workplace is under threat of being shut down: a Lacanian perspective, *Organization Studies*, 36, 987–1011.

44. Lacan, J. (1970) Of structure as an inmixing of an otherness prerequisite to any subject whatever, in R. Macksey and E. Donato (eds.) *The Language of Criticism and the Sciences of Man*, Baltimore: Johns Hopkins University Press, 186–200. The edited quotation is on pp. 190–193.

45. Sokal, A., and Bricmont, J. (1997) *Intellectual Impostures*, London: Profile Books. The quotation is on p. 29.

46. See Orwell, G. (1946) Politics and the English language, *Horizon*, April, www.orwell.ru/library/essays/politics/english/e_polit/, accessed 25 July 2018.

47. See www.denisdutton.com/bad_writing.htm, accessed 7 August 2018.

48. See www.shmoop.com/judith-butler/writing-style-report.html, accessed 7 August 2018.

49. See https://archive.nytimes.com/query.nytimes.com/gst/fullpage-950C E5D61531F933A15750C0A96F958260.html, accessed 7 August 2018.

50. See https://genius.com/Judith-butler-gender-trouble-1999-preface-annotated, accessed 10 August 2018.

51. Pinker, S. (2014) *The Sense of Style: the Thinking Person's Guide to Writing in the 21st Century*, London: Penguin, p. 36.

52. See http://faculty.georgetown.edu/irvinem/theory/Nussbaum-Butler-Critique-NR-2-99.pdf, accessed 10 August 2018.

53. Pinker, S. (2014) Why academics stink at writing, *Chronicle Review*, 26 September, https://stevenpinker.com/files/pinker/files/why_academics_stink_at_writing.pdf, accessed 23 July 2018.

54. Weick, K. (1993) The collapse of sensemaking in organizations: the Mann Gulch disaster, *Administrative Science Quarterly*, 38, 628–652.

55. Maclean, N. (1992) *Young Men and Fire*, Chicago: University of Chicago Press.

56. Weick, 1993, p. 633.

57. Ibid., p. 628.

58. Starbuck, W. (1992) Learning by knowledge-intensive firms, *Journal of Management Studies*, 29, 713–740.

59. Ibid., p. 713.

60. Ibid., p. 714.

61. Ibid., p. 715.

62. Ibid., p. 719.

63. Ibid., p. 738.

64. Walsh, J. (2011) Embracing the sacred in our secular scholarly world, *Academy of Management Review*, 36, 215–234. The quotation is on p. 218.

65. Barney, J. (1991) Firm resources and sustained competitive advantage, *Journal of Management*, 17, 99–120.

66. See Barney, J. (2005) Where does inequality come from? The personal and intellectual roots of resource-based theory, in K. Smith and M. Hitt (eds.) *Great Minds in Management*, Oxford: Oxford University Press, pp. 280–303.

67. Pfeffer, J. (2007) A modest proposal: how we might change the process and product of management research, *Academy of Management Journal*, 50, 1334–1345. The quotation is on p. 1338.

68. Mintzberg, H. (2005) Developing theory about theory, in K. Smith and M. Hitt (eds.) *Great Minds in Management*, Oxford: Oxford University Press, pp. 355–372. The quotations are on pp. 366 and 369.

69. Darwin, C. (1859) *On the Origin of Species by Means of Natural Selection*, London: John Murray, p. 425.

CHAPTER 7

1. For a comprehensive overview of research on authenticity, see Lehman, D., O'Connor, K., Kovacs, B., and Newman, G. (2019) Authenticity, *Academy of Management Annals*, 2019, 13, 1–42.

2. These are as follows:Peterson, S., Walumbwa, F., Avolio, B., and Hannah, S. (2012) The relationship between authentic leadership and follower job performance: the mediating role of follower positivity in extreme contexts, *Leadership Quarterly*, 23, 502–516.Walumbwa, F., Luthans, F., Avey, J., and Oke, A. (2011) Authentically leading groups: the mediating role of collective psychological capital and trust, *Journal of Organizational Behavior*, 32, 4–24.Walumbwa, F., Wang, P., Wang, H., Schaubroeck, J., and Avolio, B. (2010) Psychological processes linking authentic leadership to follower behaviors, *Leadership Quarterly*, 21, 901–914.

3. Walumbwa, F., Avolio, B., Gardner, W., Wernsing, T., and Peterson, S. (2008) Authentic leadership: development and validation of a theory-based measure, *Journal of Management*, 34, 89–126.

4. See https://pubpeer.com/publications/1E79BA4AA94EB722491B14AE871 B0F, accessed 15 May 2018.

5. Avolio, B., Wernsing, T., and Gardner, W. (2018) Revisiting the development and validation of the Authentic Leadership Questionnaire: analytical clarifications, *Journal of Management*, 44, 399–411.

6. Burns, J. (1978) *Leadership*, New York: Harper and Row. The following quotations are on pp. 425 and 426 respectively.

7. Ciulla, J. (1995) Leadership ethics: mapping the territory, *Business Ethics Quarterly*, 5, 5–28.

8. See Burns, 1978, p. 395.

9. Bass, B., and Steidlmeier, P. (1999) Ethics, character and authentic transformational leadership, *Leadership Quarterly*, 10, 181–217.

10. Tourish, D. (2013) *The Dark Side of Transformational Leadership: a Critical Perspective*, London: Routledge.

11. See Walumbwa et al., 2008, p. 94.

12. Luthans, F., and Avolio, B. (2003) Authentic leadership: a positive developmental approach, in K. Cameron, J. Dutton and R. Quinn (eds.) *Positive Organizational Scholarship*, San Francisco: Barrett-Koehler, pp. 241–261. The following quotations are on pp. 242 and p. 245 respectively.

13. Collinson, D. (2012) Prozac leadership and the limits of positive thinking, *Leadership*, 8, 87–102.

14. Walumbwa, F., and Wernsing, T. (2013) From transactional and transformational leadership to authentic leadership, in M. Rumsey (ed.) *The Oxford Handbook of Leadership*, Oxford: Oxford University Press, pp. 392–400.

15. The publications cited in this table are as follows:Bhindi, N., and Duignan, P. (1997) Leadership for a new century: authenticity, intentionality, spirituality, and sensibility, *Educational Management and Administration*, 25, 117–132.George, W. (2003) *Authentic Leadership: Rediscovering the Secrets to Creating Lasting Value*, San Francisco: Jossey-Bass.Luthans, F., and Avolio, B. (2003) Authentic leadership: a positive developmental approach, in K. Cameron, J. Dutton and R. Quinn (eds.) *Positive Organizational Scholarship*, San Francisco: Barrett-Koehler, pp. 241–261.May, D., Chan, A., Hodges, T., and Avolio, B. (2003) Developing the moral component of authentic leadership, *Organizational Dynamics*, 32, 247–260.Shamir, B., and Eilam, G. (2005) What's your story? A life-stories approach to authentic leadership development, *Leadership Quarterly*, 16, 395–417.Walumbwa, F., Avolio, B., Gardner, W., Wernsing, T., and Peterson, S. (2008) Authentic leadership: development and validation of a theory-based measure, *Journal of Management*, 34, 89–126.Whitehead, G. (2009) Adolescent leadership development: building a case for an authenticity framework, *Educational Management Administration and Leadership*, 37, 847–872.

16. Leroy, H., Anseel, F., Gardner, W., and Sels, L. (2015) Authentic leadership, authentic followership, basic need satisfaction, and work-role performance: across-level study, *Journal of Management*, 41, 1677–1697.

17. Yagil, D., and Medler-Liraz, H. (2014) Feel free, be yourself: authentic leadership, emotional expression, and employee authenticity, *Journal of Leadership and Organizational Studies*, 21, 59–70.

18. Hannah, S., Avolio, B., and Walumbwa, F. (2011) Relationships between authentic leadership, moral courage, and ethical and prosocial behaviors, *Business Ethics Quarterly*, 21, 555–578.

19. Walumbwa, F., Christensen, A., and Hailey, F. (2011) Authentic leadership and the knowledge economy: sustaining motivation and trust among knowledge workers, *Organizational Dynamics*, 40, 110–118.

20. Hsieh, C., and Wang, D., (2015) Does supervisor-perceived authentic leadership influence employee work engagement through employee-perceived authentic leadership and employee trust? *International Journal of Human Resource Management*, 26, 2329–2348. The quotation is on p. 2341.

21. Avolio, B., Gardner, W., Walumbwa, F., Luthans, F., and May, D. (2004) Unlocking the mask: a look at the process by which authentic leaders impact follower attitudes and behaviors, *Leadership Quarterly*, 15, 801–823. The quotation is on p. 802.

22. Contu, A. (2018) Conflict and organization studies, *Organization Studies*, DOI: 10.1177/0170840617747916.

23 See www.exed.hbs.edu/programs/ald/Pages/default.aspx, accessed 10 May 2018.

24. Spector, B. (2014) Flawed from the 'get-go': Lee Iacocca and the origins of transformational leadership, *Leadership*, 10, 361–379.

25. See George, B., Sims, P., McLean, A., and Mayer, D. (2007) Discovering your authentic leadership, *Harvard Business Review*, February, 129–138; and George, W. (2003) *Authentic Leadership: Rediscovering the Secrets to Creating Lasting Value*, San Francisco: Jossey-Bass.

26. See George, 2003, p. xxiii.

27. Erickson, R. (1995) The importance of authenticity for self and society, *Symbolic Interaction*, 18, 121–144. The quotation is on p. 121.

28. Gardner, W., Avolio, B., and Luthans., F (2005) 'Can you see the real me?' A self-based model of authentic leader and follower development,

Leadership Quarterly, 16, 343–372. The quotation is on pp. 355–357, while the following quotation is on p. 357.

29. Heidegger, M. (1953) *Being and Time*, trans. Joan Stambaugh, Albany, NY: State University of New York Press.
30. Goffman, E. (1959) *The Presentation of Self in Everyday Life*, New York: Anchor, pp. 81–82.
31. Pfeffer, J. (2015) *Leadership BS: Fixing Workplaces and Careers One Truth at a Time*, New York: Harper Collins.
32. Ford, J., and Harding, N. (2011) The impossibility of the 'true self' of authentic leadership, *Leadership*, 7, 463–479. The quotation is on pp. 465–466.
33. Fairhurst, G. (2007) *Discursive Leadership*, London: Sage.
34. Dumaine, B. (1993) America's toughest bosses: seven CEOs who make your top dog look like a pussycat, *Fortune*, 18 October, 38–50.
35. See Fairhurst, 2007, p. 104.
36. Liu, H., Cutcher, L., and Grant, D. (2017) Authentic leadership in context: an analysis of banking CEO narratives during the global financial crisis, *Human Relations*, 70, 694–724. The quotation is on p. 714.
37. Lawler, J., and Ashman, I. (2012) Theorizing leadership authenticity: a Sartrean perspective, *Leadership*, 8, 327–344. The quotation is on p. 329.
38. See Pfeffer, 2015, p. 89.
39. Algera, P., and Lips-Wiersma, M. (2012) Radical authentic leadership: co-creating the conditions under which all members of the organization can be authentic, *Leadership Quarterly*, 23, 118–131.
40. See Ford and Harding, 2011, p. 476.
41. Gardner, R. (2017) Authentic leadership through an ethical prism, *Advances in Developing Human Resources*, 19, 467–477.
42. Spoelstra, S., Butler, N., and Delaney, H. (2016) Never let an academic crisis go to waste: leadership studies in the wake of journal retractions, *Leadership*, 12, 383–397. The quotation is on p. 392.
43. The publications from which these are derived are as follows:Clapp-Smith, R., Vogelgesang, G., and Avey, J. (2009) Authentic leadership and positive psychological capital: the mediating role of trust at the group level of analysis, *Journal of Leadership and Organizational Studies*, 15, 227–240.Hsieh, C., and Wang, D., (2015) Does supervisor-perceived authentic leadership influence employee work engagement through employee-perceived authentic leadership and employee trust?

International Journal of Human Resource Management, 26, 2329–2348.
Leroy, H., Anseel, F., Gardner, W., and Sels, L. (2015) Authentic
leadership, authentic followership, basic need satisfaction, and work-role
performance: across-level study, *Journal of Management*, 41, 1677–1697.
Leroy, H., Palanski, M., Simons, T. (2012) Authentic leadership and
behavioural integrity as drivers of follower commitment and performance,
Journal of Business Ethics, 107, 255–264.Weiss, M., Razinskas, S.,
Backman, J., and Hoegl, M. (2018) Authentic leadership and leaders'
mental well-being: an experience sampling survey, *Leadership Quarterly*,
29, 309–321.
44. Gould, S. (1996) *Full House: the Spread of Excellence from Plato to
Darwin*, New York: Harmony Books, p. 30.
45. Smolovic-Jones, O., and Grint, K. (2013) Essay: Authentic leadership and
history, in D. Ladkin and C. Spiller (eds.) *Authentic Leadership: Clashes,
Convergences and Coalescences*, London: Edward Elgar, pp. 21–38.
The quotation is on p. 27.
46. Rosenzweig, P. (2008) *The Halo Effect: How Managers Let Themselves be
Deceived*, New York: Simon and Schuster.
47. Arnulf, J., Mathisen, J., and Haerem, T. (2012) Heroic illusions in football
teams: rationality, decision making and noise–signal ratio in the firing of
football managers, *Leadership*, 8, 169–185.
48. See Rosenzweig, 2008, pp. 36–37.
49. Ibid., p. 47.
50. Alvesson, M., and Karreman, D. (2016) Intellectual failure and ideological
success in organization studies: the case of transformational leadership,
Journal of Management Inquiry, 25, 139–152. Both quotations are on p. 145.
51. Walumbwa, F., Wang, P., Wang, H., Schaubroeck, J., and Avolio, B. (2010)
Psychological processes linking authentic leadership to follower
behaviors, *Leadership Quarterly*, 21, 901–914.
52. Walumbwa et al., 2010, p. 901.
53. Ibid., p. 905.
54. Ibid., p. 910.
55. McSweeney, B. (2018) Avoiding preordained conclusions in qualitative
case studies of causality – three defences against confirmation bias
[unpublished manuscript].
56. Walumbwa et al., 2010, p. 911.

57. Steffens, N., Mols, F., Haslam, A., and Okimoto, T. (2016) True to what *We* stand for: championing collective interests as a path to authentic leadership, *Leadership Quarterly*, 27, 726–744. The quotation is on p. 726.
58. See Walumbwa et al., 2008, p. 201.
59. Fredrickson, B., and Losada, M. (2005) Positive affect and the complex dynamics of human flourishing, *American Psychologist*, 678–686.
60. See Brown, N., Sokal, A., and Friedman, H. (2013) The complex dynamics of wishful thinking: the critical positivity ratio, *American Psychologist*, December, 801–813; and Brown, N., Sokal, A., and Friedman, H. (2014) The persistence of wishful thinking, *American Psychologist*, September, 629–632.
61. Fredrickson, B. (2009) *Positivity*, New York: Crown Publishing.
62. Banks, G., McCauley, K., Gardner, W., Guler, C. (2016) A meta-analytic review of authentic and transformational leadership: a test for redundancy, *Leadership Quarterly*, 27, 634–652. The quotation is on p. 634.
63. Hoch, J., Bommer, W., Dulebohn, J., and Wu, D. (2018) Do ethical, authentic, and servant leadership explain variance above and beyond transformational leadership? A meta-analysis, *Journal of Management*, 44, 501–529. The quotation is on p. 512.
64. Avolio, B., Gardner, W., and Walumbwa, F. (2005) Preface, in W. Gardner, B. Avolio, and F. Walumbwa (eds.) *Authentic Leadership Theory and Practice: Origins, Effects and Development*, Oxford: Elsevier, pp. xxi–xxix. The quotation is on p. xxii.
65. Avolio, B. (2013) Foreword, in D. Ladkin and C. Spiller (eds.) *Authentic Leadership: Clashes, Convergences and Coalescences*, London: Edward Elgar, pp. xxii–xxvii. The quotation is on p. xxvi.
66. Antonakis, J., Bendahan, S., Jacquart, P., and Lalive, R. (2010) On making causal claims: a review and recommendations, *Leadership Quarterly*, 21, 1086–1120. The quotation is on p. 1086.
67. Feynman, R. (1988) *'What do You Care What Other People Think!' Further Adventures of a Curious Character*, New York: W. Norton, p. 218.

CHAPTER 8

1. Some of the material in this chapter has been adapted from the following: Tourish, D. (2015) Evidence-based management: some pros, cons and alternatives, in A. Wilkinson, K. Townsend and G. Suder (eds.) *Handbook*

of Research on Managing Managers, London: Edward Elgar, pp. 141–160; and Tourish, D. (2013) 'Evidence based management', or 'Evidence oriented organising'? A critical realist perspective, *Organization*, 20, 173–192.

2. Rousseau, D. (2006) Is there such a thing as 'evidence-based management'? *Academy of Management Review*, 31, 256–269.

3. Barends, E., Rousseau, D., and Briner, R. (2014) *Evidence-Based Management: the Basic Principles*, Amsterdam: Center for Evidence-Based Management.

4. Learmonth, M. (2008) Evidence-based management: a backlash against pluralism in organizational studies, *Organization*, 15, 283–291.

5. Lawler, E. (2007) Why HR practices are not evidence-based, *Academy of Management Journal*, 50, 1033–1036. The quotation is on p. 1033.

6. Tourish, D., Paulsen, N., Hobman, E., and Bordia, P. (2004) The downsides of downsizing: communication processes and information needs in the aftermath of a workforce reduction strategy, *Management Communication Quarterly*, 17, 485–516.

7. Evans, S., and Tourish, D. (2017) Agency theory and performance appraisal: how bad theory damages learning and contributes to bad management practice, *Management Learning*, 48, 271–291

8. Rousseau, D. (2007) A sticky, leveraging, and scalable strategy for high-quality connections between organizational practice and science, *Academy of Management Journal*, 50, 1037–1042. The quotation is on p. 1038.

9. For an example, see Starkey, K., Hatchuel, A., and Tempest, S. (2009) Management research and the new logics of discovery and engagement, *Journal of Management Studies*, 46, 547–558.

10. Briner, R., and Walshe, N. (2014) From passively received wisdom to actively constructed knowledge: teaching systematic review skills as a foundation of evidence-based management, *Academy of Management Learning and Education*, 13, 415–432.

11. Rousseau, D., Manning, J., and Denyer, D. (2008) Evidence in management and organization science: assembling the field's full weight of scientific knowledge through syntheses, *Academy of Management Annals*, 2, 475–515. The quotation is on p. 476.

12. Pfeffer, J. (1998) Six dangerous myths about pay, *Harvard Business Review*, 76, 109–119.

13. Rynes, S., Gerhart, B., and Parks, L. (2005) Personnel psychology: performance evaluation and pay-for-performance, *Annual Review of Psychology*, 56, 571–600.

14. Guest, D., Paauwe, J., and Wright, P. (eds.) (2012) *HRM and Performance: Achievements and Challenges*, London: John Wiley & Sons, p. xx.

15. Rousseau, D. (2018) Making evidence-based decisions in an uncertain world, *Organizational Dynamics*, 14, 135–146.

16. Cooper, C., Kong, D., and Crossley, C. (2018) Leader humor as an interpersonal resource: integrating three theoretical perspectives, *Academy of Management Journal*, 61, 769–796.

17. See the following for more inspiring David Brent quotations: www.nme.com/photos/david-brent-s-best-quotes-21-of-his-most-cringe-inducing-lines-from-the-office-1419406#6RiAI2LhwhOEvY55.99, accessed 17 September 2018.

18. See Rousseau et al., 2008, p. 481.

19. Morrell, K., and Learmonth, M. (2017) Evidence-based management, in A. Wilkinson, M. Lounsbury, and S. Armstrong (eds.) *The Oxford Handbook of Management*, Oxford: Oxford University Press, pp. 419–436.

20. Hewison, A. (2004) Evidence-based management in the NHS: is it possible? *Journal of Health Organization and Management*, 18, 336–348.

21. Mingers, J. (2015) Helping business schools engage with real problems: the contribution of critical realism and systems thinking, *European Journal of Operational Research*, 242, 316–331. The quotation is on p. 321.

22. Rousseau, D., and McCarthy, S. (2007) Educating managers from an evidence-based perspective, *Academy of Management Learning and Education*, 6, 84–101.

23. Ghoshal, S. (2005) Bad management theories are destroying good management practices, *Academy of Management Learning and Education*, 4, 75–91.

24. Pfeffer, J. (2005) Why do bad management theories persist? A comment on Ghoshal, *Academy of Management Learning and Education*, 4: 96–100.

25. Evans, S., and Tourish, D. (2017) Agency theory and performance appraisal: how bad theory damages learning and contributes to bad management practice, *Management Learning*, 48, 271–291.

26. Pfeffer. J., and Sutton, R. (2006) *Hard Facts, Dangerous Half-Truths and Total Nonsense: Profiting from Evidence-Based Management*, Boston: Harvard Business School Press. For the discussion of it that took place in *AMLE*, see Book and Resource Reviews, *Academy of Management Learning and Education* (2007), 6, 139–152.

27. Learmonth, M. (2009) Rhetoric and evidence: the case of evidence based management, in D. Buchanan and A. Bryman (eds.) *The SAGE Handbook of Organizational Research Methods*, London: Sage, pp. 93–107. The quotation is on p. 95.

28. Bloom, P., and Rhodes, C. (2018) *CEO Society: the Corporate Takeover of Everyday Life*, London: Zed Books.

29. Tsang, E., and Kwan, K. (1999) Replication and theory development in organisational science: a critical realist perspective, *Academy of Management Review*, 24, 759–780.

30. Starbuck, W. (2004) Why I stopped trying to understand the real world, *Organization Studies*, 25, 1233–1254. The quotation is on p. 1245.

31. Tsui, A. (2007) From homogenization to pluralism: international management research in the academy and beyond, *Academy of Management Journal*, 50, 1353–1364.

32. Lord, C., Ross, L., and Lepper, M. (1979) Biased assimilation and attitude polarization: the effects of prior theories on subsequently considered evidence, *Journal of Personality and Social Psychology*, 37, 2098–2019.

33. Rynes, S., Giluk, T., and Brown, K. (2007) The very separate worlds of academic and practitioner periodicals in human resource management: implications for evidence-based management, *Academy of Management Journal*, 50, 987–1008.

34. Rynes, S., Colbert, A., and O'Boyle, E. (2018) When the 'best available evidence' doesn't win: how doubts about science and scientists threaten the future of evidence-based management, *Journal of Management*, 44, 2995–3010.

35. Locke, E., and Latham, G. (2009) Has goal setting gone wild, or have its attackers abandoned good scholarship? *Academy of Management Perspectives*, 23, 17–23.

36. Ordonez, L., Schweitzer, M., Galinsky, A., and Bazerman, M. (2009a) Goals gone wild: the systematic side effects of overprescribing goal setting, *Academy of Management Perspectives*, 23, 6–16. The quotation is on p. 6.

37. Ordonez, L., Schweitzer, M., Galinsky, A., and Bazerman, M. (2009b) On good scholarship, goal setting and scholars gone wild, *Academy of Management Perspectives*, 23, 82–87. The quotation is on p. 82.

38. Latham, G., and Locke, E. (2009) Science and ethics: what should count as evidence against the use of goal setting? *Academy of Management Perspectives*, 23, 88–91.

39. Adams, R., Smart, P., and Huff, A. (2017) Shades of grey: guidelines for working with the grey literature in systematic reviews for management and organizational studies, *International Journal of Management Reviews*, 19, 432–454.

40. Weick, K. (2001) Gapping the relevance bridge: fashion meets fundamentals in management research, *British Journal of Management*, 12, special issue, s71–s75.

41. Learmonth, M., and Harding, N. (2006) Evidence-based management: the very idea, *Public Administration*, 84, 245–266.

42. Applebaum, E., and Batt, R. (2014) *Private Equity at Work: When Wall Street Manages Main Street*, New York: Russell Sage Foundation.

43. Tourish, D., and Vatcha, N. (2005) Charismatic leadership and corporate cultism at Enron: the elimination of dissent, the promotion of conformity and organizational collapse, *Leadership*, 1, 455–480.

44. Hope, T. (2004) Pretend it works: evidence and governance in the evaluation of the Reducing Burglary Initiative, *Criminal Justice*, 4, 287–308.

45. Flyvbjerg, B. (1998) *Rationality and Power: Democracy in Practice*, Chicago: University of Chicago Press.

46. Tenbensel, T. (2004) Does more evidence lead to better policy? The implications of explicit priority-setting in New Zealand's health policy for evidence-based policy, *Policy Studies*, 25, 189–207.

47. Cohen, M., March, J., and Olsen, J. (1972) A garbage can model of organizational choice, *Administrative Science Quarterly*, 17, 1–25.

48. Staw, B. (1976) Knee deep in the big muddy: a study of escalating commitment to a chosen course of action, *Organizational Behavior and Human Performance*, 16, 405–433.

49. Morrell, K., and Learmonth, M. (2015) Against evidence-based management, for management learning, *Academy of Management Learning and Education*, 14, 520–533. The quotation is on p. 524.

50. Briner, R., Denyer, D., and Rousseau, D. (2009) Evidence-based management: concept cleanup time? *Academy of Management Perspectives*, 23, 19–32. The quotation is on p. 19.

51. Pfeffer, J. (2007) A modest proposal: how we might change the process and product of managerial research, *Academy of Management Journal*, 50, 1334–1345.

52. Bartunek, J. (2007) Academic–practitioner collaboration need not require joint or relevant research: toward a relational scholarship of integration, *Academy of Management Journal*, 50, 1323–1333.

53. Barger, P., and Grandey, A. (2006) Service with a smile and encounter satisfaction: emotional contagion and appraisal mechanisms, *Academy of Management Journal*, 49, 1229–1238. The quotation is on p. 1236.

54. See Learmonth, 2008, p. 284.

55. Rousseau, D. (2012) Envisioning evidence-based management, in D. Rousseau (ed.) *The Oxford Handbook of Evidence-Based Management*, Oxford: Oxford University Press, pp. 3–24.

56. Morrell, K., Learmonth, M., and Heracleous, L. (2015) An archaeological critique of 'evidence-based management': one digression after another, *British Journal of Management*, 26, 529–543.

57. Davis, G. (2015) What is organizational research for? *Administrative Science Quarterly*, 60, 179–188. The quotation is on pp. 179–180.

58. Weick, K. (2016) 60th anniversary essay: Constrained comprehending: the experience of organizational inquiry, *Administrative Science Quarterly*, 61, 333–346.

59. Clegg, S. (2009) Managing power in organizations: the hidden history of its constitution, in S. Clegg and M. Hauggaard (eds.) *The SAGE Handbook of Power*, London: Sage, pp. 310–331.

60. Mingers, J. (2000) What is it to be critical? Teaching a critical approach to management undergraduates, *Management Learning*, 31, 219–237.

61. Fairclough, N. (2005) Discourse analysis in organization studies: the case for critical realism, *Organization Studies*, 26, 915–939. The quotation is on p. 922.

62. See the following link for an account of one such conference, held in the UK in 2018: www.theguardian.com/science/blog/2018/may/02/the-universe-is-an-egg-and-the-moon-isnt-real-notes-from-a-flat-earth-conference.

63. Bhaskar, R. (1998) General introduction, in M. Archer, R. Bhaskar, A. Collier, T. Lawson and A. Norrie (eds.) *Critical Realism: Essential Readings*, London: Routledge, pp. 3–16. The quotation is on p. 14.

64. Grey, C. (2001) Re-imaging relevance: a response to Starkey and Madan, *British Journal of Management*, 12, special issue, s27–s32. The quotation is on p. s30.

65. See Morrell et al., 2015, p. 530.

CHAPTER 9

1. Acemoglu, D., and Robinson, J. (2012) *Why Nations Fail: the Origins of Power, Prosperity, and Poverty*, New York: Random House Digital, p. 182.

2. McCloskey, D. (2016) *Bourgeois Equality: How Ideas, Not Capital or Institutions, Enriched the World*, Chicago: University of Chicago Press. The following quotation is on p. 7.

3. Ridley, M. (2015) *The Evolution of Everything*, London: Fourth Estate.

4. Țițan, A. (2015) The efficient market hypothesis: review of specialised literature and empirical research, *Procedia Economics and Finance*, 32, 442–449.

5. International Labor Organization (2017) *Global Wage Report 2016/17: Wage Inequality in the Workplace*, Geneva: International Labor Organization.

6. International Labor Organization (2015) *World Employment and Social Outlook: the Changing Nature of Jobs*, Geneva: International Labor Organization.

7. Orwell, G. (2001) *The Road to Wigan Pier*, London: Penguin Classics. The following quotation is on p. 182.

8. Twain, M. (1876) *The Adventures of Tom Sawyer*, New York: American Publishing Company, pp. 11–14.

9. Trist, E., and Bamforth, K. (1951) Some social and psychological consequences of the longwall method of coal-getting: an examination of the psychological situation and defences of a work group in relation to the social structure and technological content of the work system, *Human Relations*, 4, 3–38. The quotations are on pp. 6–7 and 10 respectively.

10. See Orwell, 2001, p. 187.

11. Ng, M., and 139 others (2014) Global, regional, and national prevalence of overweight and obesity in children and adults during 1980–2013:

a systematic analysis for the Global Burden of Disease Study 2013, *The Lancet*, 384, 766–781.

12. Schumpeter, J. (1942) *Capitalism, Socialism and Democracy*, New York: Harper and Brothers.

13. Kotler, P. (2012) *Principles of Marketing*, London: Prentice Hall.

14. Schwab, K. (2016) *The Fourth Industrial Revolution*, Geneva: World Economic Forum.

15. Keynes, J. (1933) Economic possibilities for our grandchildren (1930), *Essays in Persuasion*, London: Macmillan, pp. 358–373. The quotation is on p. 3.

16. Frey, C., and Osborne, M. (2013) *The Future of Employment: How Susceptible are Jobs to Computerization?* Oxford: Oxford Martin Programme on Technology and Employment, Oxford University.

17. Lawrence, M., Roberts, C., and King, L. (2017) *Managing Automation: Employment, Inequality and Ethics in the Digital Age*, London: IPPR Commission on Economic Justice.

18. Arthur, W. (2017) Where is technology taking the economy? *McKinsey Quarterly*, October, www.mckinsey.com/business-functions/mckinsey-analytics/our-insights/where-is-technology-taking-the-economy, accessed 7 February 2018.

19. Berriman, R., and Hawksworth, J. (2017) Will robots steal our jobs? The potential impact of automation on the UK and other major economies, *UK Economic Outlook*, March, 30–47. The quotation is on p. 30.

20. Susskind, R., and Susskind, D. (2015) *The Future of the Professions: how Technology will Transform the Work of Human Experts*, Oxford: Oxford University Press. The following quotation is on p. 263.

21. Tapscott, D., and Tapscott, A. (2016) *Blockchain Revolution: how the Technology Behind Bitcoin is Changing Money, Business and the World*, New York: Random House.

22. See Lawrence et al., 2017, p. 3.

23. Nedelkoska, L., and Quintini, G. (2018) Automation, skills use and training, Organization for Economic Co-operation and Development iLibrary, www.oecd-ilibrary.org/docserver/2e2f4eea-en.pdf?expire s=1523873145&id=id&accname=guest&checksum=BA4E0D2082E128F E4FABFEC1FF5B3CB2, accessed 16 April 2018.

24. Fleming, P. (2019) Robots and organization studies: why robots might not want to steal your job, *Organization Studies*, 40, 23–38.

25. Paulsen, R. (2015) *Empty Labor: Idleness and Workplace Resistance*, Cambridge: Cambridge University Press.

26. Rothlin, P., and Werder, P. (2007) *Boreout! Overcoming Workplace Demotivation*, London: Kogan Page.

27. Harari, Y. (2015) *Homo Deus: a Brief History of Tomorrow*, London: Vintage. The quotation is on p. 375.

28. Kahenamn, D. (2011) *Thinking Fast and Slow*, London: Penguin.

29. See www.theguardian.com/technology/2017/aug/20/elon-musk-killer-ro bots-experts-outright-ban-lethal-autonomous-weapons-war, accessed 5 September 2017.

30. Pinker, S. (2011) *The Better Angels of Our Nature*, London: Allen Lane, p. 196.

31. Asimov, I., and Shulman, J. (eds.) (1988) *Isaac Asimov's Book of Science and Nature Quotations*, p. 281.

32. Dozier, R. (2002) *Why We Hate*, London: Contemporary Books. The quotation is on p. 1.

33. Pinker, 2011.

34. Pinker, S. (2018) *Enlightenment Now: the Case for Reason, Science, Humanism and Progress*, London: Allen Lane. The quotations are on p. 302.

35. Pinker, 2018, p. 302.

36. See www.bbc.co.uk/news/world-europe-41314948, accessed 16 April 2018.

37. See www.bbc.co.uk/news/business-43752226, accessed 17 August 2018.

38. Ferràs-Hernández, X. (2017) The future of management in a world of electronic brains, *Journal of Management Inquiry*, 27, 260–263.

39. Boden, M. (2016) *AI: its Nature and Future*, Oxford: Oxford University Press.

40. See extensive discussion of all these issues in Pinker, S. (1997) *How the Mind Works*, London: Penguin Books.

41. Hanson, R. (2016) *The Age of Em: Work, Love and Life when Robots Rule The Earth*, Oxford: Oxford University Press. The quotation is on p. 53.

42. Davis, G. (2016) Can an economy survive without corporations? Technology and robust organizational alternatives, *Academy of Management Perspectives*, 30, 129–140. The quotation is on p. 129.

43. Garmulewicz, A., Holweg, M., Veldhuis, H., and Yang, A. (2018) Disruptive technology as an enabler of the circular economy: what

potential does 3D printing hold? *California Management Review*, 60, 112–132.

44. Phan, P., Wright, M., and Lee, S. (2017) From the editors: Of robots, artificial intelligence, and work, *Academy of Management Perspectives*, 31, 253–255. The quotation is on p. 253.

45. See Harari, 2015, p. 379.

46. See Lawrence et al., 2017, p. 3.

47. Bregman, R. (2017) *Utopia For Realists*, London: Bloomsbury.

48. See www.wired.co.uk/article/finland-universal-basic-income-results-trial-cancelled, accessed 20 August 2018.

49. See www.ippr.org/blog/owning-the-future, accessed 7 February 2018.

50. Soete, L. (2018) Destructive creation: explaining the productivity paradox in the digital age, in M. Neufeind, J. O'Reilly and F. Ranft (eds.) *Work in the Digital Age: Challenges of the Fourth Industrial Revolution*, London: Rowman and Littlefield, pp. 29–46.

51. See Pinker, 2018, p. 119.

CHAPTER 10

1. Byington, E., and Felps, W. (2017) Solutions to the credibility crisis in management science, *Academy of Management Learning and Education*, 16, 142–162. The quotations are on pp. 143 and 147 respectively.

2. Lilienfeld, S. (2017) Psychology's replication crisis and the grant culture: righting the ship, *Perspectives on Psychological Science*, 12, 660–664. The following quotation is on p. 662.

3. Chomsky, N. (1967) The responsibility of intellectuals, *New York Review of Books*, https://chomsky.info/19670223/, accessed 5 January 2018.

4. Alvesson, M., Gabriel, Y., and Paulsen, R. (2017) *Return to Meaning: a Social Science with Something to Say*, Oxford: Oxford University Press. The quotation is on p. 85.

5. Alvesson, M., and Spicer, A. (2016) (Un)conditional surrender: why do professionals willingly comply with managerialism? *Journal of Organizational Change Management*, 29, 29–45.

6. Barker, J. (1993) Tightening the iron cage: concertive control in self-managing teams, *Administrative Science Quarterly*, 38, 408–437.

7. Marx, G. (1990) Reflections on academic success and failure: making it, forsaking it, reshaping it, in B. Berger (ed.) *Intellectual Autobiographies by*

Twenty American Sociologists, Berkeley: University of California Press, pp. 260–284.

8. Cunliffe, A. (2018) Alterity: the passion, politics and ethics of self and scholarship, *Management Learning*, 49, 8–22. The quotation is on p. 16.

9. Kerr, S. (1975) On the folly of rewarding A, while hoping for B, *Academy of Management Journal*, 18, 769–782.

10. Wright, T., Hollwitz, J., Stackman, R., de Groot, A., Baack, S., and Shay, J. (2018) 40 years (and counting): Steve Kerr reflections on the 'folly', *Journal of Management Inquiry*, 27, 309–315. The quotation is on p. 313.

11. Wright Mills, C. (1959) *The Sociological Imagination*, Oxford: Oxford University Press, p. 196.

12. Alvesson, M., and Gabriel, Y. (2013) Beyond formulaic research: in praise of greater diversity in organizational research and publications, *Academy of Management Learning and Education*, 12, 245–263.

13. Ashcraft, K., and Kuhn, T. (2018) Agential encounters: performativity and affect meet communication in the bathroom, in B. Brummans (ed.) *The Agency of Organizing: Perspectives and Case Studies*, London: Routledge, pp. 170–193. The quotation is on p. 187.

14. Davis, M. (1971) That's interesting! Towards a phenomenology of sociology and a sociology of phenomenology, *Philosophy of the Social Sciences*, 1, 309–344. The quotation is on p. 309.

15. Starbuck, W. (2010) What makes a paper influential and frequently cited? *Journal of Management Studies*, 47, 1394–1404. Both quotations are on p. 1395.

16. Barney, J. (2005) The roots of resource-based theory, in K. Smith and M. Hitt (eds.) *Great Minds In Management*, Oxford: Oxford University Press, pp. 280–303. The quotations are on p. 297.

17. Bedeian, A. (2008) Balancing authorial voice and editorial omniscience: the 'It's my paper and I'll say what I want to' versus 'Ghost-writers in the sky' minuet, in Y. Baruch, A. Konrad, H. Aguinis and W. Starbuck (eds.) *Opening the Black Box of Editorship*, Houndsmills: Palgrave Macmillan, pp. 134–142. The quotation is on p. 139.

18. LaPlaca, P., Lindgreen, A., Vanhamme, J., and Di Benedetto, A. (2018) How to revise, and revise really well, for premier academic journals, *Industrial Marketing Management*, 72, 174–180.

19. Spiegal, M. (2012) Reviewing less – progressing more, *Review of Financial Studies*, 25, 1331–1338.

20. Alvesson, M., Gabriel, Y., and Paulsen, R. (2017) *Return to Meaning: a Social Science with Something to Say*, Oxford: Oxford University Press, p. 103.

21. Lepanjuuri, K., Wishart, R., and Cornick, P. (2018) The characteristics of those in the gig economy (report), London: Department for Business, Energy & Industrial Strategy.

22. Spicer, A., Karreman, D., and Alvesson, M. (2009) Extending critical performativity, *Human Relations*, 69, 225–249. The quotation is on p. 243.

23. Hopwood, A. (2009) On striving to give a critical edge to CMS, in M. Alvesson, T. Bridgman and H. Willmott (eds.) *The Oxford Handbook of Critical Management Studies*, Oxford: Oxford University Press, pp. 515–524. The quotation is on p. 517.

24. Bloodworth, J. (2018) *Hired: Six Months Undercover in Low Wage Britain*, London: Atlantic Books.

25. Thompson, P. (2005) Brands, boundaries, and bandwagons, in C. Grey and H. Willmott (eds.) *Critical Management Studies: A Reader*, Oxford: Oxford University Press, pp. 364–382. The quotation is on p. 370.

26. See, for example, Fournier, V., and Grey, C. (2000) At the critical moment: conditions and prospects for critical management studies, *Human Relations*, 53, 7–32.

27. See Spicer et al., 2009, p. 538.

28. Ibid., p. 551.

29. Fleming, P., and Banerjee, S. (2016) When performativity fails: implications for critical management studies, *Human Relations*, 69, 257–276.

30. Butler, N., Delaney, H., and Spoelstra, S. (2018) Risky business: reflections on critical performativity in practice, *Organization*, 25, 428–445.

31. Parker, M. (2018) *Shut Down the Business School: What's Wrong with Management Education*, London: Pluto Press, p. 69.

32. Weber, M. (1946/1919) Science as a vocation, in H. Gerth and C. Wright Mills (trans. and eds.) *From Max Weber: Essays in Sociology*, Oxford: Oxford University Press, p. 136.

Index

Printed in the United States
by Baker & Taylor Publisher Services